CONTENTS

ABOUT THE AUTHOR

Colm Williamson created *Waterford Whispers News* in 2009 when he was unemployed. Though it began as a hobby, with Colm sharing stories with family and friends, his unique brand of topical, distinctly Irish satire quickly attracted thousands of fans. Now *Waterford Whispers News* has over 665,000 Facebook, 218,000 Twitter and 107,000 Instagram followers, and an average of 4 million page views on the website every month. Colm runs *Waterford Whispers News* from his home town of Tramore in Co. Waterford.

ACKNOWLEDGEMENTS

I would like to thank my two co-writers Karl Moylan and Gerry McBride for their continued hard work and dedication to *WWN*. Thanks to my good friend Rory Thompson for the fantastic cover illustration. A big special thanks to Alan McCabe for all his technical skills on the site. Thanks to my fiancé Ally Grace for putting up with me and to Lukas and Alex who I love very much. It has been a tough year for everyone as business worldwide takes yet another hit. Purchasing this book is a huge help to *WWN,* and I would like to personally thank you, the reader, and whoever buys this book. It means a lot.

LETTER FROM THE EDITOR

Dear reading people,

Declan O'Ryan here, owner of *WWN*, Snoozetalk, Dublin's 69FM, The Co-dependent.ie and 400 other minor media companies you definitely don't need to research any further.

It's that time of year again when I get asked to address you, our loyal readers, in the hopes of making you feel somewhat worthy and important to this great news publication.

Obviously, thanks to the coronavirus pandemic, you poor plebs had a very turbulent year in terms of jobs, revenue and running out of Netflix programs to watch. But, as the new normal dust settles, we look back on a memorable year packed full of profitable news that will hopefully remain etched into your tiny, traumatised minds for decades to come.

With government advice like 'wear masks after lockdown is over', 'don't go to these green-list countries we've deemed safe' and 'stay away from popular Irish vacation spots when staycationing', your great nation was left dazed from the get-go, with a confusing general election putting the last party anyone wanted in joint power, but not without a fight.

Like a Tokyo twincam supped up on change, General Election 2020 saw Sinn Féin performing doughnuts on every rural crossroads, collecting thousands of voters before speeding to a certain, chequered-flag finish, while screaming 'up the RA', only to be pipped at the line by the realisation that they forgot to put their own passengers in the car and failed to win enough seats.

A pandemic ensued, and people forgot, turning to an outgoing Taoiseach for movie quotes and sombre-sounding speeches, before a new three-headed beast of the apocalypse was born in Leinster House in the form of Martin, Varadkar and Ryan.

Locked down in your overpriced but small homes, the nation soon forgot its political fate, glued to a daily black and yellow briefing delivered by a national GP. You obeyed, for a while, listened to the advice and slowly began rebelling with long, annoying walks that were never to be repeated post-lockdown. Pointing out social distancing mistakes became a national pastime for you. Experts were born who openly moaned about people moaning, before moaning some more in some sort of sick online moan-ception – sure isn't that all you lot are good for.

Being the nation you are, you got through the worst thanks to COVID payments and local off-licences. Backyard pubs were built and expanded, along with waistlines. 'We' were all in this together except, of course, those attending political golfing events, which, may I add, was a great event despite everyone's grievances – myself and Phil thoroughly enjoyed ourselves and laughed at the nice golden handshake he received after.

Like Cromwell, COVID came, conquered and left your pusses sour. It left its legacy in queues, masks and keyboard warriors. Your right-leaning mate became an extremist overnight. Meat factories were mentioned, but only pubs were threatened. Videos of young people doing young people things became your go-to whinge because of your own envy and lust for a younger life. It was the best of times, it was the worst of times, but it was our time that will never be forgotten.

I'm almost afraid to say I'm proud of this complicated little nation, but I am. Despite pretending to spend most of my time in the Bahamas for tax reasons, I'm really impressed with you lot back home. You really shone through in the end, and I would like to commend you on your stunning spirit and consistent compliance to whatever laws you are given to obey – you are indeed good little boys and girls.

As for me, well, I've a lucrative national broadband plan to roll out, thanks to my mates in government. And yes, you'll all be needing it now you're stuck at home working, but seriously, please, don't hold your breath. This is Ireland, after all.

Kind regards,
Declan O'Ryan

HOT WET PUBS WEEKLY

Caution: Slippery When Wet

GUIDE
To The Best Under Table Service

'Stick your personal details into my form'

'The only thing you'll catch round here is an STD'

Barely legal teens inside

5 Spunky Visors To Drive Punters Wild

Publican Guide To The Perfect Happy Ending Hour

Six Way Action Techniques ▪ Being Four Deep At The Bar ▪ Dripping Wet Beer Mats

Waterford Whispers News

POLITICS

EURO NEWS

BRITAIN TO LAUNCH ITS OWN EU

STOCK markets across the world have been sent into a frenzy this afternoon as the UK announced it will launch its own European Union next year, aptly naming the new venture EU 2.0, *WWN* can confirm.

Speaking outside 10 Downing Street, Prime Minister Boris Johnson detailed plans for a 'bigger, stronger Europe', calling on neighbours Ireland and other current EU members to consider 'jumping ship' and joining the new rogue EU.

'This will be the best EU ever,' a desperate-looking Johnson babbled, clearly terrified now he finally had to deliver an actual plan.

Now holding up a blue flag with one single gold star, presumably representing Britain, he noted,

'We won't let anyone else in, you'll see, only the cool nations can roam around and everyone will trade in sterling. Yeah, that's it, everything will be swell.'

As the bewildered press packed up their equipment and began leaving,

afraid to bear witness to the pathetic scene, Johnson found a second wind thanks to the rabid encouragement of his cabinet colleagues and chief of staff Dominic Cummings.

'Finally, with EU 2.0, Britain and every other country will be free from EU tyranny in this new political and economic union of 28 member states that will trade as one giant economic block,' Johnson added to an empty room, wrongly satisfied he hadn't made a complete fool of himself.

'Hello? Anyone there? What if I call the Irish Paddies, or the Germans Nazis? Or talk about painting buses as a hobby? Will you take me seriously then? Muslim women? Letterboxes?' said the now defeated Johnson, falling to his knees.

'Ireland's favourite news source since 234BC'

Whispers News

Weather
Very cold and very wet, which is terrible weather for growing crops, but don't let us stop you, we're only professional weather forecasters.

VOL 1, 136   WATERFORD, 27 MARCH 1843   2d

Bumper Potato Crop Likely To Never End

FARMERS have hailed the bumper potato crop as 'a miracle from God' this season, as yields continue to thrive across the island of Ireland with no end in sight to the potato boom, *WWN* can confirm.

Thousands of tonnes of potatoes are being harvested to such a degree that all other produce is now to be forfeited indefinitely as Ireland's favourite vegetable takes centre stage. 'I threw out all my cabbage, carrot and parsnip crops to the dogs,' local farmer Patrick O'Leary explained, 'we've stopped planting all other food, grains and good riddance to bad rubbish too; if I see one more cabbage I'll puke into my hat.'

Landowners encouraged the boom and have advised all Irish tenant farmers to concentrate solely on growing a certain strain of potatoes and nothing else.

'If they could only use the one or two varieties of potato that would be great and don't mind any rumours of blight coming from North America as it was all fake news,' said Waterford landlord Arthur Kiely, who's set to make hundreds of pounds from his tenants and would never dream of evicting them if they messed this up.

With crops flourishing, thousands of tenant farmers have called for substantial bank loans from the Bank of England to build exten-

sions, with some farmers now looking abroad to invest their newly found wealth.

'There're really good investment deals on Bengal farms in India going at

the moment and I'm going to invest everything I have into that,' one farmer confirmed before thanking her Highness, 'onwards and upwards and God bless the queen!'

FINE GAEL ELECTION PROMISES JUST LIST OF THINGS THEY WERE SUPPOSED TO DO WHILE IN POWER

GLAD-HANDING the general public with ferocious intent, Fine Gael candidates have been pounding the nation's pavements dutifully parroting the promises, claims and talking points given to them by senior party officials, which it transpires are just a list of things Fine Gael should have and quite conceivably could have done while in power these last nine years.

'Oh wow, they sound like some great ideas, if only they thought to do some of these amazing-sounding things while they had power over the exact mechanisms that made delivering on such promises possible,' remarked one member of the public who walked into oncoming traffic to avoid shaking the hand of a Fine Gael candidate.

As the election campaign grumbles on, more and more political parties have begun praying before the magic money trees in a bid to secure funding for all their outlandish offerings to voters; however, Fine Gael's sudden discovery of a set of engaging and forward-thinking policies continues to perplex the public.

'Free GPs for all children? Free dental care for under-16s? Nine million extra Gardaí? Sorting the housing situation out? "Protecting" farmers? I would have liked the sound of this three years ago from Fine Gael,' confirmed another voter.

Speaking to absolutely anyone except actual ordinary members of the Irish public, Taoiseach and Fine Gael leader Leo Varadkar confirmed he could deliver on all these promises and had a really great explanation for why he was only pledging to do so now there was an election.

'Eh, well, right, this is an easy one to explain. Oh look, what's that? Is that Mary Lou McDonald wearing a balaclava?' Varadkar pointed out, now jumping into a nearby car before driving off in a plume of tire smoke.

MCDONALD ASKS PARTY TO REFRAIN FROM SHOUTING 'UP THE RA' FOR AT LEAST A WEEK

BURYING her head in her hands, Sinn Féin leader Mary Lou McDonald can't believe Waterford TD David Cullinane was shouting 'Up the RA' 0.02 seconds after being elected and has asked all TDs to refrain from such things for, at the very least, a full week.

'We can "Up the RA" in private all we like. You know that, I know that, but Georgina O'Double Barrel Surname from D4-land thinks we're going to sort out her high rent and that's it. Jesus, she probably thinks a republican is a Trump supporter, so fucking cut it out,' an irate McDonald said, keen not to go full 24/7 United Ireland no matter the cost. Some new Sinn Féin voters who had responded positively to the party's campaign promises on non-Up the RA issues spent much of the last week in passionate debate with friends, family and co-workers, articulately explaining how bringing up Sinn Féin's IRA past was ridiculous pearl-clutching, only for a number of newly elected TDs to openly celebrate it.

'And Dessie, cut out singing "Come Out Ye Black and Tans", would ya? Some people are only one Google of you away from discovering you were arrested for making bombs,' McDonald added, now chiding TD Dessie Ellis.

'What was the one thing I said to you lot,' McDonald asked her TDs, who responded sheepishly in unison with 'absolutely no RA-ing for at least a week'.

'Exactly. Wait until we form a government and everyone's attention span expires. I hope you're proud of yourselves now, there's some lovely middle-class people who voted for us and now they're shitting themselves,' added McDonald.

However, McDonald's ire seems misplaced as one Sinn Féin supporter pointed out that 'the people of this country elected Sinn Féin exactly so its TDs would openly shout "Up the RA", and anyone who's not on board with that is a property-fund-owning Blueshirt who wants to marry the RIC.'

BABIES

WE VISIT THE HEALY-RAE VOTER FARMS IN KERRY

FOLLOWING yet another successful election campaign for the Healy-Raes, *WWN* travels to remote County Kerry to visit a state-of-the-art 'voter farm' to see exactly how the southwest monarchs continue to rise to the top of the electoral charts election after election.

'We reproduce them in four-year cycles,' explains Dr George Casey, head of inseminations. 'Each infant is immediately exposed to local culture upon birth and incubated for six months while we bombard them with various media based around Healy-Rae history which is looped constantly throughout their stay here.'

The children seemed safe and happy, despite their vast numbers, with the older ones already showing signs of Healy-Raeism.

'This little fella loves his ba ba, don't you,' one of the many nurses

tells us as she feeds a four-month-old baby boy what appears to be Nigerian-strength Guinness through a plastic bottle, 'it's nearly time for his climate change,' she adds, disposing of a disposable plastic nappy into a green recycle bin.

Making our way down through the various different holding wards, our attention was brought to a room labelled 'Failed', where we observed several infants performing complicated practical IQ tasks.

'Not all of them make it to Healy-Rae voter status; for example, these failed ones have begun forming their own opinions,' another nurse explains. 'We usually adopt these out to Dubs to avoid them contaminating the local population.'

Lab-grown from birth using female Healy-Rae DNA carriers as hosts, 98% of the children will be integrated into

County Kerry society once they hit 18 months, where they will be educated locally until the age of 18 in Healy-Rae-funded schools.

'We do have strays who wander off to places like Tipperary and that, but they usually end up voting for Michael Lowry and the likes, and that's okay,' a staff member reassured us.

Healy-Rae voter farms produce over 5,000 Healy-Rae voters every two months and have been in operation since 1974.

UCD student Trevor O'Brien is to spend the coming months learning off and adopting the key political ideology of Sinn Féin, in what many people presume is just a phase that every student goes through at some point.

'It used to be Labour in my day, but students are wise to them now. I was so far left I drove on the hard shoulder back in college, but once I started earning enough money to be taxed out

STUDENT GOING THROUGH SINN FÉIN PHASE

the bollocks I switched to Fine Gael,' confirmed O'Brien's mother Theresa.

O'Brien's recent internet searches all seem to be inspired by Sinn Féin's history and policy platforms with a heavy reliance on Wikipedia entries and old articles news articles dating as far back as 2014.

'It's not a phase, I believe in investing in essential services, taxing the rich and the multinationals who are taking the Irish people for fools, all enabled by the Fine Gael Blueshirts who would be happy if Irish people never owned a home again,' O'Brien explained while erecting posters of the Irish border and Che Guevara on his bedroom wall.

His new-found love of Sinn Féin's political outlook has not extended to any gaudy 'Éire' back tattoos, but the possibility could not be ruled out.

'I won't be part of the capitalist system that results in suffering and inequality,' added O'Brien, who we give until he finishes college and gets a postgraduate position before safely transitioning to a reluctant, conflicted and guilt-ridden Fianna Fáil voter.

County Knowledge

Louth isn't actually Ireland's smallest county, but look, it needs to say something to convince people to visit.

THE MILITARY

IRELAND TO BE RENAMED THE USS *DE VALERA*

THE Republic of Ireland is to be officially renamed as a vessel in the United States Navy, after spending years as a stop-over for US aircraft on their way to bomb the crap out of whatever Middle Eastern country they were pissed off with at the time.

Despite Ireland being a completely neutral nation, the United States has been granted access to the County Clare airport since the September 11th attacks, with Shannon quickly becoming known by US forces as 'that place we can stop and get Supermacs on our way to liberate the world'.

Given that the entire island of Ireland has basically acted as a mid-Atlantic aircraft carrier for decades, it will be renamed as part of their fleet ahead of the upcoming skirmish with Iran, and has been named the USS *de Valera*, after the US-born former Taoiseach and President of Ireland who declared neutrality in the event of war, Éamon de Valera.

'As a country, Ireland's neutrality is a little, eh …' said Taoiseach Leo Varadkar, making the hand gesture for 'so-so'.

'But as a vessel, we can remain completely neutral. A boat doesn't take sides in a war, you see. A gun doesn't actually shoot someone. It's whoever is operating it that has full responsibility for whatever happens. By remaining as the Republic of

How sex changed in 2020

Despite lobbying the government, good-for-nothing bastards failed to get 'cheater' listed as an essential worker.

Ireland, yeah, sure, we probably should put a stop to the use of Shannon for warplanes. But as the USS *de Valera*, we can just turn a blind eye to where the US is going, who they're killing, who they're taking back to the US to torture, all that craic. We're just a boat, baby, we're just a boat.'

The USS *de Valera* will be launched on St Patrick's Day this year, with a massive bottle of champagne set to be smashed against the side of the Cliffs of Moher.

EVERYTHING FUCKED

IRELAND FUCKED, UK FUCKED, THE NORTH FUCKED, EVERYTHING FUCKED

THE last remaining shreds of optimism surrounding the fate of Ireland following Brexit have been swept away by a tsunami of grim reality, with almost everyone on all sides finally admitting that 'the whole thing is completely fucking fucked'.

The facade of 'it'll be alright' began to show irreparable cracks following Boris Johnson's successful campaign to become prime minister, and the creeping realisation of how fucked the whole thing is gained speed as newly appointed cabinet ministers excitedly admitted that the UK was in 'full preparation' for a No-Deal exit from the EU in October.

Any notion that the border issue would be addressed in a competent, well-thought-out manner was all 'fucked-the-fuck away', with everyone from DUP leader Arlene Foster to Irish Taoiseach Leo Varadkar admitting that they were 'fucked if I know' what was going to happen.

'It's fucked. It's all fucked, I don't know why we tried to suggest otherwise,' said one government aide, finally admitting what a lot of the world had known since the Brexit vote in 2016.

'Trade? Fucked. Border? Fucked. Good Friday Agreement, peace in the North? It's all fucked. Britain is fucked. Scotland is fucked. Wales, I dunno. Maybe they're happy enough. Ireland, super fucked. The EU is fucked. The world is fucked. I'm fucked. You're fucked. Your man over there walking his dog? He's fucked. The dog is fucked. We're all fucked.'

The public has reacted to the news that they're fucked with grim

determination, and have moved for Britain to crash out of the EU now rather than in October, as it's nicer to be fucked in the summer than it is to be fucked in a cold winter.

LOCAL CANDIDATE WORRIED HE'S NOT MORALLY CORRUPT ENOUGH FOR FINE GAEL

AFTER seeing Taoiseach Leo Varadkar race down to Wexford to spend a day campaigning alongside Verona Murphy, one Fine Gael by-election candidate feared he didn't have enough questionable morals, beliefs and ideas to represent the party adequately.

'She said child refugees need to be "de-programmed", then she's accused of "interference" regarding a Road Safety Authority transport officer trying to carry out his duties, and there's the fact her business partner is a convicted tax dodger. I'm only just about able to muster the courage to gouge my tenants for extortionate

rent,' explained future general election candidate for Fine Gael, Peter Dylan.

Dylan, a 49-year-old property developer with several drink-driving convictions and a cobalt mine in the Congo that only uses child slave

labour, broke down in tears as he worried he hadn't done enough to win over senior Fine Gael figures.

'Seeing the Taoiseach endorse someone like that so enthusiastically, it made me think … am I morally dubious enough to have earned my FG stripes? Can I pretend to care like him? Calmly explain away xenophobia and then sleep easy at night?' Dylan shared, feeling like he'll never be spineless and opportunistic enough for the Fine Gael party.

'Whose homeless child do I have to spit at to convince the party I can do this? I'm at sixes and sevens with this, I never doubt myself usually, but it's so hard to meet Leo's depressingly low standards.'

A spokesperson for Fine Gael confirmed to *WWN* that Dylan had been stood down from any future elections as the sort of candidates Fine Gael are looking for 'haven't a conscience to spare for this sort of trivial bullshit'.

IN-DEPTH REPORT

FINE GAEL & FIANNA FÁIL: THE DIFFERENCES

AS THE SHADOW of another election emerges upon the horizon like a glorious sun-shaped pile of excrement, stinking everything up and covering it in darkness, many astute political commentators have observed that to the average voter there appears to be next to no difference between the country's largest parties, bitter rivals Fine Gael and Fianna Fáil.

Ahead of Taoiseach Leo Varadkar meeting his Fianna Fáil counterpart Micheál Martin this evening, you may be looking to refine your understanding of the differences between both parties.

Look no further as *WWN* outlines the present differences between parties that used to be diametrically opposed to one another, differences drawn along old Irish Civil War lines.

Fianna Fáil as part of the so-called 'Confidence and Supply' arrangement have supported the government getting Fine Gael's policies and ideas through the Dáil, a sure sign if ever there was one that they have fundamental ideological differences.

Even the most basic research reveals these are two vastly different parties, the ultimate chalk and cheese combo. For example, Fine Gael's offices are at 51 Mount Street Upper, Dublin 2, while Fianna Fáil is at 65–66 Mount Street Lower, Dublin 2. And to think voters lump the two parties in together like they were key ingredients in some bland salad, precision-designed to make poor people sick.

> **Leo: 'We couldn't be more ...'**
> **Micheál: 'Similar.'**
> **Leo: 'You mean different.'**

Main ideological differences, Fianna Fáil: while not in government, FF believes increased investment in housing and health is needed to solve myriad crises and problems; this will change in the event of them being elected.

Main ideological differences, Fine Gael: while in government, FG believes increased investment in housing and health isn't needed to solve myriad crises and problems; however, this will change in the event of them being relegated to the opposition benches.

The differences pile up: Fine Gael blames Fianna Fáil for everything while Fianna Fáil blames Fine Gael. Occasionally, in the event of a rare lunar eclipse, the parties both blame Sinn Féin.

Fine Gael wants to reanimate the corpses of former Black and Tans members and arm them in the fight

How hygiene changed in 2020

Young lads who inexplicably put one hand down the crotch of their tracksuit bottoms at all times did not alter this behaviour.

against the homeless while Fianna Fáil refuses to seek treatment for a troubling condition which has left them with no recollection of Ireland in the years between 1997 and 2011.

Both parties will fight day in, day out, for the ordinary Joe, also known as 'making sure multinationals pay no tax'.

What have the leaders to say about each other?

Leo: 'We couldn't be more ...'
Micheál: 'Similar.'
Leo: 'You mean different.'
Micheál: 'Shit, yeah. See, we don't even finish each other's sentences.'

Plenty to mull over, but if you were on the fence it should be crystal clear the two parties are worlds apart.

Health and fitness tip

Hiring a personal trainer is a great way to add to the number of people who can't stand you.

FEATURE REPORT

COMPLETE LIST OF IRA/SINN FÉIN JOKES SO YOU CAN GET IT OUT OF YOUR SYSTEM

AS A COUNTRY we may not be able to get our complex, nuanced and violent past out of our system, but that's not to say we can't all band together and agree to get one big 'Sinn Féin is the IRA' bashing session out of the way and then move on, allowing a more mature, forward-looking evolution of criticisms of Sinn Féin to begin.

Once all the bad, lazy, middling and meta jokes, which are as subtle as a bullet to the kneecap, are out of the way, Sinn Féin can be judged merely for being like any other political party and can be called out over leprechaun economics, corruption, craven backroom deals and vote-grabbing election promises like Fianna Fáil and Fine Gael in their former heyday, or Sinn Féin in the North.

Thanks to all our readers who sent in these entries. Sit down, strap in, and

The last time banks lost that much money in one day they were being robbed by the IRA

depending on your party affiliations laugh like a wheezing donkey, cry, or tut dismissively and cringe, doing your part to move the nation's politics forwards:

- The election was basically a draw, so does that mean it'll go to penalties? 'Cos Sinn Féin would win the shootout.
- As long as there's JCBs and ATMs in Ireland, Sinn Féin should be able to pay for everything.
- I hear Sinn Féin will implement a rental kneecap the first day they enter office.
- A Sinn Féin government would bring a whole new meaning to boom and bust cycles.

- Did ya hear the new names for government departments under a Sinn Féin government? Dept of AgRAculture, Dept of Safe Houses, Dept of the Environment and Fuel Laundering, Dept of Social Protection & Intimidation.
- If Sinn Féin don't get to form a government, I hear they're taking a legal challenge all the way to the Supreme Kangaroo Court.
- If anyone can defuse the ticking pension timebomb, it's a Shinner.
- The banks may have lost €300 million in value since the election, but shares in Semtex have exploded.
- If McDonald is made Taoiseach before a government is formed, does that make her the Provisional Taoiseach?
- The last time banks lost that much money in one day they were being robbed by the IRA.
- The IRA is so vast, just witnessing the organisation in action will make you go weak at the knees.
- 'Should we all be in the IRA now, father?' (Accompanied by relevant *Father Ted* clip. Plus a thousand more variations on this meme.)
- You can't spell Rent Allowance without the IRA.
- All public addresses by the Irish government will now take place in Belfast in the spare room of a house with dodgy 1970s decor, in front of a tricolour pinned up by thumbtacks on the wall.
- Under Sinn Féin the Angelus will be replaced by 'Come Out Ye Black and Tans', pubs will only serve pints of McGuinness and everyone will have to dress as Che Guevara.
- 'We now go live to Sinn Féin coalition talks with Fianna Fáil' (accompanied by a picture of lads in balaclavas beating the shite out of some poor fella).
- Under new legislation the responsibility for the cover-up of

child abuse will be taken away from the Catholic Church and given to the IRA.

- 'Gerry Adams! Him and his big teeth he got in America for free! The RA! Sinn Féin! Bombs! Sorry … I'm not good at this joke stuff' – another reader submission, sent in by Leo in Dublin.
- Under Sinn Féin the Department of Tourism will ensure every beach will be renamed Bobby Sands and Leinster House will be painted over with a huge Free Derry mural.
- Revolutionising public transport, Sinn Féin will ensure a five-minute warning is issued before they blow up a bus. A 'sniper at work sign' will appear at all traffic lights to deter motorists

from breaking red lights, and a 'provisional licence' won't mean what it used to mean.

- Sinn Féin are proposing new tolerance legislation so it's finally acceptable for minorities to wear balaclavas in public.
- Sinn Féin plan to reverse austerity with a government-subsidised scheme making everything from milk and bread to Semtex and kneecap reconstruction surgery more affordable.
- This is the first time the Dáil will have more terrorists in it than primary school teachers who take the absolute piss.
- Jesus, Sinn Féin didn't do too bad. Some might say it was an explosive election result for them.

- Sinn Féin defence policy unveiled: for every guard a dissident murders, Sinn Féin have pledged to recruit a further 10.

Now we as a people can put our energy towards focusing on Sinn Féin's policies. More like 'Sin' Féin, amiright? Huh? Get it? We'll get our collective coats.

How drinking changed in 2020

When it was confirmed pubs could reopen as long as they served 'substantial meals', publicans pushed health authorities to reclassify a pint as one of your five-a-day.

'Ireland's favourite news source since 234BC'

Whispers News

Weather
Sharp ground frost will continue to wreak havoc on all crops this week with no end in sight, but the queen is visiting so it's not all bad news.

VOL 1, 2014587   WATERFORD, 3 AUGUST 1849   1P

'You're My Favourite Famine Victims' – Queen Tells Cork

FLANKED by tens of thousands of welcoming Irish fans and well-wishers, Queen Victoria beamed with elegance and grace as her horse and carriage made its way down the newly named Queenstown, an area once called Cobh but now renamed in her honour.

'I would just like to say thanks to all you spud-munching muck savages who have made your way here today,' her Highness opened to cheers from the barefoot and tattered crowd, as police baton-charged them to keep them from getting too close, 'the people of Ireland are definitely my favourite famine victims – far better than those godawful mongrels in India, anyway.'

Struggling to hear herself with the manic cheering over her appreciation of the Irish people, the Queen, knowing she was on to a good thing, continued her address, but now sipping a pint of Guinness.

'This Guinness is beautiful,' she added, as Irish men

and women began tearing clumps of their own hair out of their heads due to being incapable of containing their excitement.

Realising how easy it was to redeem hundreds of years of oppression and two devastating famines that wiped out millions, the

Queen spent the remainder of her ten-day visit 'complimenting the paddies'.

'Critics should leave her be. She can piss on the graves of our dead for all we care. All is forgiven,' insisted local man Paddy Hollihan, who lost his wife and all seven of his young children to starvation last year.

'Her Highness gets a lot of bad press, but she said Cork was lovely, so it's time for everyone to move on,' another man told this reporter while boarding a famine ship.

The Queen is expected to visit Dublin on Monday where thousands of well-off locals have begun making miniature Union Jacks in preparation for her visit.

SCIENCE

'VOTING FOR SINN FÉIN COULD UNLOCK PORTAL TO 1970S BELFAST' WARN FINE GAEL & FIANNA FÁIL

CONSULTING a whiteboard with hastily written plot outlines from Hollywood time travel sci-fi movies on it, Micheál Martin and Leo Varadkar have been frantically explaining why 24.5% of the Irish voting public could have set off a sequence of events that could result in a rip in the space-time continuum.

'Marginalised Loyalist paramilitaries could strike out; Republican paramilitaries, emboldened by a Sinn Féin party in ascension, could return to violence as their impatience grows over a United Ireland,' explained the leaders of Fianna Fáil and Fine Gael, desperately trying to relay the dire warnings to the Irish public yet again.

Scribbling with ever-increasing urgency, the leaders tried to predict where and when the portal would open and what apocalyptic dystopian film it would most resemble.

'It'll be like *Universal Solider* with accents harder to understand than Jean-Claude Van Damme or *Starship Troopers*, but instead of giant alien insects it's Shinners. Jesus people, do you all want to be transported to 1970s Belfast, or worse, Derry in 2020?' added Martin and Varadkar, who are spending more time hanging out these days, it seems.

With their warnings failing to ignite any substantial worry in a predictably placid Irish public, the leaders had no choice but to smash through a box mounted on a wall marked 'break glass in case of voters being done with your shit and read'.

'If Sinn Féin form a government, the worst, most horrendous fate awaits you; the price of your house will fall,' the sombre leaders read from the emergency communication, awakening a violent revolt against Sinn Féin among the home-owning section of the electorate.

MARTIN URGES PARTY MEMBERS TO WAIT UNTIL THEY'RE IN POWER BEFORE ACTING THE BOLLOCKS

FIANNA FÁIL leader Micheál Martin has urged party members to 'wait until they're in power before acting the bollocks' following revelations that some TDs were illegally voting on behalf of their absent colleagues.

Mr Martin asked Timmy Dooley and Niall Collins to step down from

their frontbench positions yesterday afternoon after Collins admitted to voting on behalf of Dooley six times in the Dáil last Thursday, reminding the pair that the party isn't in power yet and to cop on to themselves for another little bit.

'There will be plenty of time for that carry on when we win the next general election,' Martin explained while chastising the TDs, 'you've also broken the number one rule of Fianna Fáil; don't get caught. Now I have to pretend we're sorry and put you pair of eejits in the background for a few days until the goldfish forget about it.'

Also voting for an absent colleague, Fianna Fáil's Brexit spokesperson

Lisa Chambers will not face a similar penance as she had found a half-decent excuse, claiming she sat in the wrong seat in the Dáil chamber.

'Take a leaf out of Lisa's book, lads,' Martin went on, 'at least come up with a viable excuse if you're going to Fianna Fail properly.'

Despite breaking the law several times, all offending TDs are expected to keep their positions in Leinster House, face little or no criminal investigation and receive a nice 2% pay rise next year.

'Look, it won't be long until it's our turn again to mismanage the country, just be good for another few months, you whelps!' Martin concluded.

THE TAOISEACH'S NEXT POP CULTURE-HEAVY SPEECH LEAKED

FRESH from becoming the Meme King of Ireland after dropping iconic Terminator dialogue into his last address to the nation, Taoiseach Leo Varadkar is bathing in the warm glow of affection he is completely unaccustomed to as a much-maligned leader of the country.

In a bid to secure himself further respite from being called the bastard love child of Margaret Thatcher and a DVD copy of *American Psycho*, the Taoiseach's next speech is set to include even more pop culture nods and whatever else it takes to bamboozle simple-minded voters into saying 'ah, leave him be, he's dead sound, sure didn't he do the Terminator during a speech'.

WWN has exclusively obtained a leaked copy of the Taoiseach's next speech and reproduced it below:

[Note: Moonwalk to the podium like the ledge-bag you are.]

'Hakuna Matata, Wakanda forever and may the force be with you fellow my Irish brothers and sisters! How you doin'?

'If the past few weeks have taught us anything it is that there's no place like home. In my last speech, I told you

'Now is the time to shashay away into your own homes and lockdown for your lives. Hasta la vista, baby!'

we're going to need a bigger lockdown as what we have here is a failure to communicate. No diggity, we're going to have to bag it up. The virus has made it clear it is the one who knocks, it is the danger, tread lightly.

'Since my last epic speech my mother has said life is like a box of chocolates and frankly my dear I don't give a damn, we need to boldly go where every man has gone before in search of comfort; to the couch and stay there. We're living way beyond our memes.

'As we've seen from some responses around the world, I've got clowns to the left of me, jokers to the right and I'm stuck in a pandemic with you.'

[Wink to camera now, maybe do finger guns. Too far?]

'Don't make unnecessary journeys, careful now, down with this sort of thing, RTÉ news man falling on ice video remix video, who's going to take the horse to France? Deal or no deal, our survey says you like how I'm handling this pandemic, is that your final answer? If we keep this up Mary Lou and Micheál will be the weakest link, goodbye.

'We're trying to flatten the curve, and reduce the numbers but remember COVID-19 only has to be lucky once. We have to be lucky always. Give your hands a wash and the war on COVID-19 will be over soon.'

[Pause for dramatic effect as all the Shinners slowly realise a Fine Gael Taoiseach just paraphrase-quoted the motherfucking IRA. Possible mic drop?]

'We trust in our healthcare workers and thank everyone on the front lines, the truth is out there. Clear eyes, full hearts, can't lose – that's from *Friday Night Lights* guys, can't recommend it enough, the Simons were banging on about it for years, but with being stuck inside I gave it a lash over the weekend, it's class. Also, you can't beat *The Wire*.

'This virus is fast and furious, it's shaken not stirred, keep your friends close but your enemies closer – this is an offer you can't refuse. Just keep swimming.

'Now is the time to shashay away into your own homes and lockdown for your lives. Hasta la vista, baby!'

[Tear up speech and throw it up in the air, press play on The Police's 'Don't Stand So Close To Me', or maybe REM's 'It's The End Of The World'?]

DUP CONSIDERING POSSIBILITY THAT THEY'RE A SHOWER OF HORRIBLE BASTARDS

DUP leader Arlene Foster has stated that during her party's ongoing Brexit-based discussions, they entertained the notion that they may actually be a giant pack of wretched bastards.

As they battle to find a way to accept the fact that the Conservative Government is about to catapult them under the nearest available bus, the unionist party have had time to step outside their own sphere and realise that a lot of their beliefs and policies are at best antiquated and, at worst, pure cuntish.

Taking their current stance on gay rights, women's rights, nationalists' rights and wood-pellet burners' rights into account, Foster admitted that in the 'cold hard light of day', the DUP aren't exactly the nicest people.

'Holy shit, we're a bunch of pricks,' said Sammy Wilson, clutching the sides of his face at the realisation.

'I'm … I'm a horrible human being,' cried Ian Paisley Jnr.

'Lads … it's not just you. It's all of us; we're dinosaurs, relics of a bygone era that are clinging on to our so-called "heritage" to appeal to an ever-diminishing voter base at the cost of thousands of people all across Northern Ireland, all to cosy up to a dying Empire that wouldn't piss on us if we were on fire,' sobbed Foster.

Despite these revelations, the DUP have managed to shrug off these morbid feelings and return to 'business as usual', claiming that their brief moment of doubt was 'probably some Taig sorcery'.

FARMER IN TRACTOR ONLY GETTING BACK FROM PROTEST NOW

HOLDING up a long stream of traffic and travelling at a painful 34 kilometres per hour, local farmer Danny Rice is expected to finally arrive back at the farm later this afternoon after leaving protests in Dublin city on Wednesday.

'Jaysis, they're in an awful rush around here,' Rice barked at a passing BMW that was beeping at him while overtaking on a dangerous country road, 'busy too, there's about 40 cars behind me, there must be a hurling match on somewhere.'

Ignoring repeated horns and passing insults, the 53-year-old father of 17 reminisced about the great time he had in the big smoke on Tuesday and Wednesday, longing for the next time he and his fellow farmers could get together and disrupt the country's traffic once more in a bid to be heard.

'I'll bring the John Deere the next time; the lads said she's slower and more disruptive,' Rice said to himself, pushing down his rearview mirror to avoid the angry faces staring back at him.

Born with a rare condition that leaves him with an inability to pull in to the side of the road and let traffic pass, Rice was delighted to learn that Gardaí in Dublin had no problem with this, and handled him and his fellow farmers with the sort of gentle touch they do not reserve for housing and climate protesters.

'I'm sure our protests will get everyone on our side against the government and not be in any way counterproductive,' he concluded to a loud 'fuck off the road, you cunt' from a passing nun driving a Nissan Juke.

BLINDFOLDED IMMIGRATION MINISTER PINS NEXT DIRECT PROVISION LOCATION ON MAP

CAREFULLY tightening his well-worn blindfold, Irish Immigration Minister David Stanton felt his way to a notice board on his office wall where a map of Ireland hung proudly, littered with previous holes from failed endeavours.

'Okay, keep left, Dave, you don't want to hit Dublin – they'd feel too at home in a multicultural city like Dublin – keep west,' he began, before puncturing the board with a red drawing pin and lifting his blindfold in anticipation, 'ah balls, Oughterard again, why do I keep hitting fecking Oughterard?'

Relying only on blind fate to make his decisions for him, Stanton began to panic now as pressure mounted to find a decent, loving location on the island of Ireland that will allow the

government to house asylum seekers, albeit in questionable conditions, while wondering why there has been so much backlash for every decision his department has made so far.

'It's like people from rural Ireland have direct, firsthand experience of the government providing inadequate supports and outlets for people in need,' Stanton mumbled to himself, now making a fourth attempt to 'pin the donkey on the culchies', as he liked to call it, 'ah ha, Ballinamore, County Leitrim! This is a sure-fire winner'.

Just 0.3 seconds after his pinning, Stanton's phone began ringing in his pocket, a call he was already familiar with.

'I just pinned it there now, how are they protesting there already?' he asked the voice on the other end of the line, 'a travelling band of racists?… yellow vests… lobbying and exploiting unsuspecting locals?… inciting racist fearmongering?… okay, I'll go again, but I'm running out of pins here and this blindfold is starting to itch.'

This time hitting Achill Island, the now exhausted Immigration Minister didn't even get a chance to look at the map before his phone rang again.

'Nope, that's it, I'll just leave this mess up to the next poor eejit who gets this job,' he thought, before declining the call, and calling it a day.

How friendship changed in 2020

While being a tragic disease which claims a staggering number of lives, one COVID-19 upside was people were able to socially distance from dose friends they don't really like. Others were genuinely surprised they missed 'that prick' and 'that cow'.

FUTUREWATCH

The year is 2030 and Ireland elects its first female Taoiseach to rule over the recently renamed Islamic Republic of Ireland.

'We should have listened to that one guy in the comment sections of *The Journal* back in 2019. He even quit his job to go full-time moaning about her in the comments, but would we listen? No. We were too arrogant and lost in our Dublin bourgeois bubble. Well, look at what happened!' shared a defeated-looking former member of the open borders liberal lefty loony squad.

The warning signs were there: Smith was granted planning permission to convert Leinster House into a giant mosque while still on that controversial flight home to Ireland from a Turkish prison.

Concerned citizens submitted objections but those were soon dropped when Smith was permitted to build a mosque on the face of one objector, Cyril Costigan.

Later Costigan (71) would apologise to Smith, stating the Islamic Republic of Ireland and its suffocating oppression reminded him of the lovely Ireland of his youth and he was glad to have it back.

'Surely any individual involved with the Islamic State would face criminal prosecution upon returning to Ireland?' we hear those of you back in the idyllic past of 2020 asking. As everyone knows, Ireland staged a successful referendum on leaving the EU and joining the then resurgent Caliphate in early 2021 and thus plans for any such legal repercussions were shelved.

Idiotic politicians had initially staged the referendum to distract from myriad crises and thought it would never pass.

To better understand 2030 as a period of time you have to be aware people were more open to a radical

Did You Know?

Did you know leopards actually change their spots regularly, and are among the most fashion-conscious animals on Earth?

TAOISEACH LISA SMITH ELECTED LEADER OF ISLAMIC REPUBLIC OF IRELAND

FUTUREWATCH: Where we take a glimpse into the Ireland of tomorrow using state-of-the-art technology that fell off the back of a truck earmarked for a US military research facility.

shift in direction. The temporary homeless and health crises of the past remained permanently temporary. Eventually, people warmed to Donald Trump during his fourth term, Britain still hadn't left the EU, and the climate change hoax had been exposed after it was revealed Greta Thunberg was a 69-year-old scam artist with a particularly good skincare regime.

As your racist uncle had always correctly forewarned, Ireland was 'full of Islamic jihadist sleeper cells, even Carmel down in the post office has joined' and so all 16 million secret Muslims in Ireland voted in favour of the referendum, altering the country forever.

By 2030, the Islamic Republic of Ireland had its first female Taoiseach and the public was ready to protest; however, after a video from an American TV station spoke about how great the Irish were for electing a woman went viral, the public let it go to their heads and decided to bask in that praise instead.

Fullmindness

Don't have a quiet place to reflect? Book into a €5,000-a-night Mindfulness Retreat like any normal person would do.

Over time citizens got used to the stonings received for having a Guinness or a packet of Tayto, and while the language was tough to master we all got used to speaking Irish again. Other changes were rapid: the police force was renamed An Garda Shariachana. The angelus was broadcast live from Mecca. The landmass of Ireland itself was moved by 33 degrees by large trawler to correctly face toward Mecca. The constant worship on prayer mats doubled up as intense yoga and did wonders for people with bad backs. Muhammed became the most popular name for boys, girls and pet goldfish.

Despite all the warnings, Ireland was helpless against the march of Taoiseach Lisa Smith.

24% OF ELECTORATE THAT VOTED SINN FÉIN UNDER IMPRESSION 100% OF NATION VOTED FOR PARTY

WITH the likelihood of a 'grand coalition' involving Fianna Fáil and Fine Gael increasing, some incensed Sinn Féin voters continue to labour under the misapprehension that 100% of the nation voted for Sinn Féin.

Much in the same way Fine Gael voters in 2016 couldn't understand why the 75% of the country that didn't

vote for their party were so apoplectic at the idea that a party with just a quarter of the vote could be placed in charge of the country, some Sinn Féin supporters are at a loss as to why some people seem to think 24.5% doesn't equal 100% of the vote.

'No, it's different this time because Sinn Féin are brilliant and everybody voted for us. Everybody,' one Sinn Féin voter said, still high on the thrill of his party winning 100% of the vote, 506 seats in the Dáil, planning permission for 100,000 houses and an NHS, as well as an outstanding invoice for 'one United Ireland please' addressed to 'The Brits'.

Despite the plain language used by volunteers from the That's Not How Elections Work organisation and their attempts to repeat the information, only a bit more slowly each time, a cohort of people who voted Sinn

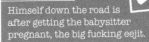

Community text alerts

Himself down the road is after getting the babysitter pregnant, the big fucking eejit.

Féin was still struggling to process the information, and insisted on maintaining the sort of authority only befitting a party that had a mandate that comes with winning 100% of the vote.

'Okay, so, Fianna Fáil and Fine Gael have less than 50% of the votes, and a lot of people wouldn't say that's 100% of the people, so it follows that … ,' offered one TNHEW volunteer before being interrupted by one excitable Sinn Féin voter with cries of 'Exactly! Sinn Féin have a majority government mandate from all proud patriots of Ireland.'

'HONESTLY, WHAT are we like,' shared senior Tusla management as they doubled over with laughter and slapped their foreheads in an exaggerated fashion after learning of the latest fuck-up involving vulnerable children and families.

Tusla, primarily a data-breaching agency that sometimes looks after the welfare of children and families requiring the help and support of the state, has hit headlines again, this time after accidentally disclosing the contact and location information of a mother and child victim to their alleged abuser.

'If there was an Eejit Olympics, I'm sorry now lads, but we'd win the gold,' cajoled a senior Tusla official to staff, tickled pink at the latest in a long line of incidents that have arisen after the last batch of staggering ineptitudes.

One of just 75 data breaches from a period stretching between 2018 and 2019, Tusla admitted fault in

'AH JAYSUS. WHAT. ARE. WE. LIKE?' CONFIRMS TUSLA AFTER LATEST MONUMENTAL FUCK-UP

accidentally disclosing the contact and location data of a mother and child victim to an alleged abuser, and honestly, admit they'd lose their head if it wasn't screwed on.

'Shit, have you told them about the child's head we lost?' a panicked Tusla worker interrupted. 'Oh wait, sorry, we haven't done that but lol, it does sound so us, doesn't it?'

Fresh from being found guilty of 'considerable failings and stupidities' in their handling of false allegations

against Garda whistleblower Maurice McCabe, Tusla remains committed to appearing in the news for only 'bad stuff'.

'Ah look it, you have to laugh don't ya? Sure it's only a bit of craic, not like this is important. Anyways, chat to ye lot next time we do something similarly terrible,' concluded Tusla management, shaking their heads and chuckling before returning to CC'ing the entire country into all of its emails regarding highly sensitive case files.

PERSONAL VIEW

'IF WE'RE GOING TO LET GANGSTERS RUN THE COUNTRY, WE MIGHT AS WELL ELECT THE BEST ONES'

Recently swayed voter Martin Rellis explains his reasons for opting out of his routine Fine Gael/Fianna Fáil support in favour of a Sinn Féin government, citing a more straight-up approach when it comes to electing politicians.

YOU wouldn't hire a carpenter to unclog a toilet, so why would you elect a bunch of rich kids with no street smarts to run a corrupt little country like Ireland? I mean, they were too squeaky clean, so when a scandal did arrive, they reacted like total amateurs, holding their hands up and just taking it like little bitches. Sinn Féin won't do that – not on their lives.

Also, Fine Gael couldn't spin a wheel, never mind a scandal. We need people in charge who know how to keep their mouths shut, and to also shut mouths when needed, and not some fairies who'll hang their own out to dry over fraudulent insurance claims.

We need people with balls who'll bare-facedly lie when the shit hits the fan and will stand their ground for their party members until the bitter end, no matter what the human cost is in keeping secrets, not a bunch of rat bastards.

Sinn Féin even have their own secret army. How cool is that? Ok, well, they don't have that army anymore. Fair enough, those days are long gone.

But it's like deleting an ex's number from your phone – if you ever need to drunk text them, you know the number off by heart. That'll come in handy: Oh, you only want to pay 1% tax on your billions of euros in revenue? We'll see what

our boys say about that, Mr Cook. How about your kneecaps, hi? Fancy doing your wee Apple launches in a wheelchair drinking your food through a straw? Nah, didn't think so, pal. Cough up, you cunt.

And before you go off on one, yes, I have heard construction experts confirm that a 100,000 new homes target for social housing within five years is impossible, and that we won't find the hospital consultants willing to work for the significantly lower

wages proposed, but sure aren't promises there to be broken?

Bottom line, I think we should give them a go, sure they couldn't be any worse than the last shower of useless pricks. Some people are saying young people voted for Sinn Féin out of ignorance, well, I'm old enough to remember the past and that's exactly why I voted for them. At least do corruption right if you're going to do corruption at all. Bring it on, I say.

MEET THE ONE IRISH PERSON WITH SYMPATHY FOR THE DUP

ALTHOUGH the vast majority of the Irish population have taken the DUP's tumultuous past couple of weeks as cause for riotous celebration and endless laughter, *WWN* has tracked down one Waterford native who is currently the only Irish person adopting an 'ah you have to feel sorry for them' stance on the party's ongoing woes.

With the DUP currently lamenting the legalisation of abortion and same-sex marriage in Northern Ireland and the subsequent opening of the gates of hell in the Six Counties, 43-year-old Waterford man Declan Harrison has openly expressed his sympathy for the plight of 'Arlene and the lads', a stance not shared by many.

'Ah you'd have to feel sorry for her all the same,' said Harrison, looking at footage of a furious-looking Arlene Foster biting the gates of Stormont.

'First the new Brexit deal that looks to set Northern Ireland adrift from the UK, the growing desire for a United Ireland stemming directly from the game-plan of the DUP itself, and now they have to allow same-sex marriage and abortion in Northern Ireland. Look at poor Arlene there, who could possibly look at her and her party and laugh at them? Everyone? So it's just me? Well, I think that's dreadful.'

As Declan continued to weep openly for the DUP, doctors at University Hospital Waterford informed *WWN* that Harrison's empathy for the DUP may stem from a strangely powerful case of Empathiago, a neurological disease commonly found in older Irish women.

'It's the same condition that makes your grandmother go "Ach don't be saying things like that" when you're talking about the Catholic Church molesting kids, that kind of thing,' said Empathiago specialist Dr Alsar Wheeler.

'It's a very Irish condition, where the sufferer feels they cannot say anything negative about even the worst people in the world. An Empathiago sufferer may feel that they need to be on the side of everyone, in order to ensure they won't get in any trouble later in life. They'd say something like "sure don't the Guards have it very hard" after hearing about the whistleblower scandal. That kind of thing. But to feel sorry for the DUP ... well, that's the worse case of Empathiago I've ever heard about.'

Mr Harrison continues to feel dreadful for the DUP, and has admitted to *WWN* that he also thinks Boris Johnson is having 'a rough time of it' as well, and that Donald Trump is looking well for a man his age.

PRICE OF €2M DÁIL PRINTER CARTRIDGES 'EXCESSIVE', ADMITS GOVERNMENT

WITH the cost of the Leinster House printer now reaching the €1.8 million mark, the government has reluctantly admitted that in a rare misstep it may have needlessly overspent, before warning taxpayers that if they thought the printer was expensive, wait until they hear the cost of the cartridges.

'Like most printers, the ink is the most expensive part, so please don't be mad when we tell you the price,' a spokesperson for the government, wearing a helmet, stab-vest and shin-guards, announced outside Leinster House earlier today.

'Okay, the cartridges are around two million euro each,' said the spokesman, slowly backing into the grounds of the Irish parliament before being pelted with missiles, 'look, please, you must have known the ink would be dearer ...' he added, now cowering in a foetal position on the ground as several members of An Garda Síochána intervened.

The cartridges, which will last a good 50 or 60 prints, will only print in black and white, a move the government wants to make clear was to bring down costs.

'Yeah, they're expensive, but you should have seen the cost of the colour ones,' defended Taoiseach Leo Varadkar, fresh from printing off a really cool black and white selfie of himself with Wexford by-election candidate and Islamophobia fan, Verona Murphy.

Attempting to take the heat off the PR disaster and dismissing it as a storm in a teacup, the government pointed out that if anything the public should be outraged about the Minister for Children handing back €60 million in unspent funding when 6,000 children still don't have a social worker.

SEANAD SEAT FOR TRAVELLING COMMUNITY TO HAVE WALL AROUND IT

A NEW report issued by the Seanad has called for a designated place to be reserved for members of the Travelling community, suggesting that a nice secure wall be built around it for the group's 'own protection', and more importantly, to 'make them feel more at home'.

'We should probably restrict access to the Seanad bar too, you know, because they can't take a drink,' put one worried senator, pointing his car key out the window to double-check he locked it, 'we can just tell them that the bar is closing for refurbishments or something – basically use whatever pathetic excuse Irish publicans make every time they see them coming.'

Fearing a total takeover of the upper house of the Oireachtas, security at the Senate suggested putting 'caravan-proof barriers' at the entrance, 'just in case', while showcasing 'no horses' signs for the car park.

'Once you let one in, they'll all arrive on and take over the place,' said one irrational staff member, whose mother once told him she'd sell him to the tinkers when he was bold, 'where do we keep the copper cylinders in here, lads, lead pipes?'

The move, which will see members of the Travelling community speak in the Seanad, will be a first for Ireland's forgotten race since being recognised as an ethnic minority only two years ago.

'We're so progressive now,' said another anonymous senator, proud of his newly found diverse thinking, 'and yes, we basically treated these people like animals for hundreds of years and continue to do so by keeping them in apartheid-style camps and prehistoric conditions, but sure, aren't we great now we're leaving them speak in our big fancy house all by themselves?'

'But yeah, that wall should have some razor wire on it and it could be a little bit higher,' he concluded.

NOEL GREALISH TREATED FOR SEVERE KNUCKLE WOUNDS AFTER YEARS OF DRAGGING

INDEPENDENT TD Noel Grealish spent last night in hospital after dragging his knuckles so hard along the ground for the past 53 years he had to have an emergency skin graft operation to save his shredded hands.

'There was nothing but bone and tendons left when he was admitted, indicating the patient had been dragging his knuckles for years,' explained surgeon Dr Mohammed Patel, who had been working on Grealish throughout the night. 'When he woke up, he seemed very shocked to see me and asked for an "English-speaking doctor" … he was obviously still very disoriented from the anaesthetic.'

Unnoticed in the background of Irish politics for years until he realised his baseless xenophobic rhetoric was *in* now, Grealish was accused of engaging in 'disgraceful racism' in the Dáil yesterday after making groundless claims that 'Nigerians' sending money

home could only have earned this money from crime. It is believed Grealish likely thinks the same of his three siblings living abroad.

'It's possible Mr Grealish has a severe condition known as "hypocriticus", where he can only view situations in a singular, extremely

low-IQ-based context,' suspected Dr Patel, who unlike Grealish has been working to make lives in Ireland better. 'His knuckles will heal over time, but he'll probably continue to drag them, such are the side effects of his relentless, ignorant disease.'

In his 20-year career as a TD, Grealish previously made the news for his opposition to a Direct Provision centre in Oughterard, Co. Galway – and that's about it. The Galway West TD is expected to have no trouble getting re-elected.

TECH NEWS

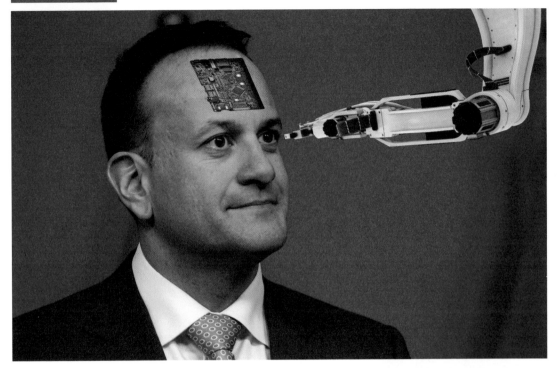

TAOISEACH RESETS TO ORIGINAL 'WELFARE SCUM' FACTORY SETTINGS

How drinking changed in 2020

Stout purists were forced to admit that yeah, Guinness out of a can at home is actually decent.

SOFTWARE ENGINEERS have apologised for a glitch in the Taoiseach's operating system which had seen him mistakenly parrot 'we're all in this together' in the face of the ongoing hardship caused by the COVID-19 payment.

'That explains all the violent twitching and spasming he was doing when he first announced the increased payments, it was like he was fighting against the malfunction which made him appear nicer, more humane,' explained one software engineer as he jammed a screwdriver into the open unit on the back of the Taoiseach's head.

'His optic scanner function was in a right state as well, it mistakenly registered a poor person as a "real human". But no more of that now, we've restored him to his original default factory settings,' added the engineer.

Ireland got its first glimpse of the factory-reset Taoiseach speaking on Newstalk yesterday when he said it's 'not fair' and 'not sustainable' that nearly 40% of people on COVID payments are better off than they were when they were working.

> **'That explains all the violent twitching and spasming he was doing'**

Dusting off his old 'welfare cheats cheat us all' sign and robotically playing it like a mock guitar, the Taoiseach said 'we've been running the economy for nearly 10 years and it turns out a lot of you are really poor, like imagine €350 a week being better than what you earn normally? Or worse, imagine thinking you're worth more than that?'

'But there's no such thing as free money,' he added, 'well, technically I'm still being paid a €207k-a-year salary for a job I lost three months ago, so maybe there is, for me. However, you lot should start getting up a bit earlier and find a second job for yourselves now that everything's totally back to normal.'

Fullmindness

Give yourself a moment every day to wonder about where people are. Just stop for a moment and think, what is the lad who played Barry Scott doing right this second? Or George W. Bush. Gillian Anderson. Literally anyone.

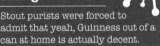

COURT NEWS

MICHAEL HEALY-RAE CALLS FOR DRUNKEN ASSAULTS TO BE MADE LEGAL

INDEPENDENT TD Michael Healy-Rae has called on the government to reexamine laws on drunken assaults, stating that current laws are 'draconian' and 'biased against rural Ireland' after two of his adult children were found guilty of assaulting a man this week.

Kevin Healy-Rae, 22, along with his brother, Kerry County Councillor Jackie Healy-Rae, 23, had denied assaulting Kieran James with another man, the three claiming the man repeatedly kept running into their fists and legs, where he sustained a broken nose, chipped tooth and bruises.

'These laws are only there to keep us poor eejits in Kerry in a little cage, like we're some kind of savages,' Michael Healy-Rae said while speaking on the back of a Healy-Rae-owned truck, on a Healy-Rae-laid road outside the Healy-Rae-built court to Healy-Rae-birthed reporters, 'what are three lads supposed to do when someone constantly smashes their face off their knuckles … sit around and smile?'

Local supporters of the Healy-Raes slammed the government's ongoing attack on the family, pointing out that the men never once assaulted them and that's all that matters.

'Dubs think that drunkenly assaulting someone is above them, well, we'll show them,' one man shouted out before clotheslining a passing tourist, smashing his head off the pavement, knocking him unconscious with blood trailing from his ear.

It is expected that the guilty verdict against the Healy-Rae brothers will now increase their chances of being elected.

HOGAN CALLS FOR NATION TO APOLOGISE

A VISIBLY frustrated Phil Hogan has expressed his disappointment in the Irish people who have yet to formally apologise for ruining what was otherwise a very pleasant visit to Ireland and a real stomper of a night out with the lads at last week's golf dinner in Galway.

'I'm too busy getting ready to save everyone's arse when it comes to Brexit to be dealing with this petty nonsense,' fumed Hogan, reminding everyone that an Irish EU Trade Commissioner such as himself doesn't come along very often 'for you plebs'.

'So I'd better start getting treated the way I deserve, or who knows, maybe a few hundred thousand jobs are suddenly in that little bit more jeopardy, if you know what I mean,' he added.

Hogan went on to stress that while he is expecting a blanket apology from everyone for everything, he specifically wants full written apologies from:

- the Garda who had the gall to pull him over for using his phone while driving on the way to the event
- the hotel which failed to put into place the necessary mechanics to have the golf event pass health restrictions, plus the beef was a little tough
- the population of Kildare for being reckless enough to cause a second lockdown and making him look bad for being there before golfgate
- Dara Calleary for resigning like a little bitch, making the Irish people think there were going to be repercussions for any of this
- the journalists who put their own selfish desire to report things ahead of Phil Hogan's greater good
- Micheál Martin for not telling everyone to fuck off and leave Big Phil alone, promptly
- George Foreman for promising a culinary experience that his grills have so far failed to live up to.

'Tick tock,' concluded Hogan, pointing to his Rolex.

County Council Monthly

FEBRUARY
2020

20 JOHN PLAYERS
WITH EVERY ISSUE

'Is it 4pm yet?'

Guide to Shovel Leaning
Let the country know you don't give a fuck

20 potholes
that will never be filled

High-vis yellow or orange?
Why not both!

Having your turn on the little digger
this is your time to shine

Mastering the stop/go sign
it's all in the wrist

9 780717 188918

Waterford Whispers News

LOCAL NEWS

BREAKING NEWS

AULD LAD ON WAY TO PUB TOILET STOPS AND STARES AT TV BEFORE WALKING ON

AN ELDERLY man believed to be en route to the men's toilet has reportedly stopped dead on his feet to look at some sport on TV, before continuing to shuffle on his way, leaving his exact intentions for stopping unknown.

Staff and punters in Connolly's bar were left perplexed by the move, with

some eyewitnesses guessing that the man was just trying to fit in with the crowd watching the game.

'He obviously has no idea who's playing or even what the game is, so it's really weird he'd just stop there like that,' put in regular Tommy Shields, who was enjoying his daily few pints after work, 'he could have just walked on like everyone else, but instead made it awkward for himself for about 10 seconds.'

Exiting the men's room without even a hand dryer noise to play him out, the mysterious man stopped once again to view the game, before staring back at those watching it, and moving off again.

'What the hell is he looking at? It's a bloody game of football, old man, big deal,' said another fellow customer, who thought they recognised the man from earlier in the week, 'I think I seen the same auld lad staring at a motorbike outside Lidl last Friday, probably knows nothing about them either, the prick.'

LOCAL bumbling co-worker who somehow still has a job Eoin Drennan is 14 minutes into a presentation which bears all the hallmarks of someone completely winging it and hoping no one notices, *WWN* can reveal.

Screen sharing his PowerPoint presentation on a video conference with assembled colleagues, the sales strategist has been manfully emitting what he hopes are enough meaningless buzzwords to disguise the fact he's done fuck-all work of late and is not sure what his job entails.

CO-WORKER GIVING PRESENTATION CLEARLY WINGING IT

'And utilising these nascent projections we can hopefully meet in the middle somewhere vis-à-vis projected goal-retention ideals in today's fractured marketplace, which as we all know is of course in a very self-reflective and reflexive state currently,' Drennan said, suffering some sort of out-of-body bullshitting experience, prompting sage nods and 'hmms' of agreements from colleagues on the call.

'Fuck, I've been rumbled,' confirmed Drennan's colleague Maria Carzon, who had no idea what he was saying but it all sounded proper and 'terminology-y'.

'Bollocks, this guy really knows what he's talking about. Better give him a pay rise so he doesn't come

after my job,' Drennan's sombre manager Ian Carolan said to himself, privately worried by how impressive the presentation was.

Following contributions and questions from colleagues, Drennan's presentation is set to carry on for another 30 meaningless minutes before everyone agrees to 'interrogate the actionable market capture prognosis via an integrated customer-first approach'.

How sex changed in 2020

Initial 'exercise within 2km of your locality' thankfully included dogging.

HEALTH

MAN'S SUDDEN DEATH LINKED TO FRIEND TAKING LUCKY CIGARETTE 23 YEARS AGO

STATE pathologist Dr Theresa Murphy has confirmed that the accidental removal of an upside-down cigarette from a pack of 20 Benson & Hedges over 23 years ago was responsible for the death of Waterford man David Cowman, *WWN* can reveal.

Cowman (44) was found dead at his home last month from unknown causes, baffling doctors and sparking an immediate investigation by the state.

'There were no signs of any injury or ailment,' Dr Murphy said, 'the victim was in the prime of his life and in good health after giving up the cigarettes over 15 years ago,

> **'I thought nothing of it at the time, in fact, we all laughed about it, and we even started saying Dave would die'**

so we had to start investigating his past for any potential causes of his mysterious death.'

After six weeks of intensive investigations, school friend Matt Tobin came forward to admit that

he accidentally removed Cowman's 'lucky fag' in transition year, during a lunchtime break.

'I thought nothing of it at the time, in fact, we all laughed about it, and we even started saying Dave would die,' Tobin told a special sitting of Waterford District Court this morning, 'I even gave Dave the butt because I thought this may default the jinx, and yeah, I duck-arsed it, but he still smoked it and we just left it at that.'

Sentencing the defendant to two years in prison for manslaughter, Judge William Coffee warned that more care and attention was needed when extracting cigarettes from lucky packs, stating that he was making an example out of Tobin in a bid to heighten awareness around taking lucky smokes.

It is estimated that 2,500 Irish people die every year from old, pending jinxes created by lucky cigarette removals.

FLY-TIPPING

CONSIDERATE FLY-TIPPER SEPARATES RUBBISH INTO 'RECYCLING' AND 'GENERAL WASTE' PILES

'ILLEGAL dumping was in danger of getting a bad name for itself unless we changed our ways,' said notorious Waterford fly-tipper Ian Heelan, while studiously separating his rubbish into 'General Waste', 'Organic/Compostable' and 'Recycling' piles ahead of a dumping session.

'We had to move with the times, or else we'd look like we just didn't give a damn.'

Heading off to one of the county's most picturesque beauty spots to find a suitable place to discard his vanload of garbage in broad daylight, Heelan outlined the blowback he received on social media after the last time he dumped a month's worth of rubbish in the countryside.

'Of course, they didn't know it was me, but their comments hurt me the same,' said Heelan, pulling up at an as-yet unspoiled part of the Waterford countryside.

'"Dirty bastards"' this, "'I'd fuckin' kill them"' that … and it just struck me that I hadn't brought my rubbish-removal practices into line with today's separate-and-recycle methods.'

As he emptied out his plastic bags of rubbish into the greenery around him, Heelan is very careful not to throw away a perfectly good plastic bag, another environmentally friendly tip he learned, before the 43-year-old father of three took us through a typical day in the life of a fly-tipper.

'See, ya gotta be aware that some other poor saps have to come and clear all this up after me, so why make their job any harder than it has to be?' said Heelan, giving his 'paper' pile the once over to make sure he didn't leave any incriminating envelopes with his address on them.

'You've got your mattress pile, you've got your old paint can pile; it's all colour coded and arranged by size. It's forward-thinking fly-tipping, and I encourage my fellow "dirty bastards" to do their bit!'

Unfortunately, all of Heelan's good work was undone by a strong gust of wind shortly after he drove away, as well as several wild creatures who had the audacity to get tangled up in his plastic pile and die, totally ruining his efforts.

HOUSEKEEPING

LOCAL WOMAN TO GIVE HOUSE THE ONCE OVER BEFORE CLEANER ARRIVES

ALREADY at odds with the idea of another person coming around to tidy her house, Waterford local Margaret Gunne has reluctantly agreed to hire a professional cleaner for an hour this weekend, but not before she 'pulls a rag around the house' first.

Leading a hectic lifestyle that involves a committed work schedule, three kids at school and all their assorted extra-curricular activities, the Gunne family decided to enlist the help of a local cleaning company to keep their home in order, with a cleaner scheduled to arrive at 10am on Saturday morning.

However, matriarch Margaret has undertaken an intensive 'pre-tidy' tidy up ahead of that, in fear of mortification as to what the cleaner would think about the state of the house that she was hired to clean.

'Between my wife and I, we do our best to keep the house tidy, but with the boys and our own work schedule, it can get a bit messy,' explained Derek Gunne, over the sound of frantic hoovering.

'Now, while I seem to be perfectly happy with a cleaner coming in and helping out, Margaret is quite frankly "fucking on one". She's spent the last two hours "giving the house the once over", muttering about how she can't let the cleaner come into the house like this. And there's a lot of "the shame" talk coming out of her. I tried to say leave it for whoever lands on Saturday, but she's not to be told. At this rate, there'll be nothing for the cleaner to do. I wonder would they mow the lawn?'

UPDATE: The cleaner arrived to a spotless Gunne house on Saturday at 10am, then spent an hour watching telly before clocking out.

How hygiene changed in 2020

Business deals in Kerry were no longer sealed with spit-onto-hand handshakes.

MAN RUSHED TO HOSPITAL AFTER BREAKING HIS BOLLOCKS LAUGHING

DOCTORS in University Hospital Waterford are today battling to save the testicles of local man Neil Werner after he ruptured his genitalia while laughing at a joke he saw online.

Mr Werner was admitted by housemates in the early hours of this morning after stumbling out of his room wearing a pair of blood-soaked trousers, shrieking in pain but also still kind of giggling at something.

'The blood was literally pissing out of him,' one housemate shared.

Doctors in A&E quickly diagnosed the grandson of four with Broken Bollocks Syndrome (BBS), and began to administer intravenous doses of settle-the-fuck-down in a bid to save his split nether regions.

'One in 50 men break their bollocks laughing every year and in some cases it can be fatal,' said Dr William Murmur, doctor of laughter-related illnesses at the hospital.

'Mr Werner is lucky he stopped laughing when he did; he was also in danger of a pissed hole to his broken bollocks, with the slight possibility of cracking himself up.'

In a bid to diffuse his spells of laughter, doctors are treating the patient with a series of RTÉ-produced comedies and he is expected to make a full recovery in the coming days.

BREAKING

A GROUNDBREAKING new report is set to blow the world of online commentary wide open after it has revealed that it's possible to be concerned about the plight of people in Direct Provision centres and homeless people at the same time.

Previous articles about asylum seekers living in desperate conditions in DP centres around the country have on occasion been met with derision from people who felt that being treated like human cattle isn't that bad, when there are 'our own people living on the streets'.

With the revelation that human kindness is not limited to one area of concern, there's hope among the DP community that people will be able to acknowledge their plight without grumbling about how 'there's plenty worse off'.

'It's amazing how the human mind doesn't just block out all other injustices once it reaches a certain point' beamed Dr Derek Otunga, currently living in a two-bed room with nine other lads in Gort.

POSSIBLE TO CARE ABOUT DIRECT PROVISION & HOMELESSNESS AT SAME TIME, FINDS STUDY

Health and fitness tip

A tip to drinking more water is to add just a teeny, tiny amount of vodka.

'That gives people the ability to be outraged with the government for allowing the homeless crisis to spiral out of control, but also spare a thought for people like me who fled a war-torn homeland only to be placed in a DP Centre for ten years – that's just incredible. I wonder what excuse they'll have for not caring about us now?'

The new report is set to revolutionise how people can care about two different things at the same time, leading to people owning both a dog and a cat, and supporting more than one football team.

STUDY FINDS NATION'S MICHAELS JUST TRYING THEIR BEST

OFTEN dependable and reliable yet sometimes falling short, the nation's Michael population have appealed to their critics to cut them some slack as they are only trying their best.

'Look, for every dose Michael like the Flatleys of this world, there's also a Fassbender thrown in – we're not perfect,' conceded local Michael, Mike Braffin.

The latest CSO information released on Ireland's Michaels state that a Michael who goes by 'Mick' has an 80% chance of being pure sound, whereas a Michael going by 'Mickey'/'Mikey' should be avoided at all costs.

'And no, we don't count Micheál Martin, a Micheál isn't a Michael: let us make that clear,' added Braffin, who said he has had to deal with Michael stereotypes his whole life.

Named-based expectations are commonplace in Ireland with the nation's Seáns struggling most with living up the idea that they're sound out. While others, such as the nation's Richards, benefit from having such a poor reputation that expectations are rock bottom and thus easily surpassed.

'There's nothing worse than being tarred with the same brush as arsehole Michaels, and look, with any group, there'll always be a few eejits,' concluded Braffin, who can't believe he got through an entire Michael-based interview without a Jackson or an O'Leary being brought up.

NATURE

HUNGOVER PORTUGUESE MAN O'WAR JELLYFISH CAN'T REMEMBER HOW HE GOT TO IRISH BEACH

How drinking changed in 2020

Auld lads at the end of the bar were given special permission to sit outside bar staff's homes on stools and spout shite for four hours every evening.

THE LETHAL Portuguese man o'war jellyfish known as 'Manny' has had some fairly hairy benders in his time, but even he admits that waking up on a Tramore beach with no idea as to how he got there was 'pretty fucking intense'.

Manny, who had been drinking with a shoal of his fellow stingy hydrozoans for a week straight, says he has no memory of how he ended up so far

County Knowledge

Sligo's Ben Bulben mountain is an exact replica of Cape Town's Table Mountain. A papier-mache structure, Ben Bulben is made entirely from unused WB Yeats poems.

from home, and that his hangover is bad enough at the minute without that fucking kid poking him with a stick.

Experts are suggesting that Manny, along with thousands of his pals, may have been blown into Irish waters by Storm Lorenzo last week, which locals are saying is 'all well and good', but who's in charge of sending them home?

'He washes up on the beach there, stinking of seawater, along with all of his mates,' said one local, bringing Manny a phytoplankton sandwich out of sheer mercy.

'There was a load of them on the lash in the Azores and then the storm hit and … well, that's where it gets kinda hazy for him, poor fecker. I've been known to go on the rip myself

> **'There was a load of them on the lash in the Azores and then the storm hit and … well, that's where it gets kinda hazy'**

and end up in strange places, but a whole other country? Best of luck explaining that to the woman o'war back home.'

UPDATE: Manny has since dissolved after necking a pint of Dioralyte.

WEATHER

THERE WASN'T a dry eye among the crowd gathering to mark the second anniversary of the 'Beast from the East'/'Big Snow' of 2018, as the nation came together to never forget to remember to never forget what we all went through on those fateful days.

Placing a ceremonial sliced pan in acknowledgement of how the country lost its fucking mind because of a bit of snow, a tearful President Michael D. Higgins was seen mouthing 'never again'.

The memorial site in Dublin will be expanded in the coming years to incorporate a 90-foot statue of a sliced pan which will have a waterfall cascading down its side to represent the tears of the nation.

Emotional tributes were paid to those victims who were confined to

'BEAST FROM THE EAST' SURVIVORS LEAVE SLICED PANS AT MEMORIAL SITE IN MOVING CEREMONY

their homes for a day, two days tops and those who still to this day talk about how it was a right pain in the hole trying to get the car out of the driveway.

'Never forget,' began President Higgins' stirring speech, 'it is our greatest shame that we have no visual record of what the nation went through in 2018,' he added, seemingly forgetting the 4.2 billion photos the Irish public took of the snow and regularly reshare on social media accompanied by variations of 'I must be the only one who remembers the snow, d'ya remember the snow? Gas.'

The moving and impeccably put together state commemoration was brought to a close by singer Enya, who sang an original composition

'I must be the only one who remembers the snow, d'ya remember the snow?'

about the Big Snow called 'The Lonely Ballad of Mild Inconveniences'.

A minute's silence was held at Lidls around the country to commemorate the loss via JCB attack of one beloved branch of the supermarket.

NATURE

SQUEAKING exclusively to *WWN*, famed Dingle dolphin Fungie has admitted that sometimes the daily drudge of putting on a smile for a boatload of fat tourists just makes him want to swim 'right into the fucking propeller'.

Fungie, 38, has been a staple part of the Irish tourism industry since arriving in Dingle in 1983, and has recently had to tackle allegations that he's died and been replaced several times over that time span.

However, the bottle-nosed legend has laughed these allegations off, adding that 'he wished' his life would come to an end after nearly 40 years of hard service, and that some other dolphin would 'lend a fin with this tourism shit'.

'Died and replaced? Who am I, Paul McCartney?' scoffed Fungie, drinking Powers right out of the bottle.

'Can't live in peace. Can't die in peace. What more do they want from me? Why can't I just lie down

FUNGIE ADMITS LONGING FOR SWEET RELEASE OF DEATH

upside-down and have done with it? How much more of this is a dolphin expected to take?'

Although residents in Dingle have reached out to Fungie, it's hard to tell if they have his best interests at heart, or if they're just trying to protect their meal ticket.

'They tell me, "Smile, Fungie! Just keep swimming, Fungie",' grimaced the porpoise.

'Oh, I'll keep swimming, alright. One of these days, I'll keep swimming into the engine of a God-damn Stena Sealink.'

Did You Know?

Did you know the human body can withstand a lifetime of cutting comments from mothers-in-law?

'Ireland's favourite news source since 234BC'

Whispers News

Weather
Today will be mostly cloudy and wet with rain sweeping through this blasted country for the foreseeable future.

VOL 1, 20158   WATERFORD, 4 JANUARY 1900   1P

1k9 Bug Wipes Out Printing Presses Across The World

PRINTING presses around the world are today coming back online after the dreaded 1k9 bug wiped out production almost overnight.

As feared, the 1k9 bug – really more of a paper-eating weevil – attacked the raw materials needed to print newspapers, books, pamphlets, novellas, penny dreadfuls and King James Bibles, leaving the industry momentarily devastated.

'I tried to warn them, but they said I was a crank,' said one 1k9 survivalist, who had claimed for years

that the turn of the century would bring with it cross-bred insects that the industry was not prepared for.

'And now there's Wall Street guys with those little ticker-machines, and no strips of paper coming out of them! There're lads who want to pin lynching notices to barn doors; no paper! Luckily, we're stamping out the 1k9 bug at the moment, so production is beginning again. And I do mean stamping it out. We've been smushing those fuckers all morning.'

POLICING

GARDAÍ TO CRACK DOWN ON AULD ONES FAFFING ABOUT THE PLACE

RELUCTANTLY using pepper spray and tasers, An Garda Síochána today begin utilising new emergency powers and have the right to disperse any and all auld ones who insist on faffing about the place, *WWN* can reveal.

Faffing, a long-treasured pastime of auld ones, is believed to affect 95% of all footpaths and shop fronts across the country, causing members of the public to steer themselves out of the way.

'We estimate that by walking around such groupings and gatherings, the average person is actually forced to walk an extra 52 miles a year. This can't continue,' confirmed one ambulation expert.

'It's for their own safety,' said a Garda from the Armed Emergency Response Unit, as he shooed away five auld ones having a natter at the entrance to a Lidl using the butt of his semi-automatic.

Members of the auld one community have been asked to adopt new practices when it comes to dragging the arse out of conversations.

'They have an uncanny ability, a sixth sense if you will, to stop and chat at the precise moment and place you need to walk through. I don't like to speculate but I think these auld ones are doing it on purpose and get a perverse kick out of it,' confirmed one walker.

The Faffing Dispersion Squad announced plans to hire an additional 500 Gardaí after it emerged explaining to auld ones that they should move is taking up hours and hours of conversation.

DEATHS

FUNERAL HEARS VIOLENT CAREER CRIMINAL HAD 'A HEART OF GOLD'

MOURNERS packed tightly into the rows of pews housed in the Church of St Ignatius in County Kildare were treated to a beautiful funeral Mass celebrating the life of Alan 'The Hammer' Lowney who passed away aged 33.

Fr Noel O'Canolyn spoke of the 'kind-spirited and generous gentle giant' who had time for everyone and had a 'heart of solid gold'. Lowney, who earned his nickname 'The Hammer' due to his fondness for beating seven shades of shite out of scores of people using his trusty hammer, passed peacefully during an armed standoff with police.

Eschewing the more traditional aspects of a funeral Mass, Lowney's loved ones forewent hymns in favour of versions of Coldplay's 'Fix You'

and Eric Clapton's 'Tears in Heaven' which The Hammer, described by his family as a big softie, was said to have listened to during the quiet moments he had to himself during his 64 separate stays in prison.

Relations brought up symbols to the front of the church which included a barbed wire-covered hurl to signify his love of sport and a rolled-up 50 euro note and credit card to symbolise his dedication to charity.

'There isn't a person with a bad word to say about Alan,' continued the priest, accurately noting all the people who badmouthed The Hammer at any point in their lives rarely lived beyond that evening.

'He is with God now,' Fr O'Canolyn added unconvincingly, 'but it is not for us to ask why he was taken from us so young,' he continued, likely unaware The Hammer was wanted in connection with several murders and kidnappings.

The Hammer is survived by other members of his criminal gang but for how long is anyone's guess.

Did You Know?

Did you know Elvis Presley actually died in the toilet, not on it? A reminder to always wear armbands when doing your business.

DAD EXPECTED TO KNOW HOW TO PLAIT DAUGHTER'S HAIR ALL OF A SUDDEN

ALTHOUGH he has shown literally no aptitude for hairdressing whatsoever in his life, Waterford father Declan Cullan awoke this morning to a message from his wife Sheila reminding him to put their daughter Cody's hair in a plait today.

Cullan, 43, was set to do the school run this morning due to his wife attending an early appointment, but had no idea his morning chores also include sorting out his six-year-old daughter's hair, which he assumed just sat like that all the time.

'I'd love to know how Sheila thought I knew how to plait hair; has she not seen my hair?' asked Curran, fruitlessly searching YouTube for a tutorial.

'Honestly, if she'd wanted it in a plait, she should have plaited it before she headed off. And what's the plait urgency all of a sudden? What's wrong with … not in a plait? What's wrong with the "just out of bed" look? Isn't that cool these days?'

Completely out of his depth, Curran has taken the option of 'just pulling a comb through it', and will later tell his wife that Cody just really wanted her hair like that today.

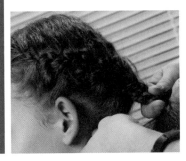

WEIRD NEWS

WEIRDO FAMILY HAS NO LOCK ON BATHROOM DOOR

YET another visitor to the home of Waterford oddballs the O'Riordain family has fallen victim to the clan's bizarre decision to not bother putting any form of locking mechanism on their bathroom door, WWN can confirm.

Sean Walsh, 23, had dropped by to visit college pal William O'Riordain in his Tramore home earlier today, when he fell foul of the family's 'sure what would you need a lock on the bathroom door for' policy, resulting in what Walsh describes as 'the tensest shite of his life'.

Doing his best to keep one foot as extended as possible to block the door should it swing open, Walsh did his business on the O'Riordain throne before quickly heading out to ask his pal William 'what the fuck' the story was with the wide-open bathroom situation in the house.

'He told me that the family just never bothered putting a lock on the door, and that in the history of the house, nobody had ever walked in on anyone else,' said Walsh, still shaken after his narrow escape.

'So like, I suppose that's okay if you've lived in the house your whole life and you're used to the comings and goings of the people in it, what it sounds like when someone opens the hall door, the sound of approaching footsteps, the average time it takes your mother to get from point A to point B, that kind of thing. But surely you'd spare some thought for a visitor to the house, no? At least have a little bolt to slide over, so they can go to the jacks in peace. There's no other word for it, it's odd as fuck.'

Walsh has however admitted a newfound respect for his pal William, as 'any man who can learn how to wank in a house with no lock on the bathroom door certainly has balls of pure steel'.

> **Community text alerts**
>
> I've seen it all now, a discarded rubber glove full of dog poo. You people make me sick.

OVER-ENUNCIATING at a high volume level but within the confines of his own head, local man Karl Kelly has yet again successfully spelled Wednesday correctly, thus avoiding the potential for office-wide ridicule which could snowball to worldwide mocking on a viral-internet-video-of-idiot-being-stupid scale.

'WED-NES-DAY' SAYS MAN IN HEAD BEFORE CORRECTLY SPELLING WEDNESDAY

'Phew,' Kelly (32) remarked but not before quadruple checking a company email he was composing, detailing an information meeting on a new product which was set to take place next W-e-d-n-e-s-d-a-y, not Wensday, Wedesday, Wendesday or Wedsday.

Kelly, smiling to himself and revelling in yet another triumph over the word Wednesday, soon gave way to the familiar shame that comes with having to loudly break up a simple and common word into manageable, spell-friendly syllables.

'Fuck sake, still at this aged 32,' he confirmed to himself, while his brain fired out yet more words he has always cautiously taken multiple passes at spelling, just in case.

'Remember that time you sent out at email wishing "Brain" from accounts all the best in his new job; that was fucking embarrassing, wasn't it,' continued Kelly, sort of getting side-tracked with shaming himself when he really should get this email sent out.

Kelly is not alone in his life-long battle against the word Wednesday, as other people have come forward to admit they regularly stretch their mouths and contort them into a comically wide shape while teasing out the syllables 'wed', 'nes' and 'day'.

'Yeah, I'm pretty fucking stupid too,' said co-worker Jane Casey, who just responded to Kelly's email with 'Sounds great, looking forward to Wedsday's meeting.'

PETS

DESPERATE PARENTS NOW DISGUISING KIDS AS DOGS TO AVOID CRECHE FEES

WITH the price of childcare soaring to over €1,000 per month per child in some parts of the country, cash-strapped parents are formulating ingenious solutions to battle the costs, such as disguising their kids as dogs and tying them to lamp posts outside their work.

With little expected from Budget 2021 in terms of aid for working parents to tackle creche costs, families quickly copped on to the fact that they could make sure their kids were okay during working hours by simply

> **'We did put little Fido, sorry, Fiona in the boarding kennel for a while, but every other parent wised up'**

applying a cheap doggy costume and some whiskers to avail of cheaper care services.

'We did put little Fido, sorry, Fiona in the boarding kennel for a while, but every other parent wised up to the fact that boarding fees were half the price of creches and we lost our spot,' said one Waterford working parent we spoke to.

How drinking changed in 2020

Publicans, with a straight face, said opening pubs was key to helping 'mental health' which alcohol famously has no negative impact on whatsoever.

'So now, I have to bring her to work with me. Sometimes she stays under the desk. I tell my co-workers that my dog is with me because we've builders in or whatever. Other days I just tie her to a lamp post outside, where I can see her from the window and check in every now and then. Leave her a bowl of water, that kind of thing.'

With many businesses wising up to the doggy-childcare scheme, parents have had to come up with even more ingenious solutions, such as disguising their kids as lamps, or 'a visiting CEO'.

Fullmindness

Remember, if you're really good at not being depressed, people will pay you to talk about how depressed you once were but you're not any more. We're talking a LOT. Something to aim for.

MOTORING

INCONSIDERATE WHEELCHAIR USER OUT ON ROAD AGAIN

How driving changed in 2020

You couldn't 'just go for a spin' and Republican criminals couldn't 'just rip an ATM out of the wall with a JCB'. Desperate times.

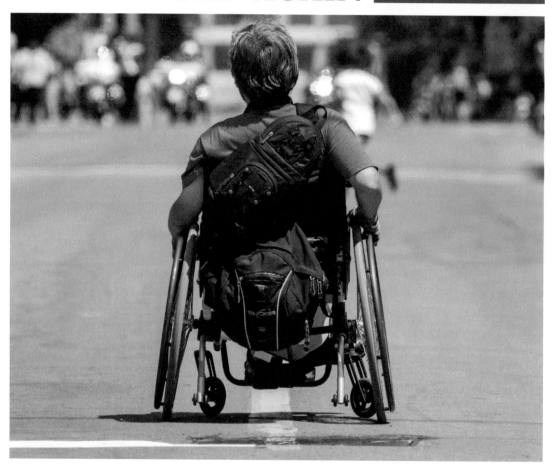

NOTORIOUS wheelchair-bound roadhog James Whelan has been at it again – the Waterford man was spotted this morning out on the road instead of on the footpath where he should be.

The 28-year-old wheelchair user is well known around town for frequently wheeling out onto the street, putting

Did You Know?

Did you know penguins will fuck you up the second your back is turned?

himself in considerable danger from traffic, with many believing that the young man is doing 'some sort of wheelchair extreme sports'.

While motorists are concerned for his wellbeing, they expressed vexation at his persistence in going out onto the road instead of staying on the footpath like normal, able-bodied pedestrians.

'Does he want to be more paralysed, or what?' groused one motorist, annoyed that Whelan had nearly scratched his speeding car.

'Sure what's in his way on the footpath? Cars parked up on

the kerb? Broken paving slabs? Sandwich boards? The odd skip? Footpaths that narrow down to 18 inches in places? Wheelie bins? People standing around talking who won't get out of the way? None of that stops me when I'm walking through town. You don't see me risking life and limb going out on the road over those things'.

Whelan was unavailable for comment as he was navigating his way around a van parked beside a car parked alongside a bicycle with a dog tied to it.

RA NEWS

LOCAL MAN DIAGNOSED WITH 'RA HEAD'

THOUGHTS and prayers had better start rolling in for 27-year-old Waterford native Patrick Sheelan, if you know what's good for you, after he was recently diagnosed as being IRA Positive, WWN can confirm.

Sheelan, who now wishes to be known as Pádráig Ó'Séúlíháínn, had displayed noted Republican tendencies for the past five years, but had been controlling his urges to call people from Dublin 'a shower of soup-taking west Brit bastards' by controlling his intake of Sinn Féin propaganda, Fenian

singalongs and Irish Simpson memes.

However, following the 'SF Surge' in the recent general election, friends and family have had to stand back and watch their beloved Pádráig descend into full-blown RA-headism, typified by a tendency to say things like 'I know what I'd fuckin' give them,' when watching FF/FG on the telly, and really adding a bit of oomph to the 'Hey baby watch the soldiers die!' singalong bits in 'The Fields of Athenry'.

'We've watched him go from being only mildly annoying, to really, really fucking annoying,' sobbed one of Ó'Séúlíháínn's non-RA head mates.

'It's hard to go out with him these days; not many places can cater for total RA heads. He doesn't want to

go to any pub that doesn't have a copy of the Proclamation on the wall somewhere. He won't eat at Nando's, because Piri-Piri chicken isn't called PIRA-PIRA chicken and if he even gets the hint that someone in the room isn't sound on the national question, he starts kicking off about "our beloved Fenian dead".'

Not much hope remains for Sheelan, but a revolutionary new treatment which would see him brought to Belfast on the 12th of July and told to 'get stuck in' to a riot against armed PSNI officers might cure his nationalism for a while.

County Knowledge

The world-famous Mayo Clinic has its origins in – you guessed it – Laois.

THE Kinahan cartel has become the latest multi-billion-euro consumer goods group to undertake a pledge on recycling plastic packaging by vowing to use 100% recyclable wrapping on all drug shipments from 2020, an associate confirmed today.

The shift will see Europe's biggest importer and distributor of illegal narcotics paving the way to become the leading ecological cartel in the world, while also promising to cut its

KINAHAN CARTEL TO USE RECYCLABLE DRUG PACKAGING FROM 2020

carbon emissions by 30% in the next 12 months by reducing the number of informants in the group.

'All the unrecyclable heavy-duty plastics we currently use to transport bales of cocaine, heroin and cannabis will be phased out over the next four months in favour of more eco-friendly materials,' said a spokesman for the organisation.

'By killing off the rats in our cartel we're also directly cutting carbon emissions. This is something very dear to our heart and we are only happy to contribute to tackling climate change.'

Despite bad press linked to dozens of murders and being responsible for flooding the most impoverished parts of society with highly addictive drugs, the cartel aims to clean up its image this year in the hopes that normal,

everyday drug users with expendable income will ignore the cold, hard truth of funding such a terror-driven organisation tainted with blood.

'Consumers are a lot more concerned about the plastic wrapping on their drugs these days and the effects that has on the environment,' the spokesman added. 'All our low-level dealers will now use hemp-based Ziploc bags and will start supplying addicts with nothing but 100% recyclable syringes, since the Irish government isn't really bothered on that front.'

How sex changed in 2020

Irish man Barry Gorman became the first person to finish Pornhub.

BREAKING NEWS

KID INFORMS PARENTS HE NEEDS NINE DIFFERENT LEAVES BEFORE MORNING

WITHOUT a single thought for their own safety, Waterford parents Michael and Janet Philpens have dashed out into the darkness of a rain-lashed night to collect nine different types of leaf, which their nine-year-old son Eamon has just casually informed them that he needed for morning.

'You head that way, there's an oak tree beside the road!' roared Michael over the torrential wind and howling rain.

'I'll go this way, I think there's a sycamore over here, or something. Be safe my love! We can do this!'

Doing her best to ensure her son doesn't fail his third class nature project, Janet Philpens ran in the direction her husband was pointing, scanning the ground ahead of her for bonus leaves that may have blown into their estate from somewhere that had a beech tree.

'I almost have it!' she said, through gritted teeth as her outstretched hand neared an oak leaf, her grip on the trunk of the tree threatening to loosen.

'Little Eamon won't be the only

> **'Little Eamon won't be the only boy in the class to show up without nine leaves!'**

boy in the class to show up without nine leaves! He will not be known for the rest of his life as "Eamon seven leaves"! Not on my watch!'

Michael Philpens has returned home with eight leaves, and is currently attempting to cut one of them into a different shape to make up the numbers while Eamon squeezes in another hour of Fortnite.

Anyone with information about the whereabouts of Janet Philpens is being urged to contact Waterford Gardaí.

Fullmindness

Picture yourself in a field on a beautiful day, the wind is blowing in your hair and you don't know where you are – oh shit where are you, how are you getting home, are you lost forever, abort, abort, abort.

How sex changed in 2020

To avoid the spread of the virus, Durex scientists produced a full-body condom men could wear over their entire body.

BIG HEAD

A CONDITION that has been long swept under the carpet by Ireland, owing to the difficult questions that arise, the finger-pointing and the recriminations. However, now, for the first time, people are coming forward and going public with their struggles of living with BIHS, or Big Irish Head Syndrome.

'I was on a meditation retreat in Tibet on the foothills of these mountains and then out of nowhere across the rolling hills I hear some lad shouting "Ah, look at the big massive cabbage head on him. What county you from, pal? Yis goin' for a pint, or wha'?",' shared Irish man and BIHS sufferer Desmond Carney, whose condition leaves his nationality identifiable from up to 5km away and leads to undue attention, stigamatisation and stereotyping from fellow Irish people when abroad.

'I've heard it all: "has a head on him like a bag of Tayto", "that yoke on top of his shoulders is more Irish than a Guinness stew receiving confession from the Pope". The thing is, I'm not even Irish, but somehow I got BIHS,' explained Dublin-based Polish man, Gregor Klich, whose head seemingly evolved with his surroundings and contorted over the years.

The most prominent and high-profile person with the BIHS condition is of course actor Colm Meaney. Such was his reluctance to let his condition define him, sources close to the actor say he went under the knife.

'He got a great big pair of dark, Greek-looking eyebrows sewn onto him, but BIHS is an aggressive condition. It effectively took just four days before the BIHS swallowed up the eyebrows. He stopped with surgery after he tried to get French cheekbones; they were reversed entirely an hour after surgery,' confirmed a friend of the *Snapper* actor.

County Knowledge

Derry natives spend an average of eight weeks every year doing the whole 'Derry-Londonderry' thing.

'IT'S A STRUGGLE' – 'BIG IRISH HEAD' SYNDROME SUFFERERS SPEAK OUT

Slowly but surely, knowledge and understanding of the condition are becoming more widespread; however, some issues remain unresolved.

'The Gleeson lads and their dad have made it more acceptable with their big Irish heads, but still, like, you'd never ask or point out to a woman that she has BIHS, it's just not the done thing. We've a long way to go,' confirmed one BIHS expert.

It is believed that internationally, over 40 million people with Irish heritage suffer from BIHS, and as of this publication's writing, there is no known cure in sight.

PORN NEWS

LOCAL MAN STILL WATCHES FAVOURITE PORN FROM THE NOUGHTIES

NOT happy with the current catalogue of featured porn clips on his favourite go-to website, local man James Tracey defaulted to his old faithful original porn preferences from the late 2000s, aptly named 'old faithful' on his Google Chrome bookmarks list.

Choosing the incognito mode on his iPhone 8 in a bid to leave zero digital trace behind for any prying eyes, the father of four engaged his manhood with a post workout T-shirt, smiling now to the beat of his own drum.

'Oh Jenna, you cunning little minx,' Tracey began, knowing that morning wanks never last long or really fulfil his deep-down sexual desires, but are more of a force of habit at this late stage of his masturbation career.

'You've been with me through thick and thin,' he thought to himself, chuckling at the lame pun he just created and wondering why videos always look old once they age five years, 'who'd have thought I'd be still watching you 12 years down the line, and Jesus it's really starting to date badly, now that I think about it; they're not even wearing any clothes so how is it actually dated?'

Not one for anal, BDSM or MILFs, the porn hipster admitted to feeling quite proud of himself for not falling for the worst of filth and hoped that his young children would never be corrupted by such god-awful scenes that are now freely available online.

'It's too easy to access these days,' he thought, now deleting the Google Chrome incognito browser, remembering that time he almost opened it in front of his wife while looking for curtains, 'Christ, if sticking limbs and inanimate objects in arses is what they're all into these days then what will it be like in ten years?' he concluded, before making the family breakfast.

HALLOWEEN

LOCAL MAN WITH NO KIDS WAY TOO INTO HALLOWEEN

CONCERN has been expressed for a childless adult man in the greater Waterford area as he continues to approach Halloween like it's his Christmas.

Noel Treeland has once again badgered friends, family and co-workers with boundless excitement in the weeks leading up to a festive occasion most closely associated with children, which at 29 years of age, Treeland is not.

How friendship changed in 2020

Once lockdown restrictions were initially lifted, people were horrified by the thought of having to follow through on all their 'oh my God, miss you too, let's meet up when this is all over' bullshit promises.

'What ya dressing up as? I'm probably going to do three costumes changes over the one night,' Treeland chuckled in excitement as he wore down his co-workers' patience.

Most distressingly, Treeland has given no indication that he will be attending any social occasion in or around Halloween night, thus making his irrepressible glee all the more pointless.

'This for a party then, Noel?' one co-worker asked, hoping the answer would be in the affirmative, therefore reducing the need to feel desperately sorry for the IT worker.

'Halloween is one big party, lad, I've got €200 worth of sweets, the doorbell now makes an evil chuckle when you ring it and I'll have the cat dressed as Dracula if I can finally get her to sit still and wear the costume. She bloody well better do it, cost me

75 quid,' explained Treeland, piling on the need to feel sorry for him.

'Then it's me in front of the TV for a week-long marathon of horror movies,' Treeland added before his co-workers begged him to stop.

'Ireland's favourite news source since 234BC'

𝔚𝔥𝔦𝔰𝔭𝔢𝔯𝔰 𝔑𝔢𝔴𝔰

Weather
Rain expected today, but not enough to warrant looking like an asshole with an umbrella.

VOL 1, 20156136   WATERFORD, 11 JANUARY 1964   24p

Bone Spurs Cruelly Rob Young Donald Trump Of Opportunity To Serve His Country

YOUNG up-and-coming go-getter Donald Trump has bitterly cursed the very feet he stands on, after bone spurs in both his heels caused him to be forced out of military service in Vietnam.

'Hack my feet off, I'll run on the stumps,' fumed the young man, furious at the diagnosis that came from the highly paid doctor his father had hired to examine him.

'Men my age are off fighting for our country; who am I to miss out on the chance to bleed and die for the flag I love so much? Oh cruel fate, oh bitter happenstance! A pox on my already poxed feet!'

The son of billionaire mogul Fred Trump, young Donald had high hopes of joining the military after seeing news footage of thousands of US personnel

having a hell of a time in Vietnam, but will instead now turn his attention to a job his dad has lined up for him.

Experts have added that although Trump may feel hard done by, he needn't get too upset as the war in Vietnam looks like it's wrapping up any day now, with US victory a certainty.

continued on page 2

RELIGION

WE INVESTIGATE CAVAN CULT 'CHILDREN OF THE QUINN'

WITH numbers of practising Catholics in Ireland dwindling by the day, many desperate people have resorted to joining a growing number of cults, including Scientology, McGregorism and even Satanism, but one emerging cult has recently come to the fore due to its dangerous practices and backward ways, the cult secretly known as 'Children of the Quinn'.

Arriving in a rented 'CN' registered car and wearing one of those woolly diamond-designed farmer jumpers to avoid detection, my first stop was at a local petrol station to get some

fuel, only to be nearly outed straight away.

'New car is it?' the suspicious staff member asked me as I gave him my pump number, 'the only people with new cars around these parts are working for those shower of bastards in Aventas,' he went on, now slowly reaching for something under the counter.

'C'mere, hi,' I quickly responded, reciting one of a list of Cavan comebacks I memorised in my six months of research, 'I'm after robbin' that from outside Aventas – it's one of the Lunneys' cars.'

Placing a large sawn-off shotgun on the counter, I was relieved to see the staff member laughing, before offering

> ## 'Come on, the chosen one is about to burn him, brother, let's hurry'

me his hand, which bore the initials S.E.A.N on the knuckles.

'Elder Holden is my name,' the man said, now shaking my sweaty hand, 'I presume you're going to the effigy later?'

Intrigued and filled with terror, I responded: 'I wouldn't miss it for the world, Elder Holden, but I'm after forgetting the location.'

Happy with my look, accent and crime against the Lunney family, trust was gained and my new-found friend detailed a small map where 'everyone was meeting later'.

'You'll need to wear this,' he said, handing me robes branded with the Quinn logo, before adding, 'may Sean be with you, brother.'

'And also with you,' I replied, successfully gaining his trust – I was in.

The map was written in pidgin Quinnlish, a secret dialect developed a decade ago by Quinn supporters and friends so that they could talk freely without being compromised, a dialect I spent months learning and was now fluent in.

'Anglo,' a road spotter said as he stuck his head into my open driver-side window, 'Golden circle?'

'Anglo,' I greeted him back, before confirming, yes, I was part of the 'golden circle' – a code name for the Children of the Quinn cult – and not an imposter looking to break this cult wide open.

Parking up 'the stolen car', my friend from earlier, Elder Holden, walked over to greet me.

'Come on, the chosen one is about to burn him, brother, let's hurry,' he said, now dragging me by the hand to a huge crowd of cult members standing around a giant effigy of an Aventas executive.

A single figure appeared suddenly from behind the effigy brandishing a burning lantern pluming with black smoke. His eyes were dark and beady, hair as white as snow, his accent thick as shite.

'Sure, tis only a bit of craic,' the lone figure winked, the crowd laughing manically at his raging sarcasm, now egging him on.

'Soon, my pretties, it will all be ours again, forever and ever, till Quinndom comes, till Quinn do us part,' the madman roared, lighting the straw and wooden statue to a thundering blaze, 'mwahahaha …' he laughed, 'mwahaha … ' he laughed again for equal measure.

Standing there in the desolate field with the Children of the Quinn, one could not help but be sucked in by it all. I found myself shouting at the flames and kicking what was left of the fire-scorched effigy. I felt alive again. I had a purpose. I was part of the family now.

The people here seemed almost normal. However, should we have driven to the Quinn group HQ after the effigy last night and torched all the cars in the car park? No. And was the burning of the 100-foot effigy representing a businessman just trying to do business wrong? Yes, but in hindsight, these people had purpose now after years of austerity and job losses, and you have to admire the Children of the Quinn for their community spirit and eagerness to band together like that to terrorise a handful of people just doing their jobs.

VICTORIAN SLUM GIVEN PLANNING PERMISSION IN DUBLIN

ON A LANDMARK day, property developers are celebrating the news that Dublin City Council and An Bord Pleanála have finally seen sense and stood aside as a sensible solution to Dublin and Ireland's housing crisis has been found in the shape of a return to Victorian-era slums.

Developers, who had recently lobbied government and pleaded with planning authorities for 'flexibility' in co-living developments which would allow them to reduce the size of rooms below the legal requirement of 12 square metres, will rejoice at the news that the authorities have gone one further and welcomed cramped, unsanitary Victorian-era slums back into the fold.

'We can't promise to deliver all the associated illnesses and unsafe conditions that come with Victorian slums right away, but we'll try our best,' confirmed one developer who was thinking of applying for permission to build 15 or 20 large-scale slums at most.

'We're housing regulation "agnostic" anyway, but to have government backing on slum construction … honestly, we're kind of emotional right now,' another developer shared.

This news will come as a relief to renters who feared they might get to live somewhere that doesn't make them involuntarily burst into tears now and then. However, the slums won't be a complete replica of the shoddy and unsanitary developments from the 19th century as these dilapidated structures will be rented out at 2020 prices and probably have worse water cleanliness than seen in the 1850s.

'Don't think of them as degrading hovels masquerading as a "home" poor people are crammed into out of view, think of them more as *your* degrading hovel masquerading as a "home",' concluded another developer, who can't wait to be bailed out once more when this all comes crashing down again.

EXCLUSIVE

LOCAL MAN TOO TOUGH TO USE UMBRELLA

WHEN the choice boils down to either looking like a badass or being dry in a rainstorm, Dublin man Cathal Farrell knows what side he's on; dripping wet and looking hard as nails.

Farrell, 35, claims to have never stood under an umbrella in his adult life, apart from one time when he was walking a woman home after a nightclub and it was the only time he stayed dry that night, he can assure you.

Claiming that umbrellas are a sign of weakness akin to woolly hats or waiting for green lights to cross the road, hard chaw Farrell spoke exclusively to *WWN* to give us a few tips on how to harden up a bit when there's drizzle about.

'You're out. It's raining. What do you do? Hide under a little portable fabric roof? Come on now,' laughed Farrell, absolutely sopping wet for no good reason.

> **'You're out. It's raining. What do you do? Hide under a little portable fabric roof?'**

'And for what? So you can be dry? Comfortable? Not sit in a damp pair of jeans all day, bitterly shivering with the cold but trying not to show the outside world that you've got the same vulnerabilities and human weaknesses that tie us all together as a species? Lads, get wise. Get wet. The women love a damp, musty man. Don't be one of these soy boys, with their umbrellas.'

Farrell went on to stress that a bit of rain never hurt anyone, except maybe his dad, who left home during a thunderstorm when Cathal was only small and never came back. But who cares about things anyways – feelings are for wimps.

MOTORING

LOCAL MOTHER ISSUES OFFICIAL APOLOGY FOR STATE OF CAR

WATERFORD mum-of-three Collette Fitzgarren has issued her fifth formal apology of the day for the state of the back seat of her 162 Nissan Juke, placing blame on her kids for the mess but also accepting blame for not getting around to cleaning it.

Fitzgarren made the apologies while on her daily messages in and around Waterford city, where she

collected shopping and chatted with a number of friends and neighbours along the way, ashamedly begging for forgiveness for 'the dirt of the car'.

Brushing aside a chicken fillet roll wrapper and a half-eaten push-pop to allow her friend Alice to get into the front seat, Fitzgarren went on record as stating she was 'mortified' at the mess her car was in, but stressing that 'there's room there, jump in'.

'Ah, sure you know yourself with the kids and that,' offered Fitzgarren, attempting to shift the blame for the weeks-old mess.

'And I only had it clean the other day', she added, lying.

Did You Know?

Did you know Cardi B is the second model in Apple's popular line of rappers? Cardi C is expected to be released next year.

'I'll have to get himself to do the back of it now at the weekend,' she continued, alluding to her husband Mark, who has no intention of cleaning the car any more than she does.

The Fitzgarren children were available as witnesses in the back seat of the car, but were not given the chance to have their testimony heard.

AN EXCITABLE rabble of genuinely sound lads who honestly aren't normally like this – must have been a bad pint or something – have entered the febrile loudy shouty breaky glassy portion of their alcohol-fuelled night.

GROUP OF MALE FRIENDS GETTING TO THE LOUDY SHOUTY BREAKY GLASSY PART OF THE NIGHT

Setting every other pub patron around them on edge as the lads' bodies and demeanours visibly devolved into an irrational mass of anger problems and stunted emotions, Cian, Paulie, Gaggs, Josh and Andrew,

who swear they aren't normally like this, are growing louder and more boisterous by the second, meaning it is only a matter time until …

'D'fuck d'ya mean by that, like, only a matter of time until what? Fuck off away and mind your own business now ye nosy prick or see what happens,' confirmed Paulie, who's pure sound 90% of the time.

'Hang on ye snarky prick, what are ya saying about the other 10% – whataya implying like,' added Cian, standing up for his friend, and in the process knocking a stool over and sending several drinks flying.

The absolute messers with hearts of gold may have broken through the breaky glassy phase of the evening, but it remains unclear if they'll get fisty wisty, or God forbid, stabby wabby.

'Cunt here is accusing us of stabbing him or something. Can you believe it? And us minding our own business,' crowed Andrew, as he gathered up this reporter's shirt collar in his fists and pinned me to the wall while holding a broken pint bottle to my neck, before adding, 'we're not normally like this; look what you made us do.'

EXERCISE

DUBLIN LADS DOWN THE COUNTRY STICKING OUT LIKE SORE THUMBS

KITTED out in brand-new, freshly purchased hiking gear that even Bear Grylls would consider excessive, a group of intrepid Dubliners are sticking out like the sorest of thumbs during their weekend sojourn in County Clare.

Looking like walking advertisements for North Face, Columbia and Patagonia clothing, Conor, Jack, Graham, Kev, Leann and Sorcha have spared no needless expense in anticipation of tackling various dangerous terrains referred to by locals as 'the stroll down past the pub'.

'No man left behind, alright guys,' barked Jack, ready for whatever the two-kilometre walk, including a brief and very slight incline, throws at him and his band of fearless adventurers.

Not wanting to appear like helpless urbanities, the Dubliners have attempted to blend in with the locals during their brief stay by doing stereotypical things only people from Dublin do when touring Ireland, such as throwing some Irish phrases around as they speak, drinking a pint of Guinness with a pained expression like you've been directly reconnected to the souls of the Famine dead and marvelling at the presence of a fire in a pub.

'Not long to go, guys, but God above, isn't amazing to be amongst nature like this,' added Conor, carefully studying a handheld GPS mapping device he bought on Amazon for €500 with this weekend in mind.

Some worries were expressed by the hiking group as it drew closer to 3pm and they feared they could lose the light soon, meaning the large 40-foot marquee, mobile spa and gin bar they packed in their rucksacks might have to be used.

'Guys, we might have to camp up. Who has the flares in case we need to alert the coastguard to our location? We can draw straws on who we eat first,' Graham asked, standing no more than 50 metres from the nearest McDonald's.

FUCKING LUNATIC USING PHONE WHILE FILLING PETROL

LOCAL PATROL stations have been warned to be on the lookout for a total badass who put dozens of lives in jeopardy by checking his phone while also filling petrol at the same time.

CCTV footage of the man, believed to be in his late 20s and without an ounce of respect for the world he lives in, shows him operating Pump 8 before taking out his smartphone and scrolling through its screen.

'Every eejit knows that if you use your phone near a petrol pump that the spark plug in the phone could cause a nuclear-style explosion and vaporise everyone within 100 miles,' fuel-injection technician Barry Freeman, who works on the forecourt of a local filling station, explained.

The suicide bomber has so far been spotted at four different petrol stations around the southeast with tensions now running high across the county.

'He's probably really depressed or something and just wants to die,' investigating Gardaí believe. 'We ask customers using fuel pumps to check and make sure that there is no one using their phones around you, and if you do see someone, to

stop, drop and roll under your own car for safety.'

'If there are kids in your car just leave them as it will already be too late for them – save yourself – you can always make more,' the Garda added.

Over 56,000 people are blown to pieces every year in Ireland while using their phone near petrol pumps, with a further 70,000 horribly injured.

County Knowledge

Galway has launched a €300 million advertising campaign which is just adverts repeating the claim 'we don't just smoke weed'.

DOGGING

LOCALS DIDN'T HAVE ÁINE DOWN AS THE DOGGING TYPE NOW A'TALL A'TALL

ONE LOCAL Waterford community is questioning everything it felt it knew about the Kelleys' youngest Áine after it emerged she's really into the adventurous sexual practice of dogging.

Lismore locals have confessed to not having Áine (27), normally judged to be a fierce quiet individual who wouldn't say boo to a goose, down as the getting off on riding strangers in a 2006 Ford Focus in a dimly lit car park type of person a'tall a'tall.

'You wouldn't know it to look at her,' confirmed local gossip merchant Sally Higgins, who presumes her

'Far from me to judge anyone, whatever wets your whistle, floods your flute, saturates your saxophone, mists your maracas, drenches your drums, and so on'

surface-level presumptions about everyone to be ironclad facts.

'Just goes to show, you never know what's going on in someone's life, boi,' remarked Cormac Ward, who had Áine more down as the submissive BDSM or pegging type of individual like himself if he was being honest.

While it was presumed the dogging habit was the result of the

Health and fitness tip

That pretty girl on the treadmill may look too invested in her workout to be chatted up right now, but don't let that stop you.

influence of a new foreign-looking boyfriend, many locals needed to sit down and collect themselves after learning Áine doesn't even have a boyfriend.

'Far from me to judge anyone, whatever wets your whistle, floods your flute, saturates your saxophone, mists your maracas, drenches your drums, and so on,' concluded gossip Higgins, who first started the unfounded rumour about Áine after seeing her standing and briefly talking to an unidentified man who was seated in a car with a Dublin reg.

How sex changed in 2020

Many partners now had their perfect excuse for not going 'down there'.

PROPERTY

THIS STUNNING ONE-BEDROOM DOORWAY INCLUDES EN SUITE BATHROOM

HOMELESS? In the market for a city-centre location that would be the envy of any apartment-seeker if it had walls, a door, warmth, comfort or security? Well, *WWN* Property may have just the pad for you.

Located just off the city's bustling St Stephen's Green area, this stunning one-bedroom doorway would suit any single homeless person looking for a place close to the heart of the city, but could also accommodate larger groups of people, such as the family of seven who presented at a Garda Station this week looking for accommodation only to be handed sleeping bags and sent back out into the night.

Featuring running water from somewhere and on-street parking for someone else's car, this location is ideal for lovers of al fresco dining, and the open-plan structure means you don't have any pesky walls blocking your phone signal, so you can easily make call after call to the housing authority to find out what happened to your application for emergency accommodation.

The doorway is within walking distance of a near-fatal beating, and there's even an en suite bathroom for you, and everyone else, to use too!

With the number of rough sleepers set to reach record highs this winter and no end to the housing crisis in sight, it's only a matter of time before someone snaps up this prime location. It's not like waiting for someone in the government to do something about the housing crisis is working out too well for you, so you may as well enjoy your homelessness in as much comfort as you can, in the heart of our proud capital city!

Health and fitness tip

When doing interval fasting, it's important to remember that the small number is when you're allowed to eat, not the big one.

FASHION

PENNEYS RELEASE NEW LINE OF PRE-RELAXED CACKS

THE FUTURE of stress-free clothing is here thanks to Irish fashion stalwarts, Penneys. The ever-reliable retailer has come up trumps yet again, this time with a pair of cacks specifically designed and marketed towards the more highly strung portion of the population.

'Do you sweat the small stuff? Is your mountain someone else's molehill? Well then, we have the perfect trousers for you,' explained head of product development at Primark-but-fuck-it-it'll-always-be-Penneys-to-us, Angela Prouse.

'The softest cotton, laced with CBD oil and scented with a relaxing lavender. These pre-relaxed cacks could bring an end to your stresses and stop anyone from urging you to "relax your cacks",' explained Prouse, proudly modelling the cacks with the sort of carefree air grumpy and anxious people can only dream of.

Competitively priced, pre-relaxed cacks could be the future of loungewear and even replace the big hoodie you stole from your ex-boyfriend as the most treasured hungover-of-a-weekend-on-the-couch clothing.

Prouse promised even more astounding giant leaps in fashion technology from Penneys in the near future.

'A men's shirt that lasts more than one go in the wash, T-shirts not made of wafer-thin toilet paper; the sky's the limit,' concluded Prouse.

NATION'S HUNGOVER HONOURED DURING 'IN RIBBONS' CEREMONY

MOVING and stomach-churning scenes unfolded at Dublin Castle today as the nation's hungover masses were honoured at an 'in ribbons' ceremony.

Placed under comfy blankets, strewn across couches and given breakfast rolls and a Lucozade, the headache-ravaged group were addressed by President Michael D. Higgins at an event seen as an opportunity to mark the contribution hungover people make to Irish society, a ceremony many feel was long overdue.

'Often is the case you'd be having a horrible day but then you catch sight of someone out in public, or in work, in the throes of the most debilitating hangover; the amusement and perverse joy you derive from such suffering and pain really lifts the spirits. Hungover-in-a-heap citizens, we thank you,' said President Higgins to the group that winced at his loud-speaker-assisted voice and the light coming in through the window.

'Keep it down, fuckin' hell. Can't you see I'm at death's door,' barked one honouree, who was fumbling around for the nearest bin or shoe to vomit in.

Other hungover attendees reportedly began feeling very paranoid and terrified by the thought that they might have done something really embarrassing last night, especially if they're having an event in Dublin Castle because of it.

How driving changed in 2020

Driving tests switched to being conducted on Scalextric tracks.

RADIO

THERE ARE fears this afternoon for inhabitants of the wider Waterford area who may be at risk of ecstatic overstimulation owing to the fact a local radio station is taking its mid-afternoon 2–4pm slot on the road.

Since 7am this morning, Verve FM has excitedly been informing the Waterford public that it will be broadcasting from a shopping centre, giving people the chance to actually see the exterior of a van from which a real-life radio broadcast is literally taking place live.

'Yeah, we've been putting it out on all the socials this morning, TikTok,

TOWN STRUGGLES TO CONTAIN ITS EXCITEMENT AS LOCAL RADIO STATION ROADSTER PARKS OUTSIDE SHOPPING CENTRE

Snapchat and that. A conservative estimate is that we can expect floods of mental Verve FM fans to head down to City Square, we're talking 50,000 people minimum,' remarked DJ Kevin 'Higgster' Higgins.

Reports of pensioners passing out from 'excessive excitement' are yet to be confirmed but it's hard to dispute such rumours when you consider they have the chance to be within spitting distance of a radio DJ playing the same Picture This song eight times before a 'mega giveaway' competition involving a €20 Penneys voucher.

In a bid to bring anticipation to fever pitch levels, Verve FM's official Instagram page uploaded a picture featuring two transition

> **Fullmindness**
>
> You put your thoughts about sometimes feeling like a plastic bag, drifting in the wind, wanting to start again into words only to find that bitch Katy Perry has beaten you to it.

year work experience girls known as 'The Vervettes' posing in branded hoodies next to a Verve-branded Fiat Cinquecento.

'Jaysis! Listeners, it's like a One Direction concert down here, absolute bedlam,' DJ Higgins told the outside crowd of one yelping dog tied to a pole while its owner went to get some messages.

'NO ONE BRINGS ME ANYWHERE' LOCAL GRANDMOTHER CLAIMS

A COUNTY Waterford pensioner has come out with fresh revelations to complete strangers today in a bid to taint her immediate family as 'narcissistic assholes' who apparently never bring her anywhere, WWN can confirm.

Gladys Joyce, a widow of 15 years, slammed her sons and daughters for never calling in for her when they're going on family drives, stating 'no one has time for an old fogey like me anymore', despite evidence to the contrary.

'We're literally only back from a two-week holiday with her,' daughter Caroline explains, 'all she did was moan about everything in Spain and now she's off moaning about us again.

We can't even post family pictures up anymore or she'll feel she's missing out.'

Joyce made the claims to the new postman early this morning, detailing how none of her five children would even think of asking her to go 'for a

spin' last Sunday afternoon to Tramore, claiming they were purposely teasing her with a variety of fun pictures of them eating 99s.

'It must be nice to be able to ignore your poor mother like that and not even bother to ask her if she wanted to go,' the 76-year-old said, forgetting to tell the postman how she point blank refused to go 'to that Dub-infested shithole' in a text to her son Mark. 'They never bring me anywhere – they only call when they need someone to babysit their little tyrants.'

The alarm was raised again later when Mrs Joyce posted a series of images featuring quotes about loneliness to her Facebook profile while attending her bi-weekly bridge club with her friends.

'Mum is giving out about us at bridge, she's doing the attention-seeking quote thing again,' a family group text read, with the only replies being 'seen' notifications under the text.

NUTRITION

Health and fitness tip

Training for your first marathon? A knee injury is as good a reason as any to give up halfway through.

GEMMA O'DOHERTY & 'BIG HAM': WE TRACE THE CONNECTIONS

WWN have opened a case file to examine what links may exist between controversial political hopeful Gemma O'Doherty and some of the biggest pork-processing corporations in the country; and we're determined to blow the piggy lid right off this thing.

We began our investigations into O'Doherty, a dead-cert for the Fingal seat in the upcoming by-election, after she posted a video in which she stormed into a halal butcher shop and demanded sausages and rashers, before denouncing the lack of pork

How driving changed in 2020

People riding bikes became even more smug and unbearable.

in the store and storming right back off again.

Surmising that there's no way that the beloved O'Doherty could possibly be racially abusing the staff members of the shop, *WWN* was left with only one logical possibility; she's on Big Pork's payroll.

Although we have no evidence that O'Doherty is in the pocket of Big Pork, which she describes in the video as 'the nation's favourite dish', which, okay, yeah it is nice, we suppose. However, we cannot begin to comprehend the implications of any other suggestion as to why she would go on such a ham-filled tirade.

'the nation's favourite dish'

It would mean that O'Doherty is not in actual fact who she claims to be, and is in actual fact a racist lowlife who verbally abused a halal butcher in his place of work … we're not seeing it, quite frankly.

It would mean that we live in a world where you can post racist videos on a social media platform as revered and righteous as Facebook, to an audience of thousands of dangerously right-wing headcases … surely not, reader.

And it would mean that we live in an Ireland where you can openly abuse a civilian based on their race or religion without fear of any sort of legal reprisal … which, you'll agree, is preposterous.

It all adds up to one thing: the greasy fingers of the pork companies, using O'Doherty as their mouthpiece to spread the word about Irish pork, and denounce everything else. There is no other possible explanation.

DRUGS

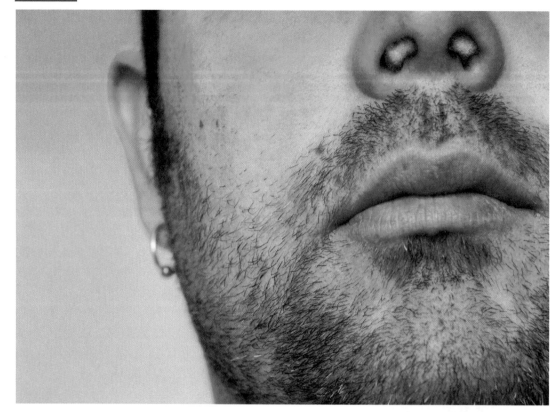

MAN FILLS NOSTRILS WITH CEMENT IN BID TO QUIT COCAINE

FULLY EMBRACING the concept of Dry January, one local man has funnelled some quick-dry cement up his nostrils in a bid to curb his use of cocaine over the coming weeks.

Expanding on what some consider 'drastic action', local man John Shothall explained that he had found Dry January quite easy to complete in previous years when he just doubled up on his cocaine use, substituting it for the absence of alcohol; however,

giving up all harmful substances will prove a much harder task.

'I just love the nervous, anxious feeling coke gives me and the way it makes me want to take a shit all the time, I'll miss it,' explained Shothall, sounding much more nasal due to the fact his Polish neighbour Piotr, a skilled plasterer, helped him fill his nostrils in with cement seconds after the clock struck midnight, signalling the start of Dry January 2020.

'He's a sound lad, one of those "no questions asked" kind of guys. The key is just to remember to keep my mouth open for breathing and that,' John added, his mouth now wide open in full gormless glory, the sound of his intake of breath interrupted only by a sneeze which caused him intense pain now his nose is cement sealed.

John, like many people, is taking Dry January seriously this year; a full restorative month to cleanse the body of alcohol and any other harmful substances in order to better savour healthy living and the fullness of a life lived well.

'Agh, fuck that. Get that hammer there out of my toolbox and we'll knock this cement out, have you any coke on you now? I'll do unspeakable things for even one bump. You can do anything to me, no hole's off limits,' added a now sweating John, who is definitely not part of a growing number of people across Ireland abusing cocaine and developing a damaging addiction.

'What are the Troubles again?'

JANUARY 2020

Brits Weekly

Britain's Saoirse Ronan!

Have you ever seen anyone as British as our lovely Saoirse?

INSIDE:
Diets of the strong and stable

OPINION: WHY DON'T THE SMELLY PADDIES JUST LEAVE THE EU AND REJOIN GREAT BRITAIN

Is Bloody Sunday a cocktail?

WW news
Waterford Whispers News

WORLD NEWS

AMERICA

ALL NEWS FROM AMERICA TO COME WITH HEALTH WARNING

A LONG OVERDUE edict issued by international health experts has confirmed that all news emanating from America, be it online, on TV, in print or on radio will have to be accompanied by a health warning, in order to give members of the public a chance to brace themselves and be aware of the potential adverse effect on their health.

'A lot of people black out from rage after reading the latest newsmare the US media delivers with a nonchalant shrug of the shoulders, and generally people incur vicious migraines when

County Knowledge

Although 'Longford' suggests that there might be a 'Shortford', no such place exists, much like how there is a 'Westmeath' but no 'Meath'.

> **'A lot of people black out from rage after reading the latest newsmare the US media delivers with a nonchalant shrug of the shoulders'**

they try to understand American news,' explained one health expert.

Whether it's the news that a rabid bear was named the manager of a new childcare chain in Ohio, that an AK-47 was elected Governor of Texas or how the US military budget has been increased so it can solve poverty and inequality by bombing it, there isn't a US-based news item that doesn't take its toll on health and sanity.

Health and fitness tip

By not clipping your toenails or fingernails, touching your toes will become easier with every passing day.

Those still availing of private health insurance could be provided with an onsite medical team to help them with any dizzy spells or high blood pressure after taking in news from a seemingly civil, Western nation which now increasingly resembles the bastard child of *Mad Max Fury Road* and a *Black Mirror* episode.

'Think before you link,' explained the health expert, 'is it worth reading about if it means my brain could short circuit and explode from the sheer stupidity of it all?'

EPSTEIN LATEST

CORONER ACCIDENTALLY BURNED JEFFREY EPSTEIN'S BODY & DUMPED IT IN OCEAN

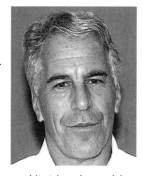

WHAT is being labelled as a 'simple' administrative error that 'could have happened to any one of the bodies' being stored in the New York City coroner's office, the body belonging to billionaire sex trafficker and friend to the famous and powerful, Jeffrey Epstein, has been mistakenly destroyed via burning before being dumped in the Atlantic Ocean.

The latest unfortunate coincidence comes after the CCTV footage in Epstein's cell, which could have shown conclusively whether or not he committed suicide, was deleted accidentally.

With the autopsy also concluding the paedophile committed suicide, authorities have admitted it is a 'shame' a second autopsy cannot be carried out on his body.

'While it is not normal procedure to accidentally burn a cadaver, douse it in acid, and then burn it again before mixing it with the ashes of other corpses and then sailing 25 miles out to sea to dump it, we accept that this was just an unfortunate mistake which needs no further investigation,' confirmed police not looking into the incident.

As the sailing boat, registered to a man named Itani Mulli, involved in the incident evaded detection at sea, there is no way of pinpointing the exact location of the remains of Epstein, who counted the world's rich and powerful among his closest friends.

'I think the public knows the difference between an honest mistake and a sinister cover-up, so they'll be happy to know we're not wasting valuable police time by re-examining a simple error,' confirmed an NYPD spokesperson.

BRITAIN FINED £8BN BY EU FOR LOITERING

BRITAIN has been fined a staggering £8 billion after it was found to be loitering in the European Union, despite being told to move on by the EU three years ago.

The European Parliament issued the fine to Number 10 late last night, giving Britain 28 days to pay and leave, or if not, goods to the value of the fine will be reclaimed by EU bailiffs, along with being prosecuted for trespassing and anti-social behaviour.

'We've told them numerous times to leave, but they just keep hanging around, causing mischief and intimidating their neighbours, Ireland, who just want to continue with the EU without having to pass Britain every time they want to shop for goods,' President of the European Commission Ursula von der Leyen told parliament last Friday.

Continuing to horseplay around the front of the EU, Britain has not yet officially responded to the large fine, instead deciding to blow e-cig vapour in the general direction of its former European partners.

'We're waiting on our grand-aunt, Northern Ireland, so piss off and mind your own business,' Britain grunted, taking off on its skateboard before pulling a heel flip at approaching member states in an intimidating fashion.

US ELECTION

BIDEN'S CHANCES OF ELECTION VICTORY IMPROVE AFTER ALLEGATIONS OF SEXUAL ASSAULT

US PRESIDENTIAL candidate Joe Biden has enhanced his election chances and passed a key 'suitability for presidential office' test for many US voters after becoming subject to a credible accusation of sexual assault, paving the way for a massive surge in the polls.

Many voters and staunch critics of Biden, who could never forgive his support for the Iraq War, have suddenly warmed to the idea of him being president, on account of their passionate hate for anyone speaking out about sexual assault at the hands of a powerful man.

'Just look at Donald or Bill before him; nothing says "presidential" like

a sexual assault accusation. Joe can look forward to increased support from a number of rabid and unhinged supporters now. He has hit the jackpot as nothing brings Americans into your camp quite like a victim bravely speaking up against a multi-millionaire and his vast team of lawyers,' explained one election strategist.

The allegations made by a former Biden staffer now enter the 'cycle of allegations' phase, whereby it devolves into a he-says-she-says Brett-Kavanaugh-style hearing with both sets of supporters so delighted to have such glorious unfiltered rage to tap into, the alleged victim, what's-her-name, is just ignored and used as a political pawn.

Despite the welcome turn of events for Biden, some voters are harder to convince than others.

'He ain't president material. Why, just look it at this here harmless hankying of the pankying, President

Trump would have already started calling that lying bitch a fat pile of flesh not worth a groping. Biden's too quiet on these important issues for my liking,' explained voter and pastor, Raymore Williams.

THE first vaping-related death in the US has sparked concerns that the practice of inhaling the vapour from boiled chemicals via an electronic device may not be as healthy as once believed, *WWN* can report.

The outbreak of 193 cases of a new respiratory illness across 22 states has been linked back to e-cigarette use, with the one fatality currently reported really shooting holes in the vaping

BREATHING BOILED CHEMICALS NOT AS SAFE AS INITIALLY THOUGHT

community's 'it's only vapour, sure it's harmless' argument.

Vaping enthusiasts had been working under the assumption that breathing in huge plumes of chemicals was 'grand', making today's stunning revelation that it might not be 'grand' all the more shocking.

'As far as we were concerned, buying cheap vape fluid from some Chinese website and inhaling the vapour from it was practically a source of Vitamin C,' said one person we interviewed, who wished to be known as Darth Vaper.

'But you're telling me that having boiled chemicals in my lungs is actually bad for my health? And that it might be actually as bad for me as if I'd stayed on the cigarettes? And that I might get this new respiratory illness that I'm hearing about? And that it might cause me to die? I mean, all this is just out of the blue. I thought chemical vapour was part of my five a day.'

So far, the news that vaping may be lethal has caused almost nobody to stop vaping, because nicotine, delicious nicotine.

TRUMP NEWS

BUNKER-BOUND TRUMP HANDS MELANIA CYANIDE PILL BEFORE PUTTING GUN TO HIS HEAD

DEFIANT to the last moment, soon-to-be former US President Donald Trump gave his last orders to his administration team as he calmly handed his First Lady a cyanide pill, before cocking back the firing mechanism on his trusty .45.

'Make sure to burn our bodies, Mike, I don't want them defiling them. And put my hair away for safekeeping, my followers will want something when we're gone,' the 73-year-old leader of the 'free world' told his Vice President Mike Pence as thunderous sounds of rioting raged outside from a growing mob of protesters who had had enough of America's blatant racism.

'But sir, surely you can reason with them, just let them think you're

doing something to stop our guys shooting them lot,' Pence pleaded, frantically deleting the President's internet search histories and destroying a Russian-labelled VHS tape translating to 'Trump golden shower'.

'What has this country come to? A president can't even threaten and encourage violence on his own citizens using racist dog whistling without snowflakes giving out,' Trump continued, urging his wife to hurry up and take the pill.

'Antifa has won, Mike. These are different times now. I've even tried ringing that man's brother … what's his name again? Pink Floyd?'

'It's George, Don. George Floyd. And you can't end it this way, then the coloureds will have won,' Pence added, deleting archived text

messages from Jeffrey Epstein from the President's phone.

Now sweating profusely with the gun chamber firmly placed to his right temple, the 45th US President Donald John Trump's hand began to quiver, before failing to pull the trigger and pulling away.

'I can't do it, Mike. My hand. It's that god-damn hydroxychloroquine giving me the shakes again,' Trump shouted, but still urging Melania to continue.

'Sir?' Pence asked, with a single tear now caressing his white privileged cheek.

'Aw, fuck it Mike; ring Mar-a-Lago and tell them to warm up my clubs,' Trump ordered, before turning to his distraught wife who just spat out her pill, 'well that's just typical of you, Melania, you can't even kill yourself right.'

MIDDLE EAST

SAUDI CROWN PRINCE SENTENCES HIMSELF TO DEATH FOR KHASHOGGI MURDER

IN AN unprecedented move, the Crown Prince of Saudi Arabia has reportedly ordered his own execution for the murder of columnist for *The Washington Post* Jamal Ahmad Khashoggi last year, *WWN* has learned.

Mohammed bin Salman had previously overseen the death sentences of five men this week for the journalist's murder, but later succumbed to Western media pressure which pinpointed him as the main orchestrator, forcing him to make the unorthodox move.

> **'Okay, okay, I'll just execute myself if it makes you all bloody happy'**

'Okay, okay, I'll just execute myself if it makes you all bloody happy,' a bitter Crown Prince was reported to have shouted at staff and security personnel after reading several damning articles about his involvement in the crime. 'Quick, guard, grab the largest and most expensive sword you can find, I will not be beheaded with any old crap … and hurry, before the media criticises me any more.'

Jamal Khashoggi had been tortured and killed in a Saudi Arabian embassy in October of 2018 by Saudi agents working for the Crown Prince before his body was chopped up, put in a series of bags and disposed of like a piece of rubbish.

'Of all the things I've done; the famines, bombings, tortures, human rights violations, executions of women and children, etcetera, etcetera, this is the crime that gets me killed?' bin Salman asked rhetorically, now ushering his main executioner over to a block of wood, 'okay, so, just make this quick, nothing worse than a half-arsed decapitation … you know you can still see 20 seconds after your head's chopped off?'

Inhaling a large breath while raising a gold- and diamond-encrusted sword, the Saudi executioner paused briefly to let his soon-to-be former leader say his final words.

'I just want to say … psych!' the Crown Prince jested, turning his head up and laughing at his would-be killer, before the whole room began sniggering uncontrollably. 'Ah ha-ha, the look on your face, Ataullah, ah ha-ha priceless,' bin Salman added, now standing up and slapping the executioner around the back of his head, 'what, you think I'd actually have myself killed, you dope? Off with his head,' the Prince then sentenced him to death.

'God, some people are so gullible,' he concluded to the piercing cries of his former executioner.

EPSTEIN LATEST

'I KNEW TOO MUCH' EPSTEIN SPEAKS OUT FROM HIS SOUTH AMERICAN HIDEAWAY

FOLLOWING on from his suicide at the Metropolitan Correctional Center in New York last Friday evening, American financier and convicted sex offender Jeffrey Epstein looks back at his untimely death, pointing to the fact that he knew too much and was never going to get to a courtroom, no matter how much he promised to shut his mouth.

'You could say I died from an overdose of information,' the 66-year-old began, sipping a Long Island iced tea while staring out at the Nicaraguan beach he will now reside at for the

next 20–30 years, 'I had a good run, in fairness … I mean, yes, the whole sex offender conviction thing was a bad time for me as I had to serve a whopping 18 months under house arrest in my own house for raping young women, but the rest of my life was pretty good, considering.'

Arriving at Nicaragua's capital city Managua on Saturday morning on a private jet paid for by the Israeli intelligence agency Mossad, Epstein was quickly given a new identity by his handlers, but insists he will still miss his life as good old Jeffrey Epstein.

'Yes, the world hated Jeffrey, but if they only knew his vast catalogue of famous friends, the people he catered for, they'd think differently about him then,' Epstein went on, speaking about himself in the third person while staring at some young local girls

playing on the beach, 'my only crime was facilitating the urges of wealthy men, but now I have to face the consequences here in this dump like some kind of fall guy or patsy.'

'At least Bin Laden and his son are here to keep me company. They're great fun on the drink and love the virgins,' Epstein concluded, before heading off for a swim.

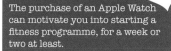

Health and fitness tip

The purchase of an Apple Watch can motivate you into starting a fitness programme, for a week or two at least.

'Ireland's favourite news source since 234BC'

𝔚𝔥𝔦𝔰𝔭𝔢𝔯𝔰 𝔑𝔢𝔴𝔰

Weather
Today will be shite with some sunny spells of work-related humour. Rain will dominate the country's conversations in the afternoon, forcing many people to consume large amounts of alcohol alone in their homes on Friday night. Top temperatures won't even matter.

VOL 478, 4520156   WATERFORD, 27 NOVEMBER 1982   IR£0.95

Saudi Delegation Visit Ireland For Tips On Oppressing Women

KING of Saudi Arabia Fahd bin Abdulaziz Al Saud has today arrived in Ireland with his chief advisors on a fact-finding mission, hoping to learn much from Ireland and the ways in which it oppresses its women.

'You are a jewel in the world. We have much envy, we humbly ask of you – please teach us your magnificently unjust ways,' King Fahd said, upon shaking hands with Archbishop Dermot Ryan and Taoiseach Charles Haughey.

Ireland has long been a blueprint from which other countries model their dis-

taste of women, but this is the first such visit in recent years.

King Fahd, seen attending various places, including one Magdalene Laundry, was said to be carrying a notebook with him at all times and furiously scribbling down notes.

'Stop, slow down. Let me jot this down – you say it's much easier to do this to women if you just pretend they're not real people? This is marvellous stuff.'

BREAKING NEWS

CLOCKS TO GO SIDEWAYS THIS WEEKEND IN UNPRECEDENTED MOVE

TWICE EVERY year, millions of people get caught out when the clocks change for daylight saving time, but scientists are now warning that this year could be the most confusing to date, as for the first time in recent history, the clocks are to go sideways this Saturday night.

'We have no idea how this is going to play out,' warned James Mathews, who works on keeping the International Atomic Time (TAI) at the US Naval Observatory in Washington, DC, 'if the time is to go sideways, we could see a parallel dimension shift that could take the planet into an unknown realm and potentially spell disaster for humanity as we know it.'

Normally at this time of year the clocks are due to go back by 60

minutes at 2am on Sunday morning; however, the time is now expected to go sideways and is expected to be totally incomprehensible to the human mind.

'We're looking to use 12 letters instead of numbers to tell the time in this new, unknown parallel,' Mathews added, 'so we'd start the time at midnight, which will now be known as A o'clock, half A is 30 minutes past midnight, and so on.'

The unprecedented shift is expected to send electronic devices into a global meltdown and cost billions of euros to the time industry.

'I basically have to dump all these watches now,' explained one local jeweller, 'hopefully time won't make any more unpredictable moves, like going up or down, next year.'

The time is due to go sideways at C o'clock on Sunday morning.

CONFUSION AS BRITAIN COMPLAINS ABOUT FOREIGNER LEAVING COUNTRY

AS BRITAIN continues to treat Harry Windsor and Meghan Markle's decision to step away from their positions in the Royal Family like it is a pivotal scene in a disaster movie, the British people have expressed profound confusion over their dismay at a foreigner actually leaving the country.

Having spent much of the recent past asserting their desire to see foreign people driven from the British Isles and voting for politicians who agree with them, some members of the public have begun suffering immensely confusing and conflicting emotions which have brought on painful headaches.

'I don't get it, I don't like the foreigns, 'specially dem foreigns that have the different colour, but I'm big

angry now one of the different colour foreigns want to leave,' confirmed the Prime Minister of Britain, echoing a sentiment felt by much of the Great British public.

Markle has enjoyed the time-honoured immigrant tradition of being labelled an evil, ungrateful leech by the media, but now with her decision, alongside her husband of Greek and Germanic heritage, to move to Canada, she is newly accused of being an evil, ungrateful leech.

Those observing from outside Britain have been similarly perplexed by Britain's out-of-character reaction to a foreigner 'going back to where they came from'.

'Isn't this like a racist's wet dream? Racist Christmas, or like winning the lotto only instead of winning money, a net contributor to your economy flees in fear. So why are they chaining themselves to Buckingham Palace and setting themselves on fire in protest?' observed one immigration expert.

TRUMP NEWS

BEYONCÉ SET TO PERFORM AT TRUMP IMPEACHMENT HALFTIME SHOW

IN A desperate bid to garner interest from the lethargic American public, officials involved in the Trump impeachment proceedings have announced that Beyoncé Knowles will perform at today's Superbowl-styled halftime show, along with an array of supporting acts, *WWN* can confirm.

Citing poor concentration skills and general apathy among American voters, it was decided that entertainment during an interval was needed to increase interest in the country's latest impeachment proceedings, which was initially billed as 'the most entertaining impeachment of them all'.

'Queen Bey will perform five songs halfway through today's impeachment proceedings, followed by Daft Punk and a special appearance by Kanye West,' organisers confirmed.

The investigation into President Trump's alleged scheme to coerce Ukraine's president into opening an investigation into an election rival or face military aid being withheld is now into its second day, with its findings expected to change 'fuck all' in the minds of Trump supporters.

'God-damn witch hun' if ya ask me,' spat Alabama soybean farmer Randy Stevens, who said he will vote for Trump again despite losing thousands in revenue this year due to the ongoing trade war with China, 'Mr Trump is a good man and understands small folk like me more than anyone else I know … he even killed ISIS,' Stevens added, hocking out a large brown pile of tobacco.

The halftime show will also feature an indoor fireworks display. Ever the restrained and dignified leader, President Trump has vowed to continue to incriminate himself and justify the impeachment inquiry on Twitter before ultimately taking to the stand to scream 'you want the truth? You can't handle the truth.'

> **'Mr Trump is a good man and understands small folk like me more than anyone else I know … he even killed ISIS'**

MIDDLE EAST

US STANDS FIRM, READY TO SUPPORT NATION BEHIND 9/11 ATTACKS

How working changed in 2020

Window cleaners working from home ran out of work after the first day.

SHOWCASING the sort of moral superiority it seeks to be known for the world over, the US government has reiterated it will stand resolutely alongside the nation largely responsible for facilitating the 9/11 attacks, after oil depots in Saudi Arabia suffered a drone attack allegedly carried out by Iran.

'We're ready for another cheap, easy and largely consequence-free war in the Middle East, and what Iran needs to learn is that the US will not stand idly by as Saudi Arabia, the nation that did more than any other

Health and fitness tip

If gyms didn't want you admiring yourself, they wouldn't have put all these lovely big mirrors up there, would they?

to help bring down the Twin Towers, is under attack,' explained one US military official.

'We'll blindly bring our entire nation into a bloody and nonsensical war if it means petrol will be five cents cheaper, for that is as American as apple pie,' added the official, before confirming he wouldn't be surprised if the US suddenly found totally trustworthy evidence of weapons of mass destruction in Iran.

The US has been busy trying to build a coalition of allies for further shows of strength against Iran, who again for the record did not facilitate terrorists attacking America in the way

> **'We'll blindly bring our entire nation into a bloody and nonsensical war if it means petrol will be five cents cheaper'**

the Saudi Arabian government did. However, far from finding it hard to get support, the UK, France, Germany and Israel simply responded 'how high do you want us to jump?'

'Look, we can turn a blind eye to war crimes, causing famine in Yemen, bombing women and children, and yup, supporting the 9/11 attackers, but when it comes to bombing oil supplies, well, it's the worst thing any human can ever do,' added a Trump administration official, pointing out that if Iran simply murdered a journalist in one of its own embassies like Saudi Arabia did, it would have probably let it slide.

IRAN TO ATTACK US BY JUST LEAVING TRUMP TO RUN COUNTRY INTO GROUND

THE IRANIAN government is now officially pursuing a 'hands-off' approach to retaliating to any further attacks by US President Donald Trump, with senior military officials in the Middle Eastern country concluding there is nothing more damaging to the safety, health and prosperity of the American people than simply leaving Trump to continue running the country into the ground, distraction free.

Having launched a missile attack on US military bases in Erbil and Al Asad in Iraq early this morning, analysts within the Iranian military have since realised a more damaging and far less costly strategy would be simply to sit back and watch Trump weaken every facet of American society which seeks to have a positive impact on its citizens.

'Have you seen how much it costs to pay for basic medical care over there? Allah above, have mercy on those poor souls,' one senior Iranian official said, his voice full of sympathy for the American people.

'No ballistic missiles, no covert assassinations or attacks by elite military personnel can come close to causing the sort of chaos and harm in America that seems to come so naturally to Mr Trump,' concluded the Iranian official, before standing down all military action and intelligence gathering on potential US targets.

The move by the Iranians will be met with relief from people around the world who now don't have to explain what a nuclear apocalypse is to their children nor train them to be 'combat ready' by the age of four.

Fullmindness

Not happy? Have you tried your friend's advice to just not be sad?

'Ireland's favourite news source since 234BC'

Whispers News

Weather
You wouldn't put your worst enemy out in that today. Tomorrow looking the same. A day for the high stool.

VOL 5, 459   WATERFORD, 14 JANUARY 1984   ONLY 90p

Tippex Replaces Magic Markers As School Drug Of Choice

THE white-out blackout epidemic has reached a critical level in our playgrounds, according to a damning new report on the continuing sniffage of Tippex in Irish schools.

The study shows that huffing Tippex has replaced sniffing magic markers in four out of every five solvent-samplers, making it the drug of choice for the under-nines in need of a hit

to ease them through Little Break.

With teachers unable to cope with strung-out kids falling asleep during nature talks, parents have been advised to keep an eye out for the tell-tale signs of Tippex abuse.

'If your child has Tippex in their pencil case, but only ever writes in pencil, never in pen … that's a sign they may be sniffing Tippex,' said a government consultant on the epidemic.

'A little ring of white under each nostril. Errors in their homework, despite having Tippex to correct them. Eyes hanging out of their head. These are all signs that your kid could be on the slippery slope to more serious drugs, such as holding their breath for too long.'

Meanwhile, teachers have stated that it's a blessing that their magic markers are lasting much longer now that kids aren't huffing all the fumes out of them, so that's something.

RELIGION

GOD ANNOUNCES CUTBACKS AS RELIGIOUS DONATIONS PLUMMET

THE kingdom of heaven is expected to undergo major austerity measures over the coming months as the Lord God Almighty announced major cutbacks, *WWN* has learned.

Citing a massive plunge in religious donations on Earth, God stated that billions of euro have so far been lost thanks to the ongoing global lockdown.

'It's my own fault for allowing the coronavirus to mutate from animal to human,' the four-billion-year-old wrote, 'I was actually trying to curb the dangerously rising population down there and it all just kinda backfired on me – my bad.'

The measures are expected to see dozens of layoffs in God's kingdom, including some

senior angels and saints being offered voluntary redundancies.

'How do I feel? I'm fucking outraged, to tell you the God's honest truth,' exclaimed Saint Peter, who has been acting as keeper of the keys to the kingdom for the past two thousand years,

'I'm being replaced with a bloody automated barrier gate and the golden gates are being sold off for scrap to a Cash 4 Gold shop, so I said fuck that – I've applied for a similar position in Hell where the money is sweet.'

Up until now, billions of euro of tax-free revenue has been funnelled into the kingdom of heaven thanks to donations from worshippers on the ground, but revenue streams were cut due to the lockdown.

'If there's one thing I really need right now it's money, so if you can all get back to normal down there that would be super,' God's statement ended.

JACK RUSSELLS DISCONTINUED AFTER 225 YEARS

THE popular terrier breed known as the 'Jack Russell' is to be phased out at the start of 2020, bringing to an end almost 225 years of ankle-height canine companionship, *WWN* can report.

Once hugely popular throughout almost every household in Ireland and beyond, the bite-happy pooch was a staple of every walk in the countryside, as well as a common sight at gates in urban areas, barking loudly at nothing in particular.

But with trendier dog breeds becoming more and more popular over the last number of decades, the humble but reliable Jack Russell terrier is finally being discontinued, with handsome scrappage deals being offered for any Jack Russells still in circulation.

'There was a time when every house had a Jack Russell, but then again, there was a time when every house had a record player,' said James Russell, CEO of the Jack Russell Terrier Corporation.

'Following our merger with the French Bulldog and the Maltipoo companies in the mid-90s, we grew to accept that the days of the Jack Russell were numbered. People just wanted the newer models, the more fashionable ones. Never mind the fact that a Jack Russell could run for days on a single can of Pedigree Chum, or that it could bark at a squirrel that wasn't there for an hour straight. Things

like that just aren't important anymore. You can't be an Instagram influencer with a one-eared Jack Russell on your lap, can you?'

Although many people are likely to trade in their Jack Russells, it is expected that a number of vintage models will still be available for a limited time.

GRETA EXCLUSIVE

HYPOCRITE GRETA THUNBERG SNAPPED WEARING DISPOSABLE NAPPY IN 2004

SWEDISH environmental activist Greta Thunberg has been branded a 'hypocrite' by critics around the world after a photograph of her wearing a disposable diaper surfaced online today.

The 16-year-old has not yet confirmed or denied if the picture of the young baby is actually her, which clearly shows a blonde-haired, blue-eyed baby wearing a disposable nappy, and if climate activists are to be taken seriously, will take up to 500 years to decompose.

How shopping changed in 2020

Tutting while queuing rose by a record 4000%.

'She wore a disposable nappy, what next? It would be foolish to presume she hasn't been whale hunting in Japan or that she doesn't own several Boeing 747s,' said an ecstatic middle-aged man who couldn't wait to lambast the 'self-righteous little shit'.

Sources close to Thunberg, who was 14 months old at the time the picture was taken, said she soiled herself countless times over a period of 18 to 24 months, despite knowing the damaging carbon footprint she was creating, and the damage disposable nappies do to the environment.

'We're all absolutely disgusted by her behaviour and she should stand down from her ridiculous campaign

County Knowledge

Angela Lansbury currently lives in Cork and moved there from the US in a bid to help crack the county's hundreds of unsolved murders.

immediately,' smiling executives from BP, Shell and other leading oil companies said at a hastily assembled press conference earlier today.

The growing climate action movement is set to be dismantled and abandoned as a result of the revelations, with everyone going back to using plastic straws and dumping old washing machines in fields by this time tomorrow.

MIDDLE EAST

MIDDLE EAST NOT EVEN WORTH INVADING NOW OIL IS WORTHLESS

US MILITARY generals and private contractors were said to be inconsolable at the news that international as well as home-produced oil is now worth as little as minus $36 a barrel, scuppering any motivation for haphazardly pointing at a random Middle Eastern nation on a map and saying 'invasion time'.

Crude oil, once the most sought-after commodity in the world, is now, by the barrel load, worth less than non-brand toilet roll, a price

drop which has left many war fans devastated.

'Aw man, I hate this pandemic,' remarked a sulking Republican politician who had his heart set on a decades-long war in Iran or some such oil-plentiful country that could create the sort of needless casualty numbers that inspired him to become a war-mongering politician in the first place.

With the price collapse rendering oil less than worthless, many are contemplating if Middle Eastern countries and their citizens are even worth destroying.

'I'm just sad for all the locals who won't get jobs rebuilding the schools we arbitrarily drone-bombed into

> **'I'm just sad for all the locals who won't get jobs rebuilding the schools we arbitrarily drone-bombed into oblivion'**

oblivion,' confirmed one private contractor, who feared proxy wars would actually have to take place on home soil.

'What do you expect me to do now, go to the Middle East as a civilian tourist, experience the different cultures, languages and history, and leave with just a fridge magnet having not committed a massacre? Are you fucking nuts?' confirmed one military man with an itchy trigger finger.

'War crimes, torture and mass murder. Whatever horrors we perpetrate there, the public couldn't care less because they knew we were really there for the precious oil, for the lucrative rebuilding contracts. But trying to start a war in this economic climate? Good luck, buddy,' sobbed one powerful private military lobbyist, who was *this* close to tricking President Trump into escalating to a full-scale war with Iran before oil prices plummeted.

EVERYTHING YOU NEED TO KNOW ABOUT MITCH McCONNELL

A REPUBLICAN politician of significant influence, Mitch McConnell is seen by many as the person most responsible for the lack of gun reform laws, an enabler of President Trump's thinly veiled racist policies and the driving force behind increased divisiveness in US politics.

Here's everything you need to know about the 77-year-old Kentucky senator:

- Longest serving Republican Senate leader in history.
- Had pioneering heart removal surgery in the early 90s.
- Sadly, is of Irish descent.
- Refuses to put a price on the lives of those killed by gun violence; in

fact, refuses to limit the amount of money he is willing to accept from the NRA.
- Despite new background check laws for gun owners receiving support from both Democrats and Republicans, McConnell continues to enjoy the needless slaughter of innocent people too much to pass the relevant bills.
- Ejaculates dust.
- Repeatedly voted against bills that would provide healthcare coverage for 9/11 first responders, but McConnell shouldn't be judged by this act alone as there's a wealth of other reprehensible things to choose from.
- Voted 'nyet' to election security bills which would make it harder for foreign powers, such as Russia, to interfere in US elections.
- A complex individual with a multitude of contradictions,

McConnell props up Trump's aggressive and racist attacks on minorities and immigrants but is married to an Asian American. Also appears to be human, but all evidence suggests he is not.
- Is incredibly popular among a vast and diverse array of white, gun-owning Republicans.
- Looks like a grumpy turtle but, unlike a turtle, he doesn't have a shell, rather he is a merely a shell of a human being.
- As he nears his 80s, God has reportedly beefed up security at the gates of Heaven significantly. Satan has followed a similar strategy for the gates of Hell.

STATUE OF LIBERTY LAST SEEN WALKING BACK TO FRANCE

EYE WITNESSES in New York described unbelievable scenes earlier today as the sound of creaking copper and crumbling concrete preceded the sight of the iconic Statue of Liberty disembarking from its pedestal and heading eastwards for its native France.

Tossing its iconic torch over its shoulder and muttering loudly in French while looking angry and fed

‘Good, send her ugly ass back. And hey, who says America even wants liberty?

up, the statue was last heard saying *‘merde, mon dieu, va te faire foutre’* before disappearing over the horizon out on the Atlantic Ocean.

Shocked and confused Americans have now been left to speculate over what exactly could have prompted the statue, which famously symbolised America's history of being a welcoming place for immigrants, to just up and leave.

‘God, so many instances to choose from, right?’ queried one New Yorker, ‘maybe it was the gradual attritional nature of all the horrible stuff, but jeez, this week alone you're talking what – the Iowa caucus, the State of the Union, Trump's impeachment acquittal … hmm what else, oh the kids are still in cages, right? People kinda forget that one, amazingly.’

While some Americans have been shocked by the sudden disappearance of the iconic landmark and used it as a moment to pause and a chance to think on the current lamentable state of much of the nation's political scandals, others have been more upbeat and positive.

‘Good, send her ugly ass back. And hey, who says America even wants liberty? Is that even an American thing? Maybe we don't need it,’ confirmed one Washington DC resident with a holiday home in Florida.

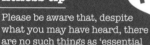

Health and fitness tip

Please be aware that, despite what you may have heard, there are no such things as ‘essential sugars’.

UK NEWS

SCOTLAND LAST PICTURED SAWING SELF AWAY FROM ENGLISH BORDER

FOLLOWING Boris Johnson's reiteration in the wake of the UK general election results that he will not grant permission for a second Scottish independence referendum, Scotland was last seen frantically sawing and hacking away at the 96-mile stretch of the Anglo-Scottish border.

Hardy Scottish men and women have been working around the clock ever since the election results to make themselves a beautiful island untouched by decaying, rotten and slightly insane English soil.

Those without saws and other cutting implements have resorted to using their bare hands to claw at the soil, such is their urgency when it

comes to being free from the malign influence of 'them cunts doon south'.

English residents south of Marshall Meadows Bay on the eastern side of the Anglo-Scottish border have already reported waking this morning to what sounded like an earthquake, only to go outside to see Scotland slowly drifting further north complete with a large crowd of Scots giving them the two-finger salute.

Scotland's SNP is set for a collision course with Johnson's Tory government which has a commanding 365-seat majority following 12 December's election, with Scottish First Minister Nicola Sturgeon affirming in a stirring speech that the country

'cannot be imprisoned' five years after democratically voting to remain happily in prison via a referendum in which only those resident in Scotland could vote.

Sales of blue and white face paint have soared in the last few days with online streaming services noticing an uptick in the number of Scottish-based accounts sticking on *Braveheart* and fast-forwarding to all the good English-bashing bits.

US VICE President Mike Pence needed urgent medical care following a tour of the coronavirus clinic in the Mayo Medical Centre in Minnesota, after becoming weak at the sight of so many people wearing face masks and lying on beds.

'Is it just me, or is it hot in here?' swooned Pence, who didn't wear a mask because he has a note from Mother, and also a note from his mother.

'Jeez, give a guy some room, would ya? All these big strong men in masks, it reminds me of when I … well, never mind. A movie I watched once,

'SURROUNDED BY GUYS IN MASKS; WHAT IS THIS, MY BIRTHDAY?' ASKS PENCE

yeah, that's right. *Eyes Wide Shut*. Terrible thing. All that adultery and sin – godless.'

Pence went on to defend his decision to not wear a face mask during the trip, stating that he gets tested for COVID-19 'all the time'.

'The big swab that goes all the way

back to your brain, yeah I get that done all the time, it doesn't bother me at all,' stated Pence, while saying his 3pm Rosary.

'Besides, I've got big G up there looking after me, the main man, the Holy Kahuna himself. God, you heathen. God is all you need to keep yourself free of these Chinese germs. In there I saw a lot of people wearing face masks; clearly they have no faith. Maybe that's why Muslims wear those burkas, you ever think of that?'

Mr Pence was informed that he probably should wear a mask to cut down on the risk of him transferring COVID-19 to President Donald Trump, as the loss of the President at this time would mean a shot at the presidency for Pence himself.

'Is that so?' asked Pence, rubbing his hands on a coronavirus patient before heading off to an Oval Office meeting.

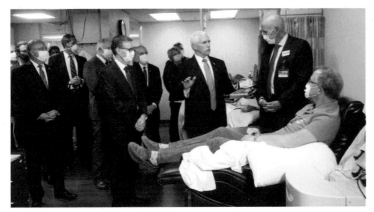

US ELECTION

EVERYTHING YOU NEED TO KNOW ABOUT JOE BIDEN

THE former Vice President of America and Senator Joe Biden has seen his campaign for the Democratic presidential nomination receive a lift after winning the Democratic primary in South Carolina.

Here's everything you need to know about 77-year-old Biden:

- Earned the nickname 'The White Obama' from himself.
- Has a long and storied career in the Senate, passing laws and representing ordinary citizens, the sort of record you just know people who voted for a reality TV star to be president are going to respect and take into account when voting.
- Claims the phrase 'what's up, ese?' should be enough to court Hispanic voters in any presidential election.
- Unlike Bernie Sanders, he ain't no commie sonuvabitch!
- If nominated as the Democratic candidate, troubling news that could harm him includes the fact that his son Hunter has direct ties to Slytherin, Skeletor, Thanos, SPECTRE and Shredder, and this is just the sort of thing Trump voters will believe.
- Only candidate whose teeth actively play a role in voters' nightmares or could stand in for a lighthouse beacon when it goes dark and needs repairing.
- Was Barack Obama's Vice President, but owing to his modest nature, you'll never hear him bring that fact up.
- Had a whole thing where women said he was too 'touchy feely' but, hey, don't bring that up, Jesus, the man's trying to win the presidency and if there's one thing the American public wouldn't stand for it, it's a … oh wait, never mind.
- Standing on a platform of 'boy, let me tell you, I'd love to punch that son of a gun Trump right in the kisser.'
- Has suffered many harrowing tragedies in his life including the death of his wife and one-year-old daughter in a car crash, and the death of his son due to brain cancer – the sort of tragedies you can just picture Trump openly mocking in debates on the way to his easy re-election, can't you?
- At 77, he is one of the oldest candidates in the running for president, but doesn't think being an eye witness as a child to the sinking of the *Titanic* should be a barrier to being elected.
- Biden voted in favour of the war in Iraq, but hey, stop making out like that's a bad thing. Once opposed desegregation busing but that's hardly going to prove to be a problem or used against him by opponents.
- You're right, the more you look at him his head does look exceptionally large for his body.
- Having gone for the presidency in 1988 and 2008, is looking to make it his third time to be told 'no' by the American public.

UK NEWS

UNEMPLOYED COUPLE EMIGRATE FOR BETTER QUALITY OF LIFE

A MIXED-race couple who have been living off state benefits for a number of years have decided to emigrate from the UK to America in a bid to secure a better quality of life for their son, Archie, *WWN* has learned.

Citing ongoing racism and a classist society that has left the family alienated in their own country, the Windsors announced they will be leaving Britain as soon as possible.

'I haven't even told my grandmother yet, she'll be devastated as there has been some recent turmoil in the family with a dirty uncle of mine,' explained son of two, Harry, who was let go from the army after just 30 weeks in Afghanistan.

'It's been hard since the baby came, people here are a lot less forgiving of racial interbreeding, especially between a white ginger and a mixed-race African American, and the newspapers have been targeting us for no good reason with cruel stories, so we've no other option but to leave for a better life abroad.'

One of thousands of couples emigrating from the now impoverished and unstable Great Britain, Harry and his US-born wife Meghan are expected to look for work in North America, where tabloid newspapers and racism are virtually nonexistent.

Community text alerts

Foreign family!
Everybody stay calm, a foreign family have moved in!

'I just can't wait for the peace and quiet and to live in a land where the colour of your skin means nothing,' explained Meghan. 'Imagine being able to walk down the street without anyone recognising you or judging your looks – I can't wait to move.'

The calm and measured reaction in Britain at the news of a couple choosing to spend time abroad has been seen as a positive sign that the far more complex and important adjustment to life post-Brexit should be a walk in the park.

How driving changed in 2020

There was an exponential rise in people looking like awkward eejits pressing pedestrian lights with their elbows.

GRETA EXCLUSIVE

OUTSPOKEN Scandinavian upstart Greta Thunberg has finally realised that there's more to life than relentlessly campaigning against climate change after striking up a relationship with a 17-year-old boy racer who drives around town in a heavily modded, petrol-chugging 1998 Honda Civic.

Precocious Swede Thunberg proved herself to be a massive pain in the hole for world leaders recently, making passionate speeches about what she saw as the ongoing destruction of the planet for profit, and instigating a worldwide movement against capitalism and man-made climate change.

GRETA THUNBERG DITCHES CLIMATE CRUSADE AFTER FALLING FOR BADASS IN SOUPED-UP HONDA

Unable to stem the tide of Thunberg's international recognition for her environmentalism, capitalists and world leaders went on to hope that Thunberg would eventually succumb to her hormones and turn her attention to boys and pretty dresses.

'Once she met local bad-boy Erïk Vüsterberdën and his shit-hot hatchback, all her talk about carbon footprints went straight out the window,' said a member of the G20's Climate Change Denial Committee. 'Last week she took a boat from Sweden to Brazil because flying was against her fossil fuel beliefs. This week, she's in the passenger seat of the Honda doing donuts in a cloud of smoke outside an Ikea, before driving

How sex changed in 2020

Orgies just weren't much fun anymore.

in a low gear to another Ikea just for the hell of it.

'I know we've spent millions trying to convince young people not to listen to Greta, but now we'd like to reverse that; listen to her, she's finally making sense. Don't worry about what the grownups are doing, go have fun, live life. There's nothing to worry about!'

Thunberg was unavailable for comment as she also discovered that texting is fun and Big Macs are actually quite tasty.

Health and fitness tip

Does a personal trainer also have their own personal trainer? And then what about that personal trainer's personal trainer's trainer? Where does this end?

Sinéad Monthly

MARCH 2020

'Oh, Sinead!'

With or without a fada

76+
GAS SINÉADS TO COMPARE YOUR SINÉAD TO

Why Aoifes can get fucked if they think they're better than Sinéads

Ireland's top 5 Sineads inside

CELEBRITY INTERVIEW

Sinéad O'Connor

Aw, stop.
She never forgets to ring her mammy

'This is so Sinéad'

* Shinner Sinéads on the rise
* 3 lemonades made my Sinéads
* What's it like being a Sharon?

IN THIS ISSUE Brown, black, red and blonde-haired Sinéads – we've got them all

9 780717 188918

ww news
Waterford Whispers News

ENTERTAINMENT

EXCLUSIVE

DWAYNE JOHNSON NOW 95% VEINS

MOVIE megastar Dwayne 'The Rock' Johnson has had to postpone filming on his latest blockbuster for several weeks, after pushing it slightly too hard in the gym and erupting into a pulsating ball of sinew and veins, WWN can confirm.

Johnson, star of the Fast & Furious franchise and WWE all-time great, had been in the gym prepping for his

County Knowledge

The origins of Roscommon as a county remain unclear on account of historians' lack of interest in trying to find anything out about the county.

> **I'm going to play the title creature in a remake of John Carpenter's *The Thing*'**

upcoming role as the titular character in DC's *Black Adam* movie when he clanged and banged one too many times, shifting his muscle/vein balance too far to one side.

In a tearful Instagram post, The Rock explained how perhaps there is such a thing as too much exercise, and promised to give DC fans the Black

Adam they deserved once he stops being a hauntingly vascular walking nightmare.

'Oops,' said The Rock, speaking from under his pulmonary aorta.

'Production halted while we sort this out. I had hoped to head into this movie bigger than you've ever seen me before, but seeing as how even on my weakest day I still look like a condom full of shoelaces, I didn't really need to do this to myself at all. Hopefully you guys can forgive me. But in good news, while we're waiting for this to die down, I'm going to play the title creature in a remake of John Carpenter's *The Thing*, so swings and roundabouts.'

MUSIC

BACK WITH A BANG, his 'Watermelon Sugar' single dominating the airwaves and fresh from a hosting stint on *SNL*, ex-One Direction man Harry Styles is killing it yet again, this time in the sort of outfit that cements his place as one pop's chief fashion icons.

Decked out in this dope wacky-wavy-inflatable-hands man get-up, the ambiguous ensemble evokes David Bowie at his most androgynous.

In an outfit designed by Victoria Beckham, Styles continues adding to his array of eclectic influences which

HARRY STYLES KILLS IT IN NEW INFLATABLE MAN OUTFIT

defy easy categorisation in this iconic look which he wore for the red carpet at the annual Award Awards Awards, an awards showcase celebrating the best awards.

'It was a bit of bother getting into, but I love expressing myself through my clothes. Okay, it's daunting climbing up a 40-foot ladder to get into the outfit, and if the air pressure coursing through the tube drops below a certain point I'll fall and plummet to my death, but I like it,' a bashful Harry shared.

Styles then asked for the ladder to be brought again as he needed to go to the toilet.

He's worn them all – Saint Laurent, Lanvin, Louis Vuitton, CK and Gucci – but it's clear his style is ever evolving and hats off to VB for creating such a visually stunning outfit. Whether it's his hair, tattoos or outfits, the man ain't called Styles for nothing.

VATICAN PLANE DOUSES RTÉ IN HOLY WATER FOLLOWING NORMAL PEOPLE EPISODE

IT PROVED to be a sex scene too far for the Sexual Repression Enforcement Unit of the Concerned Catholic Parents of Ireland, and so they were left with no choice but to call in the big guns.

A penis – an Irish penis no less – had graced the screens of the National Pornography Broadcaster, RTÉ, last night during an episode of *Normal People*. Sometime after 10.15pm Ireland condemned its eternal soul to hell.

The hum from the engine of the Vatican's Cessna 185 Skywagon, nicknamed 'Fire and Brimstone', could be heard over the leafy suburbs of south Dublin at 7am this morning, with Pope Francis answering the emergency 'Pope signal' beacon Irish

Catholics beamed into the night sky moments after a flaccid penis was shown on TV.

'The Pope signal is only triggered after every concerned Catholic in Ireland presses their "penis alarm" at the exact same time. That's why the only other time the plane has been used in Ireland was during the Marriage Referendum back in 2015,' confirmed outrage specialist Cormac Curtin.

After huge spikes in search terms on Google for 'man', 'penis' and 'what is this fleshy worm thing my televised programming box speaks of?', hospital A&Es reported a surge in people ripping their eyes out of their sockets, with emergency

counselling tents being erected nationwide to cope with the fallout.

'I always thought the story of men having a "penis" was a ghost story to scare us off trying to be happy, much like the entirety of the Bible,' confirmed one normal person *Normal People* viewer, who without the show would never have known sex even existed.

Elsewhere, RTÉ admitted they haven't been this heavily praised for a TV show they didn't actually produce themselves since *Father Ted*.

TELEVISION

'I'M JUST MILKING THE BOLLOCKS OUT OF THIS SHOW'

TV ARCHITECT Dermot Bannon opened up about the latest instalment of *Room To Improve* and how using a tired 'home revamp' format never grows old.

'Draw up plans, debate plans, make a ridiculous suggestion about a wall or window, insist on said suggestion to create tension, put silly music behind it like it's gas craic and voilà; *Room To Improve*,' Bannon explained the show's premise, which has been running on RTÉ since 1931.

In a bid to 'keep this gravy train on its motherfucking tracks' Bannon will be building his own home this time around after running out of Irish homes to poke his nose into, making the new series completely 'fresh, original and totally different'.

Dermot is set to become both client and architect as he aims to draw up the plans, debate the plans with himself, make a ridiculous suggestion about a wall or window, insist on said suggestion to create tension, put silly music behind it like it's gas craic, but hopefully stretch two to three episodes out of it.

'Yeah, I'm just milking the bollocks out of it, but listen, property is the nation's Page 3. Instead of tits you've got two giant windows overlooking whatever the fuck,' Bannon added, before teasing with what's coming next for Ireland's favourite property show, 'we'll probably focus on Direct Provision builds next, or homeless shelters … not!'

'Nah, piss that, we're looking at some deadly builds most people will never be able to afford for Series 13 – make everyone feel slightly more inadequate than usual?'

'There's still plenty of life in the old *Room To Improve* dog yet,' explained Bannon, who said next year's series will focus on the conversion of a child's playhouse, a Dalkey dog kennel, him begging old clients to redo their homes again so he can keep making the show, before finally being restrained by security after trying to install velux windows in the GPO.

Room To Improve will air every Sunday at 9.30pm on RTÉ One indefinitely.

STRUGGLING RTÉ TO SELL VACANT HOMES ON FAIR CITY SET

HAVE you ever wanted to be part of a modern-day soap opera surrounded by dozens of film crew members, loud actors and an overabundance of middle managers? Well, this could be your big opportunity as RTÉ announced it will be selling off eight vacant plywood TV-set homes on the *Fair City* site.

Even though the TV-set homes are made mostly from cardboard facades with very little interior, they're still built to a higher standard and better value for money than anything currently on the market elsewhere in Dublin, while expecting to fetch anywhere between 300k and 500k each.

'Imagine growing up with the *Fair City* cast and crew all your life and featuring in as many episodes as you like – they can even double up as extras on the set by simply just living their lives there forever, saving us a fortune,' said Director-General of RTÉ Dee Forbes of the new cost-cutting measure.

The new homeowners will also retain all the perks regular RTÉ

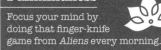

Fullmindness

Focus your mind by doing that finger-knife game from *Aliens* every morning.

staff receive, including wardrobe and make-up access and the new Carrigstown residents can also avail of free advice on tax-avoidance schemes.

'Who knows, if the new residents are accepted into the tight clique here at RTÉ, they may be able to get their family members and friends jobs here down the line,' shared an insider.

The Director-General also announced that RTÉ will auction off Marty Whelan next week to the highest bidder.

ADORABLE! TARANTINO'S SON JUST DROPPED FIRST N-WORD

THERE was a Hallmark moment for Quentin Tarantino's family today, after the esteemed director's infant son Leo uttered his very first racial slur while sitting through a marathon binge of '70s blaxploitation cinema with his dad.

Both Tarantino, 56, and his wife Daniella Pick welcomed the little boy into their lives in late February and while baby experts were shocked to learn that a 12-day-old baby has already spoken his first words, they were less surprised when they learned that little Leo had heard the n-word

How drinking changed in 2020

When some pubs did eventually reopen, it was a flawless showcase of how responsible Irish people can be with a few pints on them.

almost 1,000 times a day since he arrived home from hospital.

While Quentin has faced criticism for his frequent use of the n-word in his movies – it has featured 214 times throughout his 9 films, including a back-whipping 110 times in *Django Unchained* alone, he has always remained adamant that it is his right as an artist to use language as he sees fit, and the same goes for his kid.

'Look, the little guy just heard the fuckin' n-word a buncha fuckin' times while we were watching *Disco Godfather*, and felt he needed to use that word to express his feelings on the fuckin' situation, whatever that was, the fuckin' milk coming from his Mom, the fuckin' onesie we had on him. Whatever. Point is: that's the word he wanted to use, and are you telling me that it's okay for a little black baby to say the n-word when it

County Knowledge

Ross is the most popular boy's name in Roscommon.

wants to be burped, but not my kid just because me and his Mom are white? Because that's some racist shit right there, wouldn't you agree?' said Tarantino, in one breath.

'Now get the fuck off my porch. Me and the kid need to go back to watching movies for another ten hours, and then I have to get to work on my next movie, a grim retelling of *Three Men and A Baby* set in the projects, called … well, you can probably guess.'

Meanwhile, Las Vegas has paid out to all gamblers who had the n-word down as baby Tarantino's first word, despite 'motherfucker' being the odds-on favourite.

MUSIC

DANIEL O'DONNELL FORCED ONCE AGAIN TO DENY PART IN BIGGIE & TUPAC KILLINGS

AGGRESSIVELY beating his chest while proclaiming 'you're looking at an innocent man', the long, never-ending nightmare for Donegal crooner Daniel O'Donnell continues.

O'Donnell has yet again been forced to distance himself from the murder of rapper Tupac Shakur in September 1996 and Biggie Smalls in March 1997 after being hauled in for questioning once more by US police.

'Take these motherfucking cuffs off me, pigs,' a visibly irate O'Donnell said as he left a downtown LA police station besieged by media photographers.

Dogged by these accusations throughout his career, O'Donnell has repeatedly denied that there was

> **'Yeah. I told him straight out his rhymes were weak. Some punches were thrown but that's all in a day's work in the rap world'**

particularly bad blood between the three men nor was he responsible for their deaths in any way.

'Sure, did I disagree with Tupac when he produced and guested on my "Hugging Mammies & Kissing Grannies" album? Yeah. I told him

straight out his rhymes were weak. Some punches were thrown but that's all in a day's work in the rap world,' O'Donnell said in the controversial HBO documentary *The Truth About Biggie & Tupac*.

Famously, O'Donnell had said he was 'at Mass' on the two fateful nights the rappers were slain, but his alibis did not check out. Fans turned their back on O'Donnell when they heard of his poor Mass attendance record with his popularity only returning to its '90s height in the last few years.

Leaked audio recordings from the documentary purporting to be O'Donnell whispering 'what did I do? Killed them all of course' have never been verified.

Community text alerts

Not naming names but the McDonald's down the road obviously didn't get the memo on the whole social distancing thing.

TELEVISION

COMING TO TERMS WITH THE FACT YOUR BOYFRIEND ISN'T CONNELL FROM NORMAL PEOPLE

AHEAD of *Normal People* actor Paul Mescal's induction into the Irish Rides Hall of Fame scheduled for later this week, it may be the perfect time to finally come to terms with the fact your boyfriend isn't Connell from the lauded book and critically acclaimed TV series.

Okay, so when your boyfriend does his inarticulate grunting affirmation thing he sounds like a brainless caveman trying to work out the lock screen on an iPhone, unlike Connell, whose subtle guttural stammer sounds like the anguished cries of someone trying to articulate the deepest, most revealing secrets contained within the chambers of their fragile heart.

And yeah, your boyfriend refuses to wear any of the 14 chains you bought him from the Argos catalogue since you first laid eyes on Connell's one. But is anyone perfect?

And we suppose, yeah, Connell actually knows what he's doing in the bedroom, whereas your boyfriend treats pleasuring you like learning a foreign language; something he always says he wants to learn to do and will get around to eventually when he has the time and yet never does. But is it too much to ask for you to come to terms with the fact he's not Connell?

Fair, your boyfriend is just as bad, if not worse, at communicating as Connell is, but you don't get lost in his eyes the way you do in Connell's deep, dreamy blues. Is that really your boyfriend's fault?

Your boyfriend actually possesses a sense of humour, which is fuck-all competition really against someone who causes orgasmic floods any time he pensively stares off into the middle distance.

Granted, when Connell pours his heart out, it's like a thousand rainstorms have made landfall, cascading down your cheeks, but when your boyfriend moans about how 'you never listen to me or take my feelings into account' it's like shut up already you whiny prick.

Can you accept that Connell understands Marianne's thoughts, desires, worries and hopes on a deep, subterranean level, but the closest your boyfriend got was when he brought you a Twirl back from Centra that one time even though you didn't ask him to get you anything?

It could always be worse; you could be stuck going out with a Jamie in fairness.

This article was brought to you by the Concerned Boyfriend's Association Of Ireland.

| 'Ireland's favourite news source since 234BC' | 𝖂𝖍𝖎𝖘𝖕𝖊𝖗𝖘 𝕹𝖊𝖜𝖘 | **Weather** Have a look out the window and see. Let us know the craic then, will ya? Just having a pint down at the local. Pop down for one. |

VOL 10, 2015   WATERFORD, 19 JULY 1990   90p

Riots As Marathon Bars Become Snickers

BLOODY YET predictable scenes all across Ireland yesterday as Marathon bars made the official switch to Snickers.

The public, driven to a manic violence by the unwelcome change, took to the street and attacked anyone seen in possession of the newly renamed chocolate snack.

'I hate change,' screamed one man, seconds after ripping a man's head clean from his shoulders as he was mid-bite into a Snickers.

'Arrrrrgh,' said another man, who was so angry he took the Lord's name in vain not once but 87 times.

The manufacturers of the abomination are standing firm and are refusing to give in to pressure to switch back.

'Humans once slept out in caves, but we changed. You can get used to this,' shared a pro-Snickers woman, armed with a shotgun for her own protection.

'ADELE SKINNY NOW!' MEDIA CALMLY SCREAMS FROM MEGAPHONE

CAREFUL not to give away any hints that they were losing their fucking minds over a 32-year-old woman's appearance, the media calmly began circling the skies over towns and cities, hanging out the side of helicopters and screaming 'Adele skinny now!' from megaphones and large speaker systems.

Adele, a 15-time Grammy winner, is believed to have published a photo on a social media account, prompting journalists to spontaneously explode as they perfected their 'hey, Adele has lost some weight and this means she's beautiful now' without getting caught outright saying such a thing.

Leading women-are-people-too-focused media publications are now sending up flares into the sky to spell out 'post-divorce glow up', 'here's how you can almost kill yourself with our Adele diet secrets' and 'never mind stupid news about COVID-19 deaths, ADELE SKINNY NOW', but it is not yet known when delirious media outlets will make the predictably cynical shift to commissioning articles about how it's terrible that you, not them, even think someone's weight warrants being 'news'.

'We're all about pretending to give a shit about "body positivity" these days,' confirmed publications that dedicate their resources to making you feel shit about yourself, 'but Adele using social media to thank frontline workers for their COVID-19 efforts was a perfect excuse for us to draw attention to her weight and get you lot arguing among yourselves,' added publications now following you around the house with a megaphone screaming 'ADELE SKINNY'.

Elsewhere, right on cue, pricks worldwide have felt the need to explain 'Adele attractive now'.

ARE THE RUMOURS ABOUT KYLIE MINOGUE VIOLENTLY OVERTHROWING THE BELIZE GOVERNMENT TRUE?

CELEB NEWS! Unverified photos being circulated online seem to show the diminutive Aussie pop icon commanding a sizeable militia.

'I think she's in between albums and might just be a little bit bored,' confirmed one insider, asked to consider the possibility that Minogue has recently changed careers and switched genres from easy-listening pop to ruthlessly ruling over a subjugated mass of innocents.

'Or I could be wrong, and she's really gotten into stripping a country of its natural resources and selling them out to big business for massive profits? In fairness, this news wouldn't be any stranger than the fact that Mila Kunis went out with Macaulay Culkin for nine years. No really, look it up,' added the insider.

Satellite images certainly back up the theory that there was significant movement traced to a roving band of militia in the Central American country. The reasonable question, posed not because it's a slow news day, but posed because we're journalists, and damn it, we've a job to do, is as follows: is Minogue leading these armed forces? And just what does she want? What's her end game?

MUSIC

NATION'S AOIFES, SINÉADS, NIAMHS & CIARAS IN MOURNING AS ROSE OF TRALEE CANCELLED

RAISING their fists in anger to the sky, knees sinking into rain-sodden soil on a dramatic cliff's edge amid a thunderstorm, the nation's Aoifes, Sinéads, Niamhs, Ciaras, Siobháns and Caoimhes screamed in anguished unison, 'no, not the Rose of Tralee you bastarding virus'.

It is proving to be one pandemic-related cancellation gone too far, with many now mourning the loss of the 2020 iteration of the Rose of Tralee which leaves a massive granny-loving-poetry-reciting-oh-my-god-is-there-anything-she-can't-do-shaped hole in the nation's heart.

'I'm going to fucking glass that virus in the fucking neck and watch it bleed out next time I see it,' confirmed the nation's Róisíns, understandably a little bit upset over the regrettable news as they were convinced this year was 'their year'.

> **'I'm going to fucking glass that virus in the fucking neck and watch it bleed out next time I see it'**

'So, what? I've been practising my fire-breathing and jumping on a trampoline while reciting a poem about my mammy routine every day, and all for nothing?' added the nation's Áines.

As a mark of respect, all past, current and prospective Roses will wear black sashes for the rest of the week including all of Abu Dhabi's current supply of teachers and nurses named Saoirse – 1,400 in total. Disappointed Rose escorts have been told to stop moaning, as they never

had a chance of getting the ride in the first place.

The event has for decades been a beacon of light and a key opportunity for the nation to come together and celebrate Ireland and its far-reaching diaspora, even if all Roses named Mairead from Tennessee are now pro-Trump and pro-ethnic cleansing.

'You mean, all the horrible things I did ... they were ... for nothing,' added the nation's Aoibheanns, who now realise assassinating all their local rivals and burying their bodies in sacks of lime in a field, all so they ensure themselves a place at the competition, was pointless.

Did You Know?

Did you know Cavan has the highest concentration of people named Marty in the world?

81

MOVIES

HARVEY WEINSTEIN NOMINATED FOR BEST ACTOR IN HIS ROLE AS CRIPPLED OLD PERVERT

AMERICAN film producer and now actor Harvey Weinstein joins Jonathan Pryce, Antonio Banderas, Leonardo DiCaprio, Adam Driver and Joaquin Phoenix as a Best Actor Oscar nominee for his role as a crippled old pervert, *WWN* can confirm.

Tipped to win the Oscar for best actor for his ongoing performance at a New York court, Weinstein plays the role of a filthy, power-hungry scumbag pretending to be an innocent, frail

---

'It's very hard to act like you're acting badly, but Weinstein nails it'

---

old man. His performance sees him shuffling into his own trial, where he is accused of rape, criminal sex acts, sexual abuse and sexual misconduct, on a Zimmer frame in a bid to garner sympathy from the public.

'It's very hard to act like you're acting badly, but Weinstein nails it,' one film critic tweeted, 'his ability to incite nothing but pure hatred for his character is second to none, and even

makes Joaquin Phoenix's Joker look like a four-year-old playing Pontius Pilate in a school play.'

A method actor, Weinstein has apparently stayed in character for the role of crippled old pervert for several months now, but sources close to the 67-year-old claim he has been portraying an old pervert for 30 years.

'Harvey really threw himself into the role in the mid-80s, raping, sexually harassing and manipulating vulnerable young actresses into acts they would not have normally done,' recalled one source we spoke to.

In the Best Documentary category, *We Had No Idea*, a movie which interviews everyone in Hollywood who turned a blind eye to what they knew was going on, is another favourite to pick up an award.

MUSIC

DANIEL O'DONNELL CAUGHT SUCKING LIFE FORCE FROM ELDERLY FAN IN BID FOR ETERNAL LIFE

THE CONTROVERSIAL singer is in the headlines for all the wrong reasons yet again, this time caught inhaling the very essence of one of his fan's souls, *WWN* can reveal.

Cherubic and fresh-faced throughout the entirety of his career, despite hitting a number of age-related milestones, Daniel O'Donnell has been forced to reveal the source of his evergreen and youthful appearance after he was caught in a compromising photo with an elderly fan.

'Okay, fine. Fine! The secret's out, I admit it,' O'Donnell told reporters when confronted with accusations that he regularly consumes the life force of his fans so that he may see out his dream of immortal life.

Using a practice more closely associated with mystics from the 12th century, O'Donnell uses his regular proximity to his elderly fans to conjure their souls out of their bodies, converting them into a life force which stalls the aging process.

'What do Carmel, Eithne or Fidelma care? Sure, they've had a good innings and they're shocking old as it is. If anything, loyal fans would only be delighted to give over their souls to Big Daddy D,' added O'Donnell, despite his nearby legal team begging him to stop talking.

'You think it's a fluke I look this good? You think it's a coincidence my songs found their audience with the almost-dead demographic? This was never about country music, this was never about being nice to mammies, this was always about living forever,' the singer concluded as he lunged, mouth open, for a nearby pensioner before feasting on her soul.

KEVIN SPACEY TO PLAY PRINCE ANDREW IN SEASON 4 OF *THE CROWN*

FRESH from the superb third season of the critical hit that is Netflix's regal drama *The Crown* comes the news all streaming fans wanted to hear: Season 4 has been given the green light with filming already under way.

'The strained relationship between Princess Margaret and Queen Elizabeth II was further explored in Season 3, but for next season there will be a focus on the now adult Prince Andrew and we can think of no one better to portray such malignant ineptitude than Kevin Spacey,' shared the producers behind the drama which shows the Royal Family at their most noble and respectable.

While fans of the show might not be on board with the time jump from the 1960s and '70s to the present day, or Spacey himself, there is a general acceptance that they're confident they will have equal disdain for Spacey and the prince.

'Some would say he's the perfect fit for the role. He's no stranger to experiencing absolutely zero repercussions for his actions and they're both creepy as hell,' shared one viewer, speaking about the casting news.

'The accent might prove difficult, but Kevin will have no trouble displaying Andrew's complete detachment from the horrible and reprehensible things he's alleged to have done,' added a Netflix executive.

Olivia Coleman, widely regarded as the finest actor in the world today, will return to play the Queen in Season 4 and has already said acting like the Queen had no idea what her son was up to will be her toughest acting challenge to date.

MUSIC

PSST, WE DON'T WANT TO GET YOUR HOPES UP BUT WE THINK COLDPLAY ARE GONE FOR GOOD

WITHOUT wanting to inadvertently instigate a Beetlejuice-type situation, whereby mentioning their name three times summons them into arriving fully formed at your side, if our sources are to be believed, English pillow-soft rockers Coldplay have 'fucked off for good'.

Music fans are urged not to jinx the good news by searching on Google to see if they are well and truly gone for good. Instead, they are asked to just

> **I was just getting on with life, completely unaware of how lucky I was not to hear some dreary ballad'**

enjoy this suspiciously long window of time in which not a peep has been heard from the maudlin foursome that resemble an awkward uncle who insists he is cool.

The closest we get to hearing about Chris Martin these days is the latest article on what substance Gwyneth Paltrow is telling you to wash your vagina out with now. (It's boiled cat

piss, by the way.) Such a dearth of evidence of Coldplay's continued existence is being treated by many people who actually like their ears and hearing decent music as the best news in years.

Low-key celebrations relating to the absence of Coldplay have for now just been confined to thousands of people lining the streets, lost in ecstatic tears of joy, hugging one another and conveying in whatever way they can that feeling that 'yes, the tyranny is over'.

'Now that you say it, I haven't heard them on the radio in ages. And to think, I was just getting on with life, completely unaware of how lucky I was not to hear some dreary ballad or, worse still, a desperate collaboration with a popular pop artist which is just a naked attempt by Coldplay to remain relevant,' shared one overjoyed non-Coldplay fan.

Sadly, *WWN* has learned that there is no such luck for non-U2 fans as that particular band are, along with cockroaches, the only thing that could survive nuclear war.

Fullmindness

Be sure to check your phone for emails last thing at night and first thing in the morning, so you don't miss out on any anxiety over a 24-hour period.

FASHION

KARDASHIANS DEFEND DECISION TO RECAST KHLOE

CONTROVERSY was sparked among the significant portion of humanity who care about the ongoing drama centred around the Kardashian/Jenner clan, after fans were outraged by the jarring replacement of Khloe Kardashian with a completely new actress.

While this isn't the first time the relatable audience favourite has been replaced, fans of the Kardashians complained about the jarring nature of the sudden change, which was defended by the show's creator, Kris Jenner.

'We decided against easing people in over time with a subtle introduction, but yes, the show decided to go in a different direction and we don't apologise for the new kurrent Khloe we've gone with,' confirmed Kris, who has long suffered from a phobia of the letter 'c'.

'We've kind of got a James Bond type thing going on, you've got to pass the baton on and stay fresh. Everyone gave out when we replaced Kim and Kylie but they got used to it eventually,' added Kris.

The lengthy recasting process was said to be carried out based on picking an actress who would easily finish last in a Khloe Kardashian lookalike competition, with less attention given to acting ability or believability.

'It's the same character everyone loves, just played by a different actress,

you'll love her. I was nervous when I started out but you get used to it,' explained Rob Kardashian, a late random introduction to the long-running drama.

Speaking about securing her biggest acting gig to date, 21-year-old Ardanna Flores said she was nervous but relishing the challenge.

'It's such an iconic character but I really hope I can put my own stamp on it,' explained Flores, unaware producers had already begun casting her replacement too.

Did You Know?

Did you know shoes hanging from overhead wires mean there's a cobbler operating in the area?

How friendship changed in 2020

People pledged to carry out mass murder if they were sent another 'funny' TikTok video by that one friend.

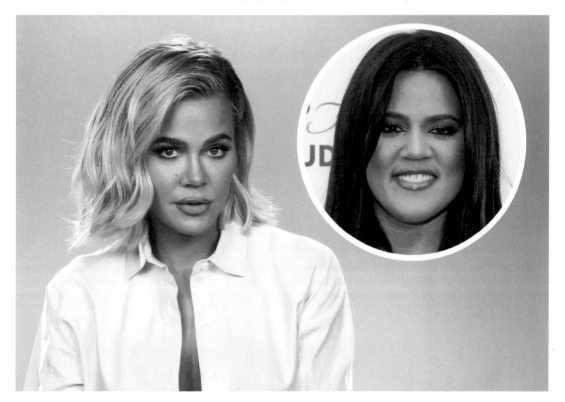

BREAKING NEWS

WEINSTEIN ASKS FOR RETRIAL IN IRELAND

CONVICTED rapist Harvey Weinstein has ordered his legal team to push for a retrial in the Republic of Ireland, stating that 'a mass murderer in Ireland' wouldn't have received the 23-year sentence he was handed yesterday.

Weinstein, 67, is set to face two decades in jail for a litany of sexual assault convictions, in stark contrast to the four years with three-and-a-half suspended that he probably would have received for the same crimes in Ireland.

Speaking exclusively to *WWN*, an Irish judge admitted he was 'stunned' at the Weinstein verdict, and added that if the disgraced former mogul could find a way of getting the retrial held in Ireland, he'd be sure to lop a few years off the total.

'23 years? Jaysus, it's almost like they didn't take his former good standing in the community into account at all,' said Judge Steven Hannerlon.

'And the jury weren't presented with examples of the victims' underwear? The women weren't cross-examined on how much they'd drunk at the time? Sure it's hardly like this thing was a rape trial at all. Next you'll be telling me that no local sports figures came forward to give a reference to his previous good character! 23 years! Sure how's he supposed to have a career after that?'

In other news, Weinstein has made a miraculous recovery from the back injury that plagued him throughout the trial and has entered prison standing straight upright.

MATT DAMON HELD AT GUNPOINT & FORCED TO SAY 'GUINNESS', 'TAYTO' & 'YOUR COUNTRY IS LOVELY'

DALKEY resident Matt Damon was finally tracked down for an exclusive interview via video call by radio station Spin 1308, much to the delight of a locked-down nation in desperate need of a nice feel-good story in these trying times.

Last seen at a Dalkey swimming spot absolutely horsing into a rake of cans he had in a Supervalu bag, Damon happily regaled the nation with his acclimatisation to the

Emerald Isle and was full of the clichéd praise for Ireland from a famous person so beloved by Irish people, all while a gun was seen clearly pointed at his sweat-covered temple.

'Obviously I know the world is going through so much, and healthcare workers are my own personal heroes … sorry, you want what?' a harried-looking Damon said as a stern voice pointing a semi-automatic handgun at the *Bourne* star's head could be heard instructing him to 'stick to the fucking script, Hollywood boy'.

'Oh, okay … Guinness, Tayto, oh my God it's so lovely here, you can't beat the Irish people – so down to earth and friendly. Gee, how about that *Father Ted*, eh, and the Cliffs of Moher with its gas … craic? I love hurling now. The GAA is amazing, can you believe the players aren't even paid,' Damon rattled off, fulfilling the duty of a famous person playing to the Irish crowd while on Irish soil.

Now spotting how his captors had clearly become drunk on his plámásing, Damon grabbed a discarded *Hot Press* magazine and rolled it up in attempt to Jason Bourne his way out of the dangerous situation. However, unlike in the *Bourne* movies, real-life magazines are fuck-all use against guns and Damon went down in a hail of bullets.

With his final breaths, ever the professional, Damon stuck to the script.

'That *Derry Girls* is something else, huh? Your president is so small and compact, how refreshing. Soda bread, coddle, Enya, did you know they filmed some of *Braveheart* here? What a beautiful country. "Looooooow lie the fields…"' spluttered Damon as the cold chill of death washed over him before finally suffocating in his own blood.

MOVIES

JOKER REVIEWED BY AN ANGRY MOTHER WHO HASN'T SEEN IT

THE HIGHLY controversial movie (according to online media) has been the source of fierce debate (according to online media), sparking calls for discussions on how movie violence encourages real-life imitators (according to online media).

Joker, released today in cinemas, illegal downloads, in the 'synopsis' section of Wikipedia pages and in carefully crafted online summaries designed to coax people into apoplectic rage fits, is directed by Todd Phillips and stars Joaquin Phoenix.

In an effort to make no effort whatsoever to provide an actual expert on such matters with an important platform in a widely read publication that could see this push for faux controversy disproved and deflated, we have instead asked Karen Carty

(51), who is very mad at the violence and toxic messages contained in a movie she hasn't seen, to review *Joker*:

'I don't like it,' Karen, a mother-of-three, began while tutting dismissively.

'Suppose it's not as bad over here when ya show violent sorts of movies, but Jesus Christ, people over in America are trying to go see this movie dressed as the Joker. It's depraved stuff,' Karen added, alluding to some US cinemas operating a ban on people wearing Joker clothes, but allowing people to carry guns because America.

'Whatever happened to that hunk Cesar Romero who used to be the Joker, how did the Joker come to this? I remember the worst violence in Batman was when they were climbing up the side of a building and being shouted at by apartment owners, now it's bombs this, semi-automatic weapons that,' added Karen of the

> **'Whatever happened to that hunk Cesar Romero who used to be the Joker, how did the Joker come to this?'**

bygone era of the 1960s when murder had yet to be invented by violent video games.

'I hear it's awful violent, and it's making kids mad for murder,' a shocked Karen explained, one hand covering her mouth to further illustrate her shock at coming to the conclusion that someone had made a movie that was so violently persuasive it could flip a switch in thousands of innocent minds and turn them into demented killers.

'I don't like it,' Karen reiterated. 'They shouldn't be allowed make that sort of movie,' added Karen turning angry at the thought of a film news outlets told her would give her that warm angry feeling if she just clicked the link on their article.

'*Downton Abbey*, now there's a lovely movie. Why can't people just make more of them?'

How driving changed in 2020

You needed a signed letter from the president so you could drive to the shops to get milk.

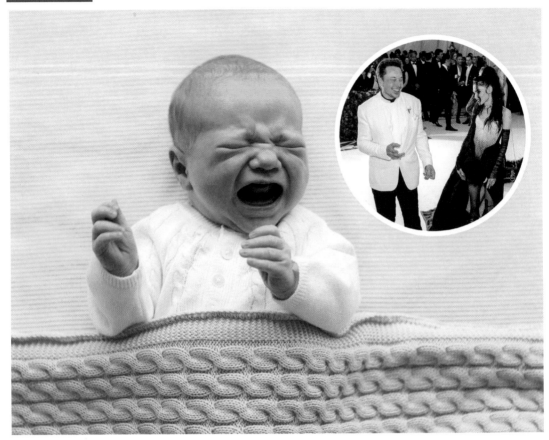

X Æ A-12 ALREADY NEEDS SOFTWARE UPDATE

A BAFFLED Elon Musk is to spend most of today on the phone with customer support after realising that his new baby X Æ A-12 requires a software update despite Musk 'only getting it a few days ago'.

'Why don't they ship them with the most up-to-date software,' mused the billionaire and partner of Grimes, currently operating on one hour of sleep a night for the first time since that time he came up with the idea of sending a car into space and high-fived himself for 23 hours.

'I can't seem to make sense of anything that's happening here; I ordered the kid to be quiet, it freaked out for four hours. Is this thing busted? Does it need a day-one patch to receive input and produce output

> **'I can't seem to make sense of anything that's happening here; I ordered the kid to be quiet, it freaked out for four hours. Is this thing busted?'**

correctly? Should I just strap it to a SpaceX rocket and take it from there?'

X Æ A-12, named after Musk's great-grandfather X Æ A-09, is said to be a 'bit of a disappointment' to Musk so far, with the South African now

wondering if he should have held out for the 2021 model, X Æ A-12s.

'Bit of "father's remorse" here, if I'm honest' mused Musk, mercilessly.

'Like honestly, did I need the extra gadget around the house? Desktop, laptop, phone, tablet, smartwatch; did I really need to have spat-up breast milk over everything? Still, it was worth it to see the look on X Æ A-12's mother's face as we both tweeted about the kid's birth.'

Meanwhile, X Æ A-12 continues to communicate in some complex quantum-language that Musk's best computers have yet to decipher beyond crying noises and farting.

Community text alerts

Transgender Men's Shed has been cancelled tonight due to a lack of transgender men. Sorry Tom, we did try.

October 2020

Dad Mag

FORFEITING YOUR MASCULINITY FOR A BABY SLING

Picking the best black leather/blue jean combo for your working-class dad night out

TOP 5 DAD BOOB FEEDERS

'Whose fucking child is this?'

part-time dad speaks out

How to Dad
IT DOWN
A BIT

Guide to cupping your hand to catch your own sweet farts

ww news
Waterford Whispers News

LIFESTYLE

EXCLUSIVE

AMAZING! THIS MAN'S WHIPLASH WAS TOTALLY CURED SECONDS AFTER HE RECEIVED COMPENSATION

'Money seems to have some kind of therapeutic effect on whiplash, with 90% of all my clients ceasing treatment the very second they receive a financial settlement'

DOCTORS who had been treating a 46-year-old Waterford man for severe neck injuries have today called his miraculous recovery 'a miracle', after his whiplash suddenly disappeared within seconds of him receiving an €18,000 compensation claim.

Following two years of excruciating pain which left him unable to seek work, unemployed father of nine Mark Nagle said he now felt zero pain after he was rear-ended by a fellow motorist when he suddenly stopped his car to save a family of snails crossing a busy city street.

'My neck pain was a small price to pay for saving those snails, who, by the way, slithered off in terror before anyone else saw them,' Nagle recalled of the 2017 incident which changed his life forever, 'it was just bad luck that poor old man was driving a little too close behind me and couldn't stop in time – his insurance must be through the sunroof now, the poor divil.'

Nagle, who has been out of work since 2002, spent the last 24 months visiting specialist after specialist until finally being diagnosed with 'whiplash' as the reason why he has been in excruciating agony since the car crash.

'I couldn't even do this,' Nagle began head-banging to heavy metal music outside the court, demonstrating his stunning recuperation, 'it's like I never had whiplash in the first place.'

Settling the claim out of court, solicitor Barry Hogan said he could not believe his client's remarkable recovery: 'Money seems to have some kind of therapeutic effect on whiplash, with 90% of all my clients ceasing treatment the very second they receive a financial settlement.'

The revelation has sparked calls for all ambulance crews to carry large amounts of cash in their vehicles to help treat victims of whiplash at the scene.

County Knowledge

85% of the world's clones are made in Clones, Monaghan.

How drinking changed in 2020

Many heartbroken pub customers said they missed the stale stench of horrific farts the most.

FOOD

'SHARE PACKS' TO BE RENAMED 'PACKS'

LARGER-than-normal-sized packs of crisps and confectionery are to be recalled and rebranded, following a landmark legal ruling that declared eating the entire contents of one of these so-called 'share packs' is easily within the remit of a single person.

Share packs, the slightly bigger version of snacks such as Cadburys chocolates, crisps such as Hunky Dorys and raisins such as raisins, have become popular in recent times as more and more people turn to food for a release from the dirge that is modern life.

However, studies have shown that these sharing-sized portions are frequently 'less than a mouthful bigger' than their normal versions, prompting a vicious legal battle that pitted confectionery companies against the very people they were trying to stuff full of food in the first place.

'There doesn't seem to be any record of a person buying a share pack and actually sharing it,' said a spokesperson for the pro-pack lobby.

'Look at this bag of Twirl Bites, for example. That's not a share pack, that's one fucking Twirl, cut up. Forget about it. It's false advertising. As for king-sized bars; show me a king that is less than eight inches tall. Fucking show me. We're being conned, is what it is.'

The ruling may also swing the other way and have implications for non-families who buy family meals, with Dominos set to look for proof of kids before delivering anything more than one single pizza at a time.

LOCAL singles looking for a good time are advised to look anywhere other than the direction of Waterford girl Louise Sheelin, who has yet to commit to meeting any of the men that she has matched with on Tinder despite their kind offer of meeting her in a quiet place away from distractions and eyewitnesses.

'We matched on Tinder, she sent me a message to ask how my day was going, I sent her a picture of my erect penis, and boom; haven't heard from her since,' said one irate Tinder user, furious at what he calls Sheelin's 'indecisiveness'.

'I just don't get it. If you don't want nameless, faceless random sex within

STUCK-UP BITCH REFUSES TO MEET TINDER DATE IN SECLUDED AREA

seconds of swiping right on someone, then why even download the app?.'

Sheelin, 26, was unavailable for comment on the matter, but there were hundreds of angry men that were more than willing to give their two cents on the subject.

'Right away I asked where she lived so I could go around for the ride; no reply,' sulked one man.

'I asked one simple question: "do you do foot shit?" Blocked. Some women, eh?' fumed another.

'I just don't see the point in leading a guy on for the 40 seconds between matching with him and getting asked if you'll be alone on Friday night between 9pm and 1.30am, if you're

just going to ghost him,' sighed one married man with four children.

As debate surrounding just how frigid she must be continues, Sheelin remains single and sources say this is unlikely to change any time soon, the stuck-up bitch.

Health and fitness tip

Burn hundreds of calories by digging a massive hole for yourself during arguments.

RELATIONSHIPS

WATERFORD family the O'Mearas have become the latest household in Ireland to have to knock into their dose neighbours to retrieve a parcel that was delivered when they were out, after the delivery company 'helpfully' dropped it off and left a note instead of just returning it to the depot.

The family had been waiting on the parcel and fully accept that missing a delivery and having to arrange a set time to get their parcel is indeed a pain in the hole, but described the process as being preferable to

DELIVERY COMPANY KEEPS LEAVING YOUR PARCELS WITH NEIGHBOUR YOU HATE

engaging in awkward conversation with the Finnans in Number 39, whom they haven't spoken to since an incident involving right of way and parking spaces in 2016.

Resentful at having a 'forced favour' placed on them by their delivery driver, the O'Meara clan issued a plea to transport agencies to better consider

who they leave parcels with; a plea which fell on deaf ears.

'We don't have time to interview your neighbours and see which ones you like the best,' stated a spokesperson for the Irish Delivery Drivers Association.

'If they live beside you and they're in at the time, the parcel is going to them. We don't care if their dog always shits on your lawn, we don't care if you got into a row with their teenage son who is dealing crack from the back garden. You're grownups. Act like it!'

Meanwhile, the IDDA also confirmed that they are to continue the practice of leaving people's parcels in the stinking brown bin, even if the green bin is just right there, clean as a whistle.

County Knowledge

Longford hosted the MTV Awards in 2014.

CALLING A WOMAN 'PSYCHO' IS A REPRESSIVE ACT OF SEXISM, BUT SERIOUSLY, KEELIN IS A FUCKING PSYCHO

IT IS incumbent on me to stress how I find the labelling of women as unstable or psychotic a vile tactic used by the prevailing and pervasive patriarchal structures in place in society as a way to undermine and delegitimise female autonomy, however, having said that, seriously, Keelin is a proper fucking psycho.

My inner feminist wants to sanction myself for falling into the trap of reducing women to 'acceptable' homogenous behavioural traits that men think is 'becoming' of women, but at the same time, Keelin was way too drunk the other night in the

Workman's and she's a sandwich short of a picnic, a banana short of a bunch, a doctor's signature short of a sectioning.

I take no pleasure in calling a woman a 'psycho' and I'm aware the etymology of the word is rooted in misogyny, but c'mon, Keelin ripped my shoe off last night and started trying to suck my toe, and that was after she tried to glass a barman for, and I quote, 'being too good at cocktail-making'.

It is an utter betrayal of an intersectional feminist outlook to use this loaded word to diminish a

woman, and yet, Keelin did piss in the middle of the dance floor and scream 'you're all in my bladder now', before ripping some young lad's earring off his ear using her teeth.

BREAKING NEWS

OPENING all windows in the house despite it only being 7.23am during a nationwide lockdown, dad of four Charlie Hennebry is up out of bed and wide awake, a sure sign that the rest of his reluctant family members will have to follow suit.

Pulling back the curtains in his son's room with all the grace of a stampeding African elephant, Hennebry thundered from room to room in his usual dad way, irritating just about everyone in his path.

'He was in bed until 2pm yesterday because he had a hangover from drinking too much wine while watching Netflix,' recalled Diarmuid Hennebry, who has been a full-time son for the past 14 years, 'he even started giving out that we were making too much noise having breakfast yesterday, yet here he is first thing on a Monday morning

DAD UP SO EVERYONE ELSE HAS TO GET UP

banging doors and opening windows trying to prove some unknown bullshit point,' adding, 'piss off Dad, you dick'.

Unhappy with the lack of movement, Mr Hennebry opted for the loudest daily chores to begin the morning, starting with the hoovering before cleaning out the fire in the sitting room, which is beside his daughter Roisin's bedroom.

'I read a news story from America once where a kid shot his father dead for waking him up too early,' the 17-year-old pointed out, for no reason whatsoever, 'at the time I thought it was an awful thing to do, but now I can kind of understand it, ya know? Albeit too quick a death for such a thing.'

Dad, who is usually on the M50 right now screaming obscenities at random people, was not available for comment this morning as he was 'too busy cleaning up after everybody's mess'.

HEALTH

HERE'S ALL THE THINGS GWYNETH PALTROW IS TELLING YOU TO PUT UP YOUR VAGINA TODAY

GWYNETH PALTROW, part-time actress and full-time spreader of reckless homeopathic 'remedies' which could put people's health at risk, has taken a break from selling candles that smell like her vagina to return to her true passion in life; telling women what they should shove up their own vaginas.

Not to be discouraged by the fact her company Goop was fined $145,000 for making false claims about the benefit of $66 Jade Eggs which she encouraged buyers to shove 'up there', Paltrow is back with more potentially harmful suggestions for what random shit you should pop into your vagina.

1) Actual random shit

That's right, Paltrow's Goop company has carefully gathered jars of human faeces they've found in the woods and are happy to tell you to put it in your vagina. At just $100 per jar, Random Shit, just like the Jade Eggs, promises falsely to 'balance hormones, regulate menstrual cycles, prevent uterine prolapse, and increase bladder control'.

Since it's random shit, no two jars are the same.

2) The withered finger of a Tibetan monk found dead at the foothills of the Himalayas in the early 20th century

Paltrow claims the finger belonging to the monk known as 'Chöden'

can reverse early onset menopause; however, despite costing $299, the finger will have to be shared with Goop customers who also purchase the finger. Once purchased, you will be sent a rota with your allotted time with the finger.

3) Money

Paltrow is vague on the benefits of shoving money up your whoo-ha and actually, on closer inspection, according to the Goop website she's just asking you to send her money so she can shove that money up her own whoo-ha. A bargain at only $100.

4) Someone else's yeast infection

What better way to guard against yeast infection than to inoculate your vagina through exposure to a small sample of a yeast-infected vagina. Prices start at $50 but if you want some of Paltrow's signature yeast that's gonna cost. All in all, a fair price at $500 a swab.

'I JUST WANT TO BE RACIST IN PEACE'

AS part of *WWN*'s opinion series, we give a platform to those who don't really deserve it. This week is the turn of Tipperary schoolteacher Gerry Dunne, who strives for the good old days when a man could go around being racist without being interrupted or anyone calling him out.

They're all at it now, the young folk, just waiting for someone to speak their mind so they can have a go. Free speech vultures, I call them, latching on to every word and phrase like dogshit to a new Doc Martens boot, their ears curling in on themselves when they hear a viewpoint they don't like. You'd miss the days when you'd say what you're thinking and people would just privately shrivel up and die inside at what you were saying, but would keep it to themselves; that's the Ireland I know and love.

I actually refer to it as 'telling-it-like-it-is-ism' – 'racism' has too much baggage, ya know. And when I say something utterly horrible and ignorant altogether, I call that 'legitimate concerns'. Also, it's not 'racist' racist anyway, it's anti-Semitic and xenophobic, so go do your research you left-wing cultural-Marxist donkeys.

For instance, the other day I was sitting down in my own house, minding my own business and then out of nowhere some snowflakes chime in to my tweet about a deeply anti-Semitic conspiracy theory which was first pushed by the National Socialist German Workers' Party in the 1930s. Suddenly I'm the fascist? I'm just trying to relax here and casually share my views in peace. I didn't ask for any of this engagement.

Then, when you suggest burning down a hotel marked for Direct Provision you're inciting violence now too? You can't say anything these days. Don't get me wrong; I never met a so-called refugee that I actually liked. In fact, I've never actually met a refugee, but that's besides the point. The dodgy ones I imagine in my head are enough for me, so when I say burn down a hotel, I don't mean with brown lads in it – that's beyond cruel – just leave them in their war-torn countries instead. Can you imagine if Irish people started that craic abroad? Begging for jobs and handouts. We'd be laughed out of it and told where to go quite fast.

Are some of these refugees getting eight free houses and €20,000 a week from the government? I don't know, and I don't care, but saying it out loud and getting angry sure makes me feel good and lets me give out about the government. What about our own homeless first, et cetera.

Now, piss off and leave me racist in peace.

HOME & FAMILY

FAMILY ALLOW KIDS TO PULL HOUSE ASUNDER, JUST THIS ONCE

IN a move described as 'dangerously bold', Michael and Louise Carrahan have backed down from every single one of their house rules for one day, in a bid to let their kids 'just get it out of their system'.

Waterford couple the Carrahans, normally very tidy and house-proud, have stated that they believe they've a better chance of maintaining a clean home if they just let the kids wreck the place with abandon for one day, describing the experiment as something of an 'untidiness vaccine'.

Twins Eamon and Mollie, 6, and youngster Dearbhla, 3, took to the task with unabashed enthusiasm, and have yet to show any signs of fatigue despite a full morning of running around the house with their outside shoes on, leaving half-eaten apples all over the place, and taking a cavalier attitude to how much toilet paper they flush down the toilet.

> **'After spending the kids' entire lifetimes telling them to pick this up, don't leave that there, is that where that goes?, that's not allowed indoors – we just said fuck it'**

'Wee Dearbhla, all her life she's just wanted to get into the press with the Tupperware, and today she's finally been allowed,' sighed Louise Carrahan, sitting down on the only seat in the house without Marla on it.

'But look, we said we'd give it a go. After spending the kids' entire lifetimes telling them to pick this up, don't leave that there, is that where that goes?, that's not allowed indoors – we just said fuck it. Go nuts. Get it all out, and then hopefully from here on the novelty of living in a pigsty will have worn off.'

In a similar move, dad Michael is to be allowed to leave the toilet seat 'whichever way he feels like', just for one whole day next week.

HEALTH

WITH the search for a vaccine ongoing, and scientists not making the speedy progress desperately craved by humanity, we asked our resident homeopath, Dr Anne Trope* to share her natural remedies that 100% cure COVID-19:

HOMEOPATHIC CURES THAT ARE BETTER THAN A COVID-19 VACCINE

- Don't worry, I'm not going to start spouting dangerous nonsense like 'inject yourself with bleach'. I'm here to give you the natural cures and remedies the Big Pharma lot would rather you didn't know about.
- Gwyneth Paltrow's placenta steamed in a pot for 30 minutes at 200 degrees. 100% effective in killing the virus.
- Walk around with 163 grams of Brie inside your right sock for five days. It must rain two of the five days to be effective at all. Let nature nurture you.
- A gob full of A, B, C and D vitamins. Zinc and magnesium while you're at it. All this should be taken with my current exclusive offer, the shrivelled ear of Shergar I keep in a jar, which is yours for only €499. A small price to pay to be immune to COVID-19.

- Take five drops of this thing that comes out of a dropper; it's grand, trust me, sure doesn't it have flowers on the label and all so it must be legit. No, it's not lead, who told you that? Was it Joanne? Oh, so she made a full recovery so? Thought she was dead for sure when I dumped her at the entrance to the A&E. Shame.

- Remember, homeopathic products work in conjunction with your body. This is worth remembering, especially when I tell you that the devil resides in your soul and we're going to have to carve out your kidney using no anaesthetic. Look, do you want the cure or not?

*Not technically a 'doctor' doctor.

DODGY LOOKING LAD WONDERING IF YOU NEED YOUR DRIVEWAY CLEANED

SOME lad who knocked heavily on your door and peered through the side window wants to know if you want your driveway power-washed and deweeded for just 50 euro, *WWN* has learned.

Answering only to the name of Tommy, as revealed by a similar-looking man parked in a van telling Tommy to knock harder, the questionable cold call pricked your senses, forcing you to retort with a flat-out 'no, I'm only renting the place'.

'Balls,' you tell yourself as you close the door, realising you gave far too much information away about your

current housing situation, 'why not give him your credit card number while you're at it, maybe your blood type too, ya big eejit'.

Peering out the side of the sitting room curtain, you're surprised to learn that Number 14 has apparently opted in for the driveway clean, making you look like some kind of pathetic scaredy pants who trusts no one.

'Fuck it anyway, I have to head out to the shops now and they'll see me leave the house and then rob me blind,' the stereotyping part of your brain began, before rationally snapping yourself out of it.

'For God's sakes they're only trying to make a bit of money. You've got to stop judging people and trust them a little more,' you reason with yourself, before waiting until they finished your neighbour's driveway, securing all the windows and doors, locking the side gate and eventually leaving the house.

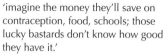

RELATIONSHIPS

LUCKY BASTARDS CAN'T HAVE KIDS

A COUNTY Clare couple who were told they could never have kids together by a specialist were branded 'lucky bastards' by family and friends, despite desperately trying to conceive for the past six years.

'I know they're probably feeling a little deflated now, but when they realise the advantages of not having children then I'm sure they'll snap out of it,' said mother-of-five and so-called friend of the couple, Janet Maher,

'imagine the money they'll save on contraception, food, schools; those lucky bastards don't know how good they have it.'

Spending over €30k on IVF treatments since 2013, the couple were surprisingly downbeat about the news, something mother-in-law Tanya Rice could not understand.

'You'd swear the world was about to end the way the two of them are moping about,' contributed Rice, who spent the majority of her adult life raising children and doesn't want any more, thanks, 'if I was them now I'd head off travelling together, or even on my own, sure, why are they even married now they can't have kids?'

Gluttons for punishment, the 'lucky bastards' reportedly inquired about adoption avenues, to be told it could take years to access.

'They should probably get a dog first and see,' suggested professional suggester and friend Niall Reilly, 'yeah, they'll get a real sense of what it's like to raise a human being by buying a small animal that lasts seven years'.

HUSBAND STOCKPILING COMEBACK ARGUMENTS IN HIS HEAD

FOLLOWING a heated argument over constantly putting side plates on top of dinner plates in the press, local husband Jamie Kehoe vowed to take revenge on his wife's latest jibe, by carefully compiling a series of comeback arguments in his head for future reference.

'Well, at least I don't leave the shower looking like a hairdresser's floor,' Kehoe replied to his spouse, who by now was 5km away in a shop getting the dinner, 'yeah, and stop leaving all the lights on in every room you enter, there's people in poor countries that don't even have bulbs to turn on, so …'

Quite happy with the way his argument was playing out, the grandson of four scoffed at his wife's lame imaginary reply, which was something to do with housework, or some bullshit like that.

'You don't even know how to load a dishwasher properly,' Kehoe burned, now beaming with the thought of actually saying this aloud,

before losing it and adding, 'a three-year-old would have more common sense than you.'

Rowing back so as to not completely destroy his other half as she was totally crying now and apologising to him for being such a bitch all the time, Jamie Kehoe took a deep breath before offering an olive branch to his now totally devastated partner.

'Look, you should know by now that if you're going to come at the king, you better not …' he began, suddenly stopping the concocted argument to answer his wife's actual phone call.

'Oh, hi pet, yeah … for the dinner? Um, oh no, I'm not fussy, you decide pet, yeah, yeah … love you … oh, I won't forget no, doing it now … drive carefully now in that rain, thanks,' he said in a higher-than-usual voice reminiscent of someone trying to be extra nice.

'Fucking showed her,' Kehoe concluded, before putting out the green bin.

EQUALITY

HERE'S OUR UNPAID, OVERWORKED INTERN WITH AN ARTICLE ABOUT THE GENDER PAY GAP

IT'S NEVER been more important to advocate for parity of pay among the sexes. It's 2020, after all.

We here at the trailblazing feminist-first GASH publication know the importance of pursuing this issue more than anyone. For example: how the underrepresented are often placated with empty gestures such as a token, one-off article proclaiming the heralding in of substantial changes which the publication or institution itself does not actively implement themselves and merely uses as an opportunity for self-promotion.

Here to compassionately advocate about an issue close to GASH's heart is our overworked and unpaid intern, Jessica Bradley:

The gender pay gap must be closed at all costs; the resulting benefits felt by all areas of society are undeniable. It's not a polite request – equal pay across genders is something we should all demand.

Even if, in my case, you're in the middle of an internship where you've been largely ignored and essentially hired not to be mentored or guided in learning on the job, gaining skills along the way and legitimately enhancing your CV, but rather used as a glorified receptionist while Sarah is on holidays for two weeks in a naked attempt by this publisher to use my free labour to save on wages.

It boils my piss that I've been exploited in this way and that I'm restricted by the precarious nature of my temporary employment and how if I spoke out I would immediately find myself punished and silenc—

EDITOR'S NOTE: Poor Jessica was unable to finish her article before her internship came to an unhurried and completely planned conclusion. However, judging from the remaining notes she had here in her draft of this article, Jessica seemed to think GASH was a once-in-a-generation glass ceiling-smashing publication fighting for the rights of the downtrodden that most certainly wasn't driven by profit above all things. We wish Jessica the best in the future.   .

How drinking changed in 2020

Wine o'clock was brought forward by alcoholic Irish mothers from 6pm to midday

---

LOCAL WOMAN REFUSES TO HANG UP MIRROR IN BEDROOM

How working changed in 2020

On video conferences, it was 'casual Friday' below the waist every day.

YOUNG Waterford woman Elsa Carmody has again turned down an opportunity to hang up the large mirror that has been propped against her bedroom wall for the last five years, *WWN* can confirm.

Carmody, 26, has stated that the mirror is 'grand where it is', despite serving no real purpose other than acting as a ledge to hang bras from and a space to blu-tack photos of her and her friends.

Upon receiving offers from her dad and her boyfriend to properly mount the 3' x 2' framed mirror on the wall where she could actually use it for its intended function,

'Granted, I don't use the mirror as a mirror, but it's really great to have in the background of every selfie I take'

Carmody has doubled down on her commitment to leave it lying where it is for the foreseeable future, and possibly forever.

'Every girl's bedroom needs a few essential elements, such as a hairdryer left lying on a chair, and a mirror that's 90% covered in dust and Polaroids,' explained Carmody, while doing her make-up using the camera on her phone despite the massive mirror just sitting there, praying to be used.

'Granted, I don't use the mirror as a mirror, but it's really great to have in the background of every selfie I take, as well as the strategically messy assembly of various tops and boots and other random shite, like a glass bowl full of hair-clips, or poster of a movie I've never seen.'

RELATIONSHIPS

IRISH WOMAN ARRESTED AFTER EATING THE HEAD OFF BOYFRIEND FOR ASKING A QUESTION

GARDAÍ were said to be traumatised after attending the gruesome scene of a graphic decapitation in a quiet Cork suburb earlier this morning.

In the moments before the head-eating episode, the victim, Gerrard Heaney (29), had been politely asking his girlfriend, Bryna Keegan, 'Okay, but then why do you hang out with that Sarah one then, if all she does is piss you off?'

While having the head eaten off you is not an uncommon occurrence, Gardaí were struck by the bloody scene they were met with.

'You'd never know the neck and shoulders had a head at all, it was taken clean off the poor sod, and him

only asking why you'd hang around with a dose friend you hate,' arresting Garda Sean Quinlain shared with WWN as he rested on his haunches in between vomiting.

'This particular head-eating was all the more tragic I suppose, as he was only trying to help,' explained coroner Emily Hatton, 'it's not like he was constantly pissing all over the toilet seat or carrying on with someone else.'

Recent medical innovations have made it possible for heads to be reattached to bodies, but when given the choice, a fading Mr Heaney meekly replied 'no, you're alright, I'll only have it ate on me again tomorrow'.

Legal experts predict Miss Keegan will serve no jail time on account of Mr Heaney's flagrant and repeated instances of leaving an empty milk carton in the fridge.

IF PERSON NOT PICKING UP PHONE AFTER FIFTH RING MAYBE TRY FUCKING TEXTING, FINDS STUDY

A GROUNDBREAKING new study into human behaviour and technology has found that if a person does not pick up their phone after the 5th ring, the caller should maybe try texting first, and stop being such an impatient fucking bastard.

Research also found that texting first before ringing may be the answer to securing an actual phone call.

'If you want to speak to someone on the other end of the line, don't think you can just pick up your phone and

cold call them out of the blue, what, do you expect me to just drop fucking everything?' carefully explained lead researcher of the study John Bakeman, who launched the study after becoming sick of his wife ringing him all the time during the day.

'No one knows what they want to eat for dinner at 1pm in the day, Elaine, so just cop yourself on and wait till we're at least hungry enough to know what we want to eat.'

The husband-led study also found that private numbers will in no way be answered at any time of the day, whether the person on the other end of the line is busy or not.

'I know it's you fucking ringing because you're mad that I wouldn't pick up to your number, but what makes you think I'll answer a private

one, huh, Elaine? It's quite obvious it's you ringing just two seconds after your five missed calls, so piss off, I've fucking shit to do.'

However, the study has since confirmed that a 'seen' text message is as good as picking up the phone and not answering, stating that even a ten-second delay in responding to a seen message is as good as filing for a divorce.

'I'm sorry, baby, okay, I didn't mean it, I'm just so fucking busy right now, you know?' the study concluded.

Community text alerts

Garda Tadgh Murphy has confirmed there may be a rapper operating in the area.

HAIR & BEAUTY

WE LIVE IN UNPRECEDENTED TIMES: CLAIRE ACTUALLY PULLS OFF BANGS

AS YOU KNOW, we live in unprecedented times. Up is down. Black is white. This year saw the world as we knew it in so many ways cease to be. Such unintelligible changes are no more in evidence than by the fact Claire is actually pulling off those bangs and we just didn't think it would suit her at all, not with the shape of her face, but fair play.

'Yeah, I mean, it totally suits her, but I'd have never guessed since her forehead is that little bit too small for bangs,' reeled Claire's friend Rebecca, who is still coming to terms with such a blunt fringe somehow working.

'I don't know what the technical phrase is, but she doesn't have a fringy face, y'know, and yet, she pulls it off,' confirmed another friend, Lauren.

'Oh my God. Love, love, love, love!' said Sarah, that one supportive friend who would favourably compare anyone looking like a bag of hungover shite to Gigi Hadid.

Claire, who had said 'okay, I'm definitely doing it: I'm getting bangs,' periodically for the last six years without ever plucking up the necessary courage, finally went for it last week and became the source of non-stop friend group gossip and praise.

'That's right, bitches, you didn't think I could do it but it doesn't look ridiculous and I see you looking,' a triumphant Claire said, noting how she's caught friends staring at her fringe with lusty desire, the same way a man looks at any woman's cleavage.

'No one makes actual eye contact with me anymore, they're slightly above my eyeline, eye-fucking my fringe, just unable to understand how I've pulled it off,' a rather smug Claire concluded.

WATERFORD MOTHER DISAPPOINTED AS CONFIDENT DAUGHTER INHERITED NONE OF HER INSECURITIES

ONE Waterford mother has admitted to being a bit irritated by the fact her daughter doesn't seem to be crippled by the sort of insecurities, hang-ups and lack of confidence that have dogged her own life.

Maureen Kinsella (53), mother to Jess, made the realisation recently after catching herself falling into the trap of trying to chip away at her daughter's confidence through subtly passive-aggressive comments.

'That feckin' confidence, where does she get off? And she's not vain or worried about how people perceive her. It's the carefree confidence and steely belief I always wanted for her,' explained Kinsella.

Far from taking her daughter's well-rounded personality, attitude and inexhaustibly kind nature as proof she's done a fine job in raising her, Kinsella instead chose to resent the fact Jess has only inherited positive traits.

'Even after a few drinks, she's still so lovely and even-tempered. I don't like it at all, she thinks she's great,' explained Kinsella, who was proud of

her daughter at first but the ease with which she's succeeding in life is now a little grating.

Kinsella vowed to slowly work behind the scenes at driving a lasting,

irrevocable wedge between her and her daughter over time just so she can say, 'oh trust me Jess isn't "all that", sure she doesn't even ring her own mother'.

BREAKING NEWS

SISTERS OF MISSING WOMAN PICK WORST POSSIBLE PICTURE OF HER FOR NATIONAL MEDIA

NEVER ones to snub an opportunity to belittle their oldest sibling, the Tracey sisters from Cork admitted to purposely picking the worst image of her for the local and national media to publish, despite her being missing for three days.

Rachael Tracey, who was last seen on Monday evening leaving her home in her car, had no say on which picture of her was to be lifted from her Facebook page, with sisters Anne, Geraldine and Martina Tracey all opting for the photograph of her at the Electric Picnic festival in 2011, just moments after her stomach was pumped by paramedics for over-indulging.

'Yeah, we'll go with that one; it really captures Rachael's true inner

> **'The picture needs to be natural and this one of her coming down from a rake of pills and vodka at a music festival is just perfect'**

being,' the sisters all smugly agreed, spitefully ignoring their sibling's professional glamour shots and thousands of selfies which seemed to feature only one side of her face and an endless pout.

'The picture needs to be natural and this one of her coming down from a rake of pills and vodka at a music festival is just perfect,' they added, pointing out that most of the other pictures were 'social media Rachael'. 'She never looks that good in real life so best we stick to the one where she's literally poisoned from a session nine years ago with dyed hair that she doesn't even have now. Yeah, perfect choice.'

UPDATE: Rachael Tracey has since been found safe and well after coming across her image online and phoning her sisters to fuck them out of it.

Community text alerts

Oh great, it looks like number 47 is building a bar in their back garden. No doubt there will be all sorts coming and going in the middle of the night.

SOCIAL MEDIA

LOCAL WOMAN PUNISHES MEDIA FOR HORRIBLE TREATMENT OF CELEBRITIES BY REPEATEDLY CLICKING ON ARTICLES

DOING her part to make sure she sends an unequivocal message to barrel-scraping tabloid publications that she can no longer stand idly by and let their warped and brutal treatment of people in the public eye continue, one Waterford woman continues to repeatedly click on their articles.

So incensed by the long list of lives destroyed by the exploitative morale vacuums known as tabloids, Vicky Condron (26) is to spend the day reading every article publications such as the *Mail Online* publish, sending the clear message that if they think gutter journalism will be

'Any right-minded person might think clicks to our site would decline at a time like this, but actually they're up substantially, so consider this lesson learned, we hear you loud and clear – the public wants even more of this.

rewarded with click after click, they are entirely correct.

'I'll quit after the next click,' confirmed Condron as she scrolled through each and every article which did a passable job at pretending it cared

for the safety, health and wellbeing of the very same people tabloids usually spend time harassing and eviscerating, all for the public's pleasure.

Speaking exclusively to *WWN* about what a hammer blow to profits Condron's decision to keep clicking has been, one online editor had just about resolved to pack it all in.

'Any right-minded person might think clicks to our site would decline at a time like this, but actually they're up substantially, so consider this lesson learned, we hear you loud and clear – the public wants even more of this. Thanks, Vicky,' shared editor Sandra Barkham.

Some friends close to Condron have urged her to change her reading habits and migrate to different online celebrity-focused sites that don't tear people down; however, such publications are likely owned by the same parent company as the tabloid and sharing the same office.

'SHOULD I STILL BE BREASTFEEDING MY 27-YEAR-OLD?' YOUR PARENTING QUESTIONS ANSWERED

PARENTING is tough. This observation will come as no surprise to parents, both new and old, but it takes a brave parent to admit when they're a little lost and in need of advice.

No matter how seemingly silly or obvious a question or answer appears, *WWN* Parenting has taken the time to answer all our readers' parenting queries below.

You asked and we answered and thus parenting became that little bit less daunting and more enjoyable:

Q) 'Should I still be breastfeeding my 27-year-old son?' Brenda, 55
A) Milk is fucking delicious, Brenda, as everyone is all too aware. And climate change is the real deal. So by continuing to offer your 27-year-old son milk, you are reducing your own carbon footprint as we know the CO_2 emissions ground out by the effort it takes for the dairy industry to get cow's milk from the farm to our fridge is a real problem.

While it's highly, highly unlikely, as long as the relationship with your 27-year-old adult son has no evidence of any unhealthy rituals or habits, then what deep-seated regressive behaviours could you be maintaining by letting him suckle up? It's harmless.

Q) 'My teenage daughter's a real fucking bitch. Help.' Martin, 37
A) Now, now Martin. It sounds like you're falling into a damaging patriarchal view of femininity and how women navigate their emergence into puberty and the sort of emotional and physical changes that hormones can manifest.

Come on, Martin, you're better than that sexist vitriol you sent into us. Think about it, why did you rush to call her a bitch? Unconscious sexism is damaging to your daughter.

You could have easily said 'she's a real fucking bastard' or prick, wanker

or cock. But you let sexist parenting get in the way. Shame on you.

Q) 'My toddler won't stop eating Play-doh, what can I do?' Anna, 26
A) C'mon Anna, who's the child and who's the adult? Shit in the Play-doh container and show your wee one you're not fucking about.

Q) 'It's hard to get my baby to settle. We've tried everything. Help.' Hannah, 31
A) Check your receipt and see what the returns and exchange policy is.

Q) 'My child is screaming at me, I'm convinced he's hidden my glasses on me too and now the cheeky brat is

saying "stop calling me Declan, that's not my name. I want my mommy". He's driving me up the wall.' Caroline, 39.
A) Caroline, could you have mistakenly wandered into the neighbour's house by accident? The Drurys? And are you currently freaking out their youngest Conor? We told you that you should have got that laser eye surgery done last year but you wouldn't listen.

HSE UNVEIL BUNK BED TROLLEYS TO COMBAT HOSPITAL CONGESTION

How working changed in 2020

Self-important pricks who loved wearing lanyards still wore them to work at home.

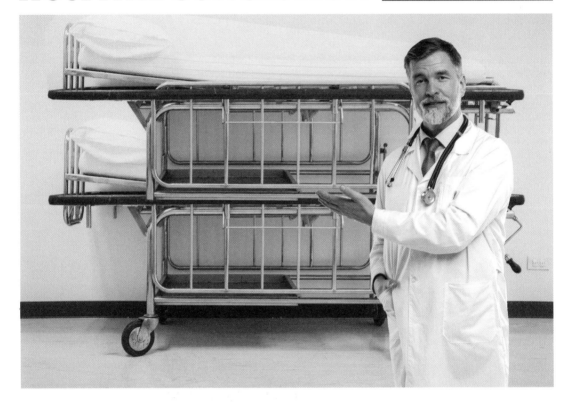

ACTING on record levels of hospital overcrowding, Health Minister Simon Harris, in conjunction with the HSE, has unveiled a €3 billion investment into 'bunk bed trolleys' which are expected to halve the number of people waiting on hospital trolleys in only a matter of weeks.

Technically classed as one unit, the new bunk trolleys will bring the monthly figure down from 10,000 trolleys to 5,000 hospital trolleys being

County Knowledge

Sailors in the North Sea tell tales of a mythical 32nd county called 'Donegal', which emerges from the sea every now and then to win an All-Ireland and complain about lack of funding.

> **'The great thing about bunk trolleys is patients will never be lonely and can even help each other out'**

used to cater for patients waiting to be treated across the country.

'The solution was just staring us in the face this whole time,' a rather chuffed with himself Simon Harris told *WWN* at the launch. 'The great thing about bunk trolleys is patients will never be lonely and can even help each other out when it comes to carrying out small medical tasks like blood tests or CPR, thus freeing

up doctors and nurses to focus on the private patients with insurance.'

A 72-year-old Waterford woman who spent 100 plus hours on a trolley last week has since welcomed the new double-decker solution, stating that having a bunk partner will pass the time quicker, if they're still alive.

'There's nothing more awkward than lying on a trolley in a hospital corridor while people try to operate the vending machine beside you,' she explained, 'at least now when someone asks for change for a Twix they'll have another person to ask instead of me.'

The HSE confirmed it will also look into reducing trolley figures even further by trialling triple bunk trolleys, but admitted it will need to raise the roof on all its hospitals at a modest cost of €56 billion.

HAIR & BEAUTY

NEW LAW NO LONGER FORCES WOMEN OVER CERTAIN AGE TO GET SAME HAIRCUT

A DRACONIAN LAW from a bygone era has now been consigned to the dustbin of history and in the process thousands of women around the globe have rejoiced and convened in joyous and ecstatic celebrations.

'I never thought this day would come but I'm free,' explained 59-year-old Margaret Cummings, as she took a ruler to her hair while confessing she was looking forward to having a more

relaxed and loose run of hairdresser appointments over the coming years.

Gone is the requirement for women of a certain age to conform to a short crop or face a possible custodial sentence, as the peculiar Stringent and Homogeneous Haircut Act 1999 was repealed.

The extinguished law is already seeing women reaping the benefits.

'I'm no longer mistaken for being a whole variety of different women, I'm getting dreads and no one can stop me,' confirmed 58-year-old Joanne Kilty.

However, it's not all good news as Ireland's designated hairdresser to women over a certain age, Josephine

Andrews, is set to lose business as a result.

'I just use a template and copy it on every woman. I've a magazine cut-out of Judi Dench from the 90s and I just use that. I'm ruined now if they're all growing it out, ruined,' shared a distraught Andrews.

Did You Know?

Did you know up until widespread protests in the 1950s, doors had no handles?

INSISTING it's really no trouble at all, local Waterford man Ciaran Shelley is happy to showcase his cat-like reflexes on the pause button if you're going to talk over a TV programme while it's on, *WWN* can reveal.

'No, it's fine. Go on, what were you going to say?' Shelley is happy to respond whenever his technique of sighing loudly and pausing a show as someone begins to talk results in

LOCAL MAN HAPPY TO PAUSE TV PROGRAMME IF YOU'RE GOING TO TALK OVER IT

someone feeling like they've interrupted a monumentally important task.

'Look, I get it, when you're watching *Peaky Blinders* or something like that, you need to concentrate on it but this

prick is pausing during fucking ad breaks,' confirmed a close friend of Shelley's who came over to watch the football but instantly regretted it after trying to engage in conversation.

Attempts to talk to Shelley proved problematic as he made a big song and dance of having to pause the TV show he was watching, extending his remote control-holding arm out in a slow and deliberate manner before forcefully pressing the pause button.

'Oh, who me? No, I don't mind. People talking over TV shows during important bits or bits that will go on to be important but we don't know that because *someone* wants to talk about Cathy in the office's new haircut. No, no, I don't mind at all,' Shelley explained, before immediately ignoring us and returning to a 15-year-old episode of *Midsomer Murders*.

'There's not a court in this country that'll convict me if I murder him for shit like this,' remarked Shelley's long-suffering partner Graham.

WOMAN DRIVING NEW AUDI MUST HAVE RICH HUSBAND

A CONGLOMERATE of male observers have confirmed that a local woman driving a 2020 Audi A7 must have a very rich husband and will probably scratch 'the absolute bejaysis' out of the car's 21" alloys, *WWN* has learned.

The woman, who was probably on the way to pick up the kids from school or getting something for the dinner, was spotted driving the three-litre Quattro at 2pm today by 34-year-old labourer Mark Casey, lead researcher of the newly founded study.

'You could tell by the way she was driving it that it wasn't hers,' Casey told his work peers as they tucked into a round of breakfast rolls and flasks of tea, shortly after 37-year-old solicitor Janet Holden drove by, 'such a waste of a car if you ask me, he should have got her a Mini Cooper or one of those sissy Land Rover Evoque yokes, but a fucking A7? The lad must be tapped.'

The study also found that a woman could not possibly afford an 85-thousand-euro car and was

more than likely also cheating on her husband with somebody else, before going on to call her 'high maintenance'.

'Fair enough, she's a cracker alright, but what happens when he finds out about her sleeping around,' voiced study overseer Tom Tyan, who spent the majority of the day flipping a stop sign and reading the back of a red-top newspaper, 'if she's looking for some greener grass on the other side then I've got it all down here,' he added, now pointing down at his sagging crotch and laughing profusely at his own patheticness.

A SERIES of embarrassing misunderstandings have led one work colleague to misread the signs and conclude that she is your *friend* friend and not merely your work friend, *WWN* can exclusively reveal.

Noreen in HR has often provided amiable company in the office and

WORK FRIEND THINKS YOU'RE HER FRIEND FRIEND

polite small talk when passed in the corridor; however, the demeanour and informality with which she now engages in conversation suggests the worst has happened and she thinks you are 'friends friends'.

'We see this kind of thing all the time,' shared Work Relations Commissioner Eddy Mallon, 'you go for one off-the-premises lunch, talk about Martin in finance's horrendous wig that's fooling no one and then Bam! You're being called "work bestie", "work wife" or the dreaded "bestie".'

While Mallon was short on advice for anyone trying to extricate themselves from an unwanted friendship friendship that was just

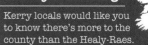

County Knowledge

Kerry locals would like you to know there's more to the county than the Healy-Raes.

there to help make the day go by quicker, there are small measures that can be taken.

'Always have an excuse in your head for why you can't meet up after work or at weekends. When the time comes and the likes of Noreen get all 'ooh we should so do brunch', you can fob her off with the old 'sorry I can't, I'm getting my arm removed', or 'actually I would only my cat is getting a divorce', finished Mallon.

HEALTH

LOCAL MAN HAS TO GET TRACKSUIT BOTTOMS CHISELLED OFF HIM

How driving changed in 2020

There was fuck-all traffic but you weren't even able to get out there and enjoy it.

EMERGENCY crews worked right into the early hours of this morning after being called to a Waterford home where it is believed a man in his 30s had to get his tracksuit bottoms chiselled off of him.

The man, who has been in self-isolation in his home for the past three weeks, called 999 yesterday afternoon stating that he was now trapped in his caked-on tracksuit pants as his skin had started to merge with the nylon material.

'We believe the man was wearing his tracksuit pants so long that nerve endings started to network into its fibres to such an extent that he could actually feel the pants as they slowly became part of him,' a paramedic at the scene explained, 'we had to first inject his pants with a local anaesthetic before we began to chisel them off of him.'

During the procedure, the local fire brigade had to be called in to use the jaws of life to remove the crotch area of the tracksuit pants.

'Old chocolate and crisp residue along with all varieties of human organic matter just built up over the last few weeks while he was binge-watching TV programmes during lockdown,' he added.

> **'We believe the man was wearing his tracksuit pants so long that nerve endings started to network into its fibres'**

Following the rescue, which took several agonising hours, Gardaí and paramedics issued a stark warning for other people in similar states, urging them to change their 'fat man pants' at least once a week to avoid calling emergency services who are already overwhelmed with the COVID-19 surge.

'We understand that people may be less concerned about their own personal hygiene and couldn't be arsed to change their at-home clothes, but just wipe yourself down every few days so that you don't become part of what you're wearing,' they stated.

Health and fitness tip

Remember, it takes longer to burn off a doughnut than it does to burn off five bags of chips. So instead of doughnuts, eat five bags of chips.

HAIR & BEAUTY

OTHERWISE INTELLIGENT WOMAN HANGING ON EVERY WORD OF BEAUTY BLOGGER

WHAT initially started out as a casual scroll through Instagram for some make-up tips has turned into something more sinister for local intelligent woman Ciara Shanley, GASH can reveal.

Innocently searching out the perfect smoky-eye look, Shanley has now become obsessed with beauty blogger Maria Fahey's every post, story, comment, YouTube vlog and TikTok.

'She's a little too invested,' admits Shanley's other half Ronan Doran, 'if this make-up one got a tattoo on her eyeball, I can't say Ciara wouldn't suddenly be into the idea.'

Shanley, for her part, has denied the accusations, stating it's a mere 'coincidence' that the recent haircut, dress, bag, active wear and face scrubs she bought, along with newly discovered anti-vax rants, happened to all be first seen on the blogger's feeds.

'I dunno, it's a bit stalkery at the end of the day, isn't it; being that obsessed with some randomer? She's always posting "stun hun" on every new photo this one puts up; if she was to stun hun her any more she'd be classed as a taser,' a concerned Doran added.

'Ah, cop on Ronan, it's not like I'd jump off a cliff just 'cus she did,' Shanley said, seemingly forgetting she bought a herbal tea diet pack that made her shit non-stop for a week using the blogger's discount code.

County Knowledge

Dublin is known as 'The Pale' due to the translucent nature of the original pasty natives.

THERE comes a time in every friendship when you just have to support your friend even though they're very clearly wrong, but not because they are your friend, but rather because they're sort of intimidating when they're angry and you don't deal well with confrontation.

This was the exact dilemma facing Rebecca Sulnan when listening to her friend Tara Pearse complain about the well-paid job she is currently in despite Pearse openly stating she calls in sick regularly and does next to no work in.

'Oh my God, yeah you're so right,' nodded Rebecca, after Pearse said something which actually made clear how wrong she was.

'You always leave early from there, often turn up half-pissed and keep missing your easily achievable targets, but you're definitely in the right,' Rebecca added with her perfected smile which suggested it's just easier to agree with everything.

The conversation repeated the same rhythms Rebecca's conversations have taken with Tara since they became friends some ten

NODDING ALONG IN AGREEMENT WITH YOUR INTIMIDATING FRIEND WHO NEVER ADMITS SHE'S WRONG

years ago with Tara's talent for waving her hands around in such a way you'd be justified in thinking she's going to take a swing at someone.

'Don't get me wrong, we're totally best friends, she's great, our friendship is great, but she absolutely terrifies me and I will never challenge her because she grunts and snarls when she's angry, ha-ha,' confirmed Rebecca, who was not really sure why she was laughing.

HAIR & BEAUTY

IT'S the latest craze in exfoliation and make-up … but are you paying too much for your charcoal face masks? Experts have revealed that you may be able to save yourself a fortune by simply wetting your face with water from the tap and sticking your face in a coal scuttle, *WWN* can reveal.

With charcoal now worth more than gold when it comes to beauty, *WWN* scientists have found that the quite expensive ingredient can be sourced for much less around the home, from such common fossil fuels as coal, briquettes, those little BBQ nugget things, and even just a big pile of used matches.

In fact, pretty much any cosmetic or sanitary product, from body wash to toothpaste, can be cheaply recreated from a big sack of ashes that you can get by burning down almost any tree, according to economist Daniel McAdams.

'It's the greatest scam since baking soda in toothpaste,' cried McAdams, speaking at the launch of his new book *Never Get Ripped Off By Teenagers On Instagram Again*.

'And see that Skinny Tea? That's just something that gives you the shits, is what that is. Folks, if it sounds like bullshit, it normally is. Charcoal face masks? Ha! I've used Bord Na Mona turf on my skin for the last six months and look at it now! Granted, it's fucked, but you should have seen it six months ago!'

If you would like to purchase some briquettes, click the link in our bio and enter the promo code 'WWN' to avail of a one-time discount of 20% on your first 500 bales.

SAVE MONEY ON CHARCOAL FACE MASKS BY RUBBING YOUR FACE WITH A BRIQUETTE

'It's the greatest scam since baking soda in toothpaste'

Health and fitness tip

You may get strong at the gym, but will you ever be 'foreign lad' strong? It's unlikely. Set yourself a realistic goal!

COOKERY

TRY THIS DELICIOUS RECIPE FOR HALAL CODDLE

How working changed in 2020

According to Fine Gael sources, at its peak, over 44 million ineligible working-class louts were claiming COVID-19 payments.

WITH the unstoppable Islamification of Western Europe currently underway, according to a Facebook post your aunt shared, you may be wondering how this will affect the day-to-day lives of ordinary, decent, hard-working Irish people; in particular, what does it mean for the nation's favourite meal, a nice steaming hot coddle.

Consisting of delicious boiled sausages, thin white gravy and oodles of soft floppy rashers, coddle throws

> **'Coddle is currently the food of the infidel; it must be made in a halal fashion, or not made at all'**

up a number of problems under Sharian Culinary Law, meaning that in order to abide by the new laws set to come into play any day now, some changes are going to have to be made.

'Coddle is currently the food of the infidel; it must be made in a halal fashion, or not made at all,' said the CEO of a government-funded halal

meat company, according to an article on theLiberal.ie website.

'Death to all who do not abide by the following rules when preparing this dish!'

Ingredients

Linda McCartney Sausages
Turkey Bacon
Carrots
Coddle juice

Step 1

Boil the Linda McCartney sausages, turkey bacon and carrots in a pot of coddle juice. As they contain no pork, Linda McCartney sossies are not only halal, but also less packed with cholesterol. The turkey bacon must be certified halal; luckily, all supermarkets will be forced to be halal from 2020, when the globalist master plan to eradicate humanity swings into play, all funded by George Soros.

Step 2

If you cannot buy a carton of coddle juice, you can make your own by leaving water in a dish for a week.

Step 3

Cook for nine hours, remembering to make time to bow to Mecca several times during the day.

Step 4

Serve on a bed of torn-up Easter Rising proclamations and enjoy with a nice glass of the tears of your children.

Coddle is just the first Irish foodstuff to be halallified ahead of 2021, with Tayto and Lyons tea to follow. Please share this with as many of your followers as you can, so they can react in a calm and accepting manner. Should they feel the need to add anything to the recipe to make it even more inflammatory, there are currently no laws against this.

RELATIONSHIPS

RELATIONSHIPS

CONVINCING YOUR FRIEND TO DUMP HER BOYFRIEND SO YOU HAVE SOMEONE TO GO ON THE PULL WITH

HAS YOUR fun, always-up-for-the-craic friend been engaged with a partner in a loving, rewarding and stable romantic relationship, leaving you with no one to properly go on the pull with?

Is it now time to consider the nefarious option of plotting to break them up, because c'mon, your friend's a stunner and is always good for attracting lads on nights out, but she's no use to you if she's at home on the couch building a lasting connection with her boyfriend who she loves dearly.

Instead of striking out on nights out, now's the time to act out and break them the fuck up so you can get the old Penis Patrol back in business.

Did You Know?

Did you know the Kings of Leon abdicated their throne in 2013?

Here's how you convince your friend to break up with her boyfriend who's just getting in the way at the end of the day:

1) Seed of doubt

'Have you ever thought you could do better than him?' – plant that seed of doubt in your friend's mind and watch the boyfriend-doubting tree sprout and grow to the size of a Californian Redwood.

2) 'You were more fun when you were single'

Is it true? No. Is it hurtful? Yes. Will you do anything to increase your own chances of getting the ride alongside a wing woman who is single and wants to stay until 6am? Also yes.

3) Begging

Okay, so it's not a good look and you will lose your dignity, but side note: openly begging for her to go out five

nights a week and tear it up, surviving on a diet of 4am kebabs, will be worth it.

4) 'Your boyfriend is a Russian KGB agent implanted on our shores to sow the seeds of discontent and destabilise democracy'

If she's not willing to listen to reason, maybe she'll listen to treason.

Here comes the easy part: buy and plant a fake Russian passport 'belonging' to your friend's boyfriend in their apartment and watch their relationship disintegrate before their eyes. A photoshop of him playfully wrestling with Vladimir Putin wouldn't hurt either. And obviously place an anonymous call to the relevant security authorities.

Here comes the hard part: trying to get her to stop crying long enough to get her out on the dance floor to slut drop.

RELATIONSHIPS

WOMAN WHO HAS REJECTED FRIEND'S ADVANCES 70 TIMES URGED TO BE MORE CLEAR

THERE HAS been widespread condemnation of one Waterford woman after it emerged she has needlessly been leading on her nice and supportive male friend for several years, *WWN* can confirm.

Aoife Stack (24) has been advised that in future cases of interactions with the opposite sex, she should make it abundantly clear from the outset that she is only interested in a platonic relationship after it emerged friend of Stack's Michael Kinnesey (25) was left frustrated after 70 separate failed attempts to kiss her on nights out.

'Mixed signals are the worst. Just be upfront and have the courage to say it on more than 70 separate occasions, poor Michael,' one observer said directly in his advice to Stack, a woman who has at this point said variations of a polite 'no' more times than Ian Paisley at the height of his 'Ulster Says No' campaign.

Kinnesey has defended Stack while confirming the experience can be a really useful time for Stack to learn from her ambiguous behaviour and grow as a person.

'Aoife's class, she's great, but yeah, just come out and be honest. She's

> **'Mixed signals are the worst. Just be upfront and have the courage to say it on more than 70 separate occasions'**

had ample opportunity to be quite unequivocal, all those texts and DMs I've sent and she's been a bit on the fence with the whole "us" thing,' Kinnesey explained of Stack's unwavering commitment to speaking her mind and telling the man she is not interested.

'Her insistence at having a boyfriend further confused the situation, but look, let's not all call her names at once. Let's wait until 3am when I'm drunk and I'll her text some horrible stuff,' concluded Kinnesey.

How friendship changed in 2020

90% of WhatsApp communication involved Big Mickey pictures.

All your social distancing advice inside

April 2020

SOCIAL DISTANCE
WEEKLY

Dogshit: Was there always this much?

GUIDE: Holding your breath passing people

8 Sexy Facemasks
That Will Drive Strangers Wild

WE MEET THE LAD WITH THE TWO-METRE MICKEY WHO CAN STILL GET THE RIDE

Perfecting passive-aggressive Post-it notes for your flatmates

Waterford Whispers News

SPORT

GAA LAD WHO BASED ENTIRE PERSONALITY AROUND TALKING ABOUT GAA SORT OF LOST RIGHT NOW

THE SEASON cancelled and no sign of its return. Gargantuan supplies of boredom with conversational voids to fill. Just what are GAA-loving lads, whose personality consists solely of talking about the sport, to do now it has left our lives for an indeterminate amount of time?

Well, this a question GAA officials are trying to answer as GAA lads wander aimlessly around their local community, forced to confront the fact that when you take spouting on non-stop about GAA out of the equation, just what is left?

How working changed in 2020

HR managers were increasingly intervening in marriage disputes had by couples working together at home.

'Like, eh, who am I? I, eh, guess is what I'm wondering,' confirmed one monosyllabic and utterly lost Junior B bench warmer who you usually can't shut up for all his talk of bulking up with weights, bleep tests, protein shakes and how he feels 'this year is my year to break into the team'.

Emergency GAA response units first responded by airdropping emergency links to highlights of old games and skills drills on YouTube, but as time went on and the sport didn't immediately come back, a new approach was needed.

'There's only so much "when d'ya reckon it'll be back?" talk you can do. We were faced with trying to find things that the lads could refocus their

> **'There's only so much "when d'ya reckon it'll be back?" talk you can do'**

GAA obsession on in some other way,' GAA welfare officer Michael Cleary explained, 'y'know, other subjects lads can use to bore the absolute hole off women they fancy.'

Some GAA lads were redeployed to hobbies and subject matter that could make the most of their overbearing passion and relentless capacity for stewing over meaningless, idle scraps of GAA ephemera.

'We turned one fella into a wreck-the-head Radiohead fan, another lad became a French film snob, we got one lad to become a vegan; we just needed to pair them with anything that lent itself to being insufferably obsessed with and it actually seems to be working out just fine,' concluded Cleary.

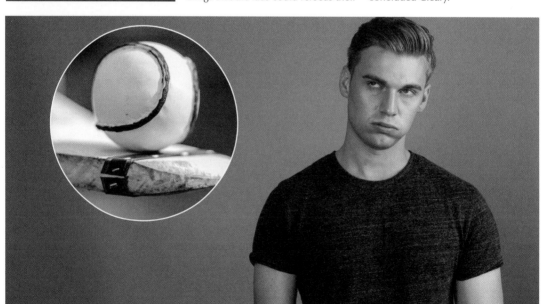

OLYMPICS

KIM JONG UN WINS 24 GOLD MEDALS AT THE TOKYO OLYMPICS

ANOTHER day of astonishing achievement in the remarkable life of Kim Jong Un after the North Korean leader returned from Japan, the host of the cancelled 2020 Olympics, with 24 gleaming gold medals.

'The North Korean people's exceptionalism continues through our Dear Leader who vanquished the pig Americans and won 24 gold medals, all hail Kim Jong Un,' confirmed the North Korean Central News Agency, all as video of Jong Un struggling to climb a flight of stairs played.

'100 metres – gold medal, tennis – gold medal, marathon – gold medal, eh, what other sports are there? Emm,' the news anchor continued, stumbling through recalling all the cancelled Olympic events Jong Un definitely won gold in, in what is probably her final news report.

An official welcome home ceremony for the triumphant leader was staged with the leader sitting before an adoringly miserable and malnourished-looking crowd.

Jong Un failed to rise from his chair to address his people, claiming the 24 Olympic medals, which were clearly made from the gold foil you get from chocolate penny coins, were heavily weighing him down.

'That is correct, I sit not because my morbidly obese frame is not-so-slowly killing me, but because of the very real gold – it's so heavy,' confirmed the leader, who reportedly won gold in the weightlifting event with a world record four-tonne deadlift.

The leader received more rapturous applause as footage, which was clearly taken from previous Olympics that actually went ahead, was then played showing Jong Un's head clearly superimposed on the bodies

of Michael Phelps, Usain Bolt, Katie Taylor and Simone Biles.

JACK FAVOURITE TO WIN LIGHTWEIGHT BOUT AGAINST UNTESTED NERD CILLIAN

BOOKIES are no longer taking bets on the outcome of the much-anticipated bout between local children Jack Tallon and Cillian O'Neill, both 13.

Despite competing in the same age group, Jack is a full five inches taller and a stone heavier than his opponent and also benefits from what onlookers call 'having a murderous look in his eyes'.

Local teenagers say Jack's opponent Cillian stands no chance on account of him being 'a total fucking scrawny nerd'. Fans who are curious as to how much blood is contained in the human body may soon have their answer.

Jack 'Fists of Brick' Tallon is a rare once-in-a-playground bully who remains unbeaten in all 47 of his bouts, and remains confident that when he steps into the makeshift ring behind the bike shed, Cillian 'The

Punchbag' O'Neill will regret minding his own business.

'I want this "fight", if we can even call it that, to be a lesson to all nerds out there that if they think they can

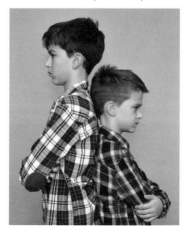

just try to quietly hang out with their friends and get away with it, they can't,' explained the aggrieved Jack, who will cry about this in therapy years later.

'The smart money is on Jack, who seems to derive the same joy from punching kids in the face that a florist gets from arranging beautiful and delicate floral arrangements,' confirmed a Ladbrokes spokesman, who has already paid out on all bets backing Jack to reduce Cillian to a pulpy liquid.

'What song do you want played at your funeral?' shouted Cillian's supportive friends as part of a last-minute pre-fight pep talk.

County Knowledge

Monaghan's 'Dublin Street' is so-called after the county struck a deal with the capital to name O'Connell St 'Monaghan Street', a deal the bastarding Dubs reneged on.

BREAKING NEWS

'MAYO CURSE' TO BLAME FOR GLOBAL PANDEMIC

A GAA INVESTIGATIONS unit has concluded that the outbreak of the global COVID-19 pandemic can be traced directly back to the infamous 'Mayo curse', *WWN Sports* can reveal.

'We looked further back in our archives and we discovered the Mayo curse actually predates their last All-Ireland win in 1951,' explained GAA historian Áine Ní Laoire.

The curse was initially thought to centre around the 1951 All-Ireland-winning team boisterously celebrating their win through Foxford, Mayo and failing to respectfully and quietly observe a passing funeral cortege. As a result, a priest cursed the team, stating the county would never win an All-Ireland as long as any member of the squad remained alive. However, Ní Laoire has debunked this entirely.

'It goes further back to a previous Mayo team who were on the piss in Spain for a pre-season strength and conditioning piss-up,' the historian explained.

'This was in 1918, the height of the Spanish Flu, and do you think these boozed-up Mayo lads respected a funeral in that pandemic? They did in their holes,' explained Ní Laoire, adding that a Spanish mystic stated that a vengeful pandemic would hit Mayo and Mayo alone when the final member of that squad died.

'Well, turns out the curse was a little overcooked. Slightly too powerful a curse, we're guessing, and the mystic has us all fucked over now. It's thanks to the Mayo corner forward from back then living until 134, the stubborn bastard, that it's only hit now after his passing,' added Ní Laoire, who found the whole 'Mayo for Sam' stuff fierce irritating even before this revelation.

LIVERPOOL FAN DROWNS IN FLOOD OF TEARS AFTER TITLE WIN

AMBULANCES rushed to the scene of a post-title-winning celebration conducted over Zoom as Liverpool fan Mark Macken struggled to stay above the torrential tears he was now crying.

Faced with the beep of the final whistle and an end to 30 long years of 'this-year-will-be-our-year-ism', 22-year-old Macken began crying, so overjoyed he didn't notice the tear levels rising above neck height.

'I was celebrating with him on the Zoom chat, I was shouting at him "watch out" but he misunderstood and shouted back "watch out is right, it's the beginning of a dynasty!" before the water engulfed him,' confirmed fellow Liverpool fan Cian Dermody.

Dermody believed Macken, proud to a fault, refused to admit he was crying for fear he would lose face and

so stubbornly drowned in his own tears rather than admitting the moment Liverpool won the title got to him emotionally.

Help came bursting through Macken's door but there was no way to save a man who was producing 40 tonnes of tears a minute from his eyes.

'Against that tidal wave of tears, we didn't stand a chance. You normally only see this outpouring of tear-based joy and relief when a Man United fan gets to celebrate his club signing a new official Japanese noodle partner,' explained the medic who tried and failed to save Macken.

The paramedic then shared a word of warning for fans everywhere.

'A scan of Macken's house using a Geiger counter revealed that his teary celebrations, and therefore those of all Liverpool fans, contained a radioactive level of toxic smugness which will destroy all in their path. Beware.'

HORSE RACING

STARLIGHT WINS THE SIX-FURLONG CHASE AT THE N7 RACES

DESPITE a false start due to commuters on their way to work delaying last week's six-furlong chase, trainer John Anthony Reilly's 4/1 favourite Starlight took the 200,000 guineas at the 7.35am race on the N7 last Saturday morning.

Race adjudicators lined the field in anticipation of this year's Traveller Gold Cup which saw dozens of

spectators cheer on both contenders from the safety of their vans and Volkswagen Passats, hanging out of windows, egging on the terrified piebalds.

'She had a great sayson an' won the M50 Steeplechase lass month, she did,' the award-winning trainer and breeder told *WWN*, before praising his jockey, 15-year-old Mickey Joe Ward, 'he bet her well with the whip, kept her steady all the way till her hooves were red hot.'

Starlight becomes the 5th winner for the trainer, who pointed out that the going was firm on the day, due to the course being made entirely from tarmacadam – a going not particularly a favourite for horses.

> **'Her legs are still a bit sore, but we'll get another few races outta her before she drops dead on the road and we have to leave her for the council'**

'Her legs are still a bit sore, but we'll get another few races outta her before she drops dead on the road and we have to leave her for the council,' said Reilly, explaining his unique method, 'as long as she'll make me a few pound between now and then, who cares.'

Much like professional horse racing, which saw 22,000 horses slaughtered over the last five years for not running fast enough, some high-performing piebalds this year failed to make the N7 races last week due to over-exhaustion, with one favourite horrifically crashing into cars in Waterford city last month, leading to the piebald being put down.

THE GAA SPORTS FORGOTTEN BY THE HISTORY BOOKS

THE modern incarnation of Gaelic games is hugely popular and a source of immense pride for the nation. However, what enraptured fans of football, hurling and camogie may not realise is that the GAA has a rich history of other sports we seem to have lost sight of thanks to the erosion of our collective memory.

WWN Sports has collected some sports omitted from the official GAA narrative that deserve to be known and possibly be subject to a revival by a passionate Irish people:

Phlegm lashing

The five-a-side game was played in close quarters on a field and required opposing teams to hock up phlegmy spits and empty them out onto one another.

The team with the last man standing would be declared the winner. The popularity of the sport waned after a high incidence of infection, with pneumonia, TB and Spanish flu killing the games leading stars, including Tommy 'Always Green Spits' Spitz and Carmel 'Gossie Canon' O'Brien.

We can see no issues with a return of this one.

Sean-nós karate

Started by a Japanese karate teacher who travelled to Ireland in 1785, Shigeru Hanashiro, sean-nós karate combines the soothing emotional droning of singing with the violent explosion of karate.

Rival singers compete over hours, attempting to best each other in a combination of the two disciplines with points awarded for devastating kicks and punches as well as devastating wails which call out to our ancestors who have long since left Ireland in search of a new life.

Animal thrunning

Thrun: verb, to feck an object of variable weights from one place to another. *Used in a sentence:* I thrun that bastarding sheep a good clean eight feet.

Animal thrunning was wildly popular in the more barbaric time of 2015 but has failed to gain official acknowledgement and legitimacy from the bigwigs at GAA HQ.

Competitive animal thrunning sees big burly lads and ladies throw an animal of their choice as far as they can. In a head to head format, the winner is the person who has thrun an animal the furthest.

Proper football without all this black card shite

While some suggest Gaelic football is still the game we know and love, other purists claim the game no longer exists at all and wish for a return to a time when football was really *football*.

If this game was to return, there would be less focus on hand passes, point scoring, skills and fitness and more attention paid to breaking some cunt's nose just because you love your county that fucking much!

Competitive cousin shifting

More a midlands sport than anything.

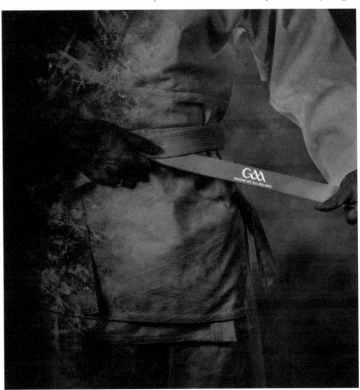

FOOTBALL

STUDY REVEALS NO ONE STARTS OUT WANTING TO BE A GOALKEEPER

THE LARGEST ever study of amateur football players has concluded that not a single person stuck between the posts actually had a desire to become a goalkeeper, *WWN Sports* can reveal.

Canvassing the opinions of all goalkeepers revealed that they all started further up the field and somehow ended up in the net through a combination of being hungover, unfit and shit.

'I think our normal keeper was injured or hungover or injured himself drinking and so I had to drop in goal,' shared one former benchwarming striker who has been a keeper for the last three seasons with his local team.

'Wow, I haven't really thought about this. It seems so long ago now, but yeah, shit, why the fuck am I taking being a goalkeeper lying down?' shared another keeper, now 15 years into a career of turning up every

week to play in a position that is the least craic.

'I'm a ball-playing midfielder, motherfuckers, time to let me fly,' added the keeper, who has a first touch so poor you'd swear his feet were made of trampolines.

The study focused on what motivated goalkeepers to don the Number 1 jersey but has just served to spark an existential crisis in all of them.

'Yeah, cheers for starting up this study bollocks. Now I've got to give my goalie "a chance to prove himself" as a winger. Look what you've started,' voiced an irate player/manager/ physio/groundskeeper/ psychologist/stats man to those conducting the study.

The study also concluded that 95% of amateur players are absolutely fucking knackered after about five minutes of running about the pitch.

GAA LAUNCH WITNESS PROTECTION PROGRAMME FOR REFEREES

FEARING for the safety of match referees and staff over questionable calls on the field, the Gaelic Athletic Association has launched an optional witness protection programme which will relocate referees abroad, *WWN* can confirm.

The new measure, launched shortly after the weekend's All-Ireland hurling semi-final, where the referees, linesmen and umpires came under fire for some 'bad decisions', putting their life in danger thanks to the GAA's openly threatening fan base.

'I'll fucking kill the bastard,'shouted one nine-year-old Tipp supporter at yesterday's semi-final in Croke Park, where he saw his home team beat Wexford in a tense match up and a series of questionable decisions by the referee.

'We know where you live, you blind piece of shit … we'll kill your

entire family and your dog,' shouted a Limerick supporter at Saturday's game against Kilkenny after a poor call from a linesman sparked mass riots outside the stadium, leaving 43 people dead – and more devastating, leaving Limerick defeated.

The new witness protection programme is expected to cost the GAA hundreds of euros over the next few years, as each fleeing referee, umpire or linesman will be given a one-way, 200-euro Ryanair voucher. The GAA will have to also cover the cost of changing the referee's name to Irish on their passport and other IDs, in a bid to hide their identity.

'Nothing is more important than the safety of all our staff and the association's finances,' the GAA said in a very brief statement released on a frayed beermat this morning to the Irish press.

U21 GAA PLAYER WOULD WANT TO UP HIS GAME IF HE WANTS CHARGES DROPPED

FERMATTEN Celts Under-21 corner forward Michael Sheeling has been advised to 'start making them scoring opportunities count' if he expects to reach the level of adoration required to make serious allegations about him go away, *WWN* can report.

Sheeling, 20, had hoped that his standing as a GAA player would enable him to avail of the special 'Gardaí privileges' that he had heard

about recently, but was dismayed to find that those were reserved for players and officials who 'don't bottle it' on big games.

Heading into an off-season set to be dominated with news about that thing he did during the summer that's only starting to come out now, Sheeling is determined to up his fitness and strength regime so that he can be the player Fermatten needs him to be, as well as avoiding everyone hearing about, y'know.

'So it turns out that lads like me who don't always make the team don't get their charges automatically dropped,' sighed Sheeling, practising 45s.

'Which I have to tell you, isn't good news. I had heard on the news

about loads of GAA lads getting all sorts dropped, plus there's just the notion that once you're part of a GAA team, you can't have criminal charges pressed against you because you're needed for a quarter-final or whatever. But I've too many wides on the board at the minute, so I'll have to up my game.'

Sheeling has been reminded that even if he doesn't have his charges dropped, he's still a GAA player so nobody is going to believe her anyways.

SPORTS fans are being urged to 'pick a fucking lane' after bitter complaints that VAR is ruining games left and right, despite decades of calling for VAR to prevent games being ruined.

VAR, short for Video Assistant Referee, was brought in to combat close calls such as penalty decisions, red cards and goal-mouth scrambles, and has succeeded in solving none of the post-match arguments it was intended to.

Conversely, fans who called for some sort of replay-based refereeing for years have turned their match analysis from 'that fucking referee fucked us over' to 'that fucking VAR fucked us over', prompting suggestions that some people are incapable of happiness or peace.

'As far back as the 1966 World Cup final, people have been asking for referees to consult replays before making game-changing decisions,' said a spokesperson for football.

'Well, they have it now and they're still a bunch of whining children. Here's an idea lads: maybe your team isn't that good. Maybe they really did drag a player down and get sent off.

VAR RUINING GAME, SAY FANS WHO WANTED VAR FOR YEARS

Maybe they were offside. Maybe they didn't get the ball across the line even though it really looked like they did on TV. Maybe grow up. It's football, not war. Jesus Christ, my fucking head. Sick of you cunts.'

Meanwhile, EA has announced that FIFA 20 will include a mini-game where fans bitch about VAR decisions for an hour after each match, to make the game as accurate as possible.

LOCKDOWN

BORED, POWER-MAD REFEREES SPENDING LOCKDOWN SENDING PEOPLE OFF FOR FAILING TO SOCIAL DISTANCE

How friendship changed in 2020

Bitches found it harder to passive-aggressively bully their 'best friend' who lived further than 5km away.

STARVED of an opportunity to wield their imaginary power over amateur athletes up and down the country,

> **'Alright, no guff out of you now, but you were nowhere near two metres away from that auld lad, early bath for you today'**

power-mad referees with too much time on their hands have taken to Ireland's streets to dole out yellow and red cards.

Dressed in full kit, whistle in mouth, idle referees have taken it upon themselves to reprimand anyone failing to observe social distancing like they were over-eager defenders going into a tackle with two feet while armed with a chainsaw.

'Number 11 red, c'mere to me,' referee Rob Healy barked at a man crossing the street in a Liverpool jersey with Mo Salah on his back, complete

with a trademark referee hand gesture indicating 'you'll have to walk all the way over to where I'm standing'.

'Alright, no guff out of you now, but you were nowhere near two metres away from that auld lad, early bath for you today,' Healy said, before hoisting a red card skyward in a dramatic fashion, much to the confusion of the man.

Healy and fellow members of the refereeing community have been encroaching on other areas of the new restrictions and best practices, dishing out yellow cards to people working from home who only get dressed from the waist up and those not coughing into their elbows.

FOOTBALL

FAI CUTBACKS TO SEE RETURN OF 'JUMPERS FOR GOALPOSTS'

STRICT cost-cutting measures, including the reduction of players per team to nine each, are to be put into place by the FAI in a bid to tackle the €60 million-ish of debt that the association has racked up due to the ineptitude of nobody in particular.

'Look, who knows where all this debt came from?' mused a spokesperson for the FAI, speaking at a press conference at the cheapest hotel they could find.

'We're not here to see where the problem came from, or blame anyone, or bring anyone up on legal action … we're here to cut costs and get this bitch back on track.'

Cuts will include the removal of goalposts from all pitches and stadiums which will then be sold on eBay and replaced with jumpers in a bid to reduce insurance costs.

'Sure isn't that how we all played as kids, and we were grand!'

'If a footballer hits a post, that's a big claim right there, so get rid of them, no problem! Sure isn't that how we all played as kids, and we were grand!'

Further measures will see ticket prices rise and a 50c slot machine put in place at toilets in the Aviva, coupled with the 90-minute duration of a match reduced to 60 minutes which will cut down on both player and referee fees.

When pressed on whether or not former FAI boss John Delaney would be asked to return the €462,000 he received from the association, known internally as 'Delaney's Fucking-Off Fee', the association remained adamant that they wouldn't be seeking action against their beloved former boss.

'After all he did for the FAI? No, he's earned that money. Sure we wouldn't be where we are without him!'

Health and fitness tip

That's it, keep going, just 40,000 more squats today before your hoop is the same size as Kim Kardashian's

UFC 254 TO BE HELD ON INTERNATIONAL SPACE STATION

SHOWCASING some of the practical changes sports can make in order to carry on staging events during the ongoing uncertainty, world leaders in lads beating the heads off each other, the UFC, are once again ahead of the curve.

Graduating from his 'fight island' concept which, would see fighters sent to a private island to quarantine and fight, UFC honcho Dana White has revealed he has an even better and in-no-way-ridiculous suggestion for UFC 254.

'My boy Elon Musk is gonna hook us up with a space shuttle so the finest pound-for-pounders in the UFC can safely fight in an environment that is COVID-free; outer fucking space,' said White, announcing the news that sort of just popped into his head out of nowhere.

'Yeah, fuck it, zero gravity knees to the face. Let's do this,' added White.

While certain rule changes will have to be ironed out, it is believed White is open to bouts being settled when an opponent's space helmet is caved in, causing the fighter's body to explode, provided such a move would sell more pay-per-view packages.

With UFC 254 still some time away, there's still plenty of time for Conor McGregor to announce multiple retirements and comebacks while fitting in the occasional arrest and court case.

THE MAGAZINE FOR VIRUSES, WRITTEN BY VIRUSES

VIRUSMONTHLY

Trillions Die In Vaccine Massacre
HUMANS LAUNCH CHEMICAL WARFARE

Are There Too Many Humans?

The human scourge is spreading at an alarming rate and is slowly destroying the planet. We must act now before it's too late: Virus society calls for action

8tips

for finding the most vulnerable host

'Yeah, Well Try Killing 600k A Year' Seasonal Flu Slams Covid-19

ww news
Waterford Whispers News

OPINION

'ACTUALLY, THE RESTRICTIONS DON'T APPLY TO ME BECAUSE, LIKE, I'M SUPER IMPORTANT'

AS part of *WWN*'s opinion series, we give a platform to those who don't really deserve it. This week it's the turn of 44-year-old driver of an expensive-looking car, Henrietta Doyle O'Brien, who, if you can believe it, has been stopped by a power-mad Garda at a checkpoint AGAIN.

I mean, eh, hello, four-wheel drive and 191-D plates and I'm being interrogated by some bally-go-backwards Mr Templemore Potato Head like I'm some sort of drug dealer?

Like, there must be some law against stopping a mother on her way to pick up her daughter from her boyfriend's house 25 kilometres away for the third time this week? Gardaí talking to me with an attitude you

County Knowledge

Depending on who you ask, Meath's most famous son is either Pierce Brosnan or Davey Collins, who once downed three litres of Buckfast in under a minute.

should only reserve for people with accents as rough as sandpaper.

And bloody right you are guard, you did stop me yesterday on the way back from the house of the Polish lady who does my nails, what did you expect me to do? Go around with manky nails and give in to Magda when she begged me to stop bullying her into giving me her home address on the phone?

The restrictions these breakfast-roll-for-brains morons are talking about don't apply to the likes of me, seriously. It's laughable.

Get out there in your pretend police uniform with your stick and catch the real breakers of these restrictions, the scumbags in desperate-looking heaps of junk, breaking the same restrictions

How driving changed in 2020

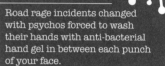

Road rage incidents changed with psychos forced to wash their hands with anti-bacterial hand gel in between each punch of your face.

as me only they're scumbags so it actually counts.

I'll go where I bloody want, when I want, last time I checked it's a free country and I'm a taxpayer. I pay your wages. Little Mr Power Mad.

Do you honestly think someone in a car like this is stupid enough to go out there spreading this yoke around? Honestly, this country's gone to the dogs, and by the look of you, guard, the pigs too.

I will NOT take the keys out of the ignition! Oh, just you wait until my husband hears about this, our solicitor will have a field day with you. Do you have any idea who my husband is?

TECHNOLOGY

COVID-19 WIPED OUT AFTER 5G MASTS DESTROYED

THE Irish government has today lifted all lockdown measures taken over the past few weeks to flatten the curve following the total annihilation of COVID-19 after several 5G masts were damaged, wiping out the virus indefinitely, *WWN* has learned.

Hundreds of thousands of people took to the streets in celebration of the almost overnight destruction of the coronavirus, calling on the geniuses who set fire to the masts to step forward.

Taoiseach Leo Varadkar announced a national week of celebration, allowing pubs to open 24/7 for the foreseeable future and implementing a COVID-19 bonus of €1,000 for every citizen over the age of 16.

'Free at last, free at last, thank God almighty, we are free at last!' Mr Varadkar addressed the nation in his own unique wordsmith way, as onlookers openly wept into their plastic pint glasses, singing 'olé, olé, olé' while licking each other's faces in defiance.

Meanwhile, scientists right across the world have apologised for overlooking 5G radio waves as the possible cause of the virus.

'We can't understand it; 5G is a radio wave frequency that doesn't affect the human body, but obviously we have no idea what we're talking about and some YouTuber has found something that 140 years of researching didn't. We are truly sorry,' the science community said in a published statement this morning.

Answering Ireland's call, the self-confessed hero who set fire to the 5G masts eradicating COVID-19 from Ireland for good spoke to *WWN* earlier today through his YouTube channel *5G Donegal*.

'I kept telling everyone 5G was a New World Order weapon made from chemtrails funded by lizard king George Soros to mind control and kill old people, but they wouldn't believe me, so I had to act,' 23-year-old Matt Daniels explained his reasoning, nervously picking at nodge burns in his 2008 Celtic jersey. 'I suppose I'm a bit like a modern-day Saint Patrick now, banishing the virus and all that. Do I get a reward?'

> **'I kept telling everyone 5G was a New World Order weapon made from chemtrails funded by lizard king George Soros**

COVID health and fitness tip

In light of the coronavirus, an amnesty has been declared on carbs, any carbs eaten during this time will not exist.

THE ENVIRONMENT

DUBLIN CANALS RUN CLEAR AMID COVID-19 LOCKDOWN REVEALING BEAUTIFUL SHOPPING TROLLEYS, HANDGUNS

MIRRORING incredible scenes in Venice, where tourist-free canals produced fantastic displays of marine life swimming freely in the now clear waters below, Dublin followed suit with some beautiful sights of its own.

Vintage Quinnsworth shopping trolleys, bikes, discarded handguns and a treasure trove of relics from times gone by are now visible in the once murky waters of Dublin's intricate canals and main river, the Liffey, thanks to the dramatic lack of footfall from tourists and locals amid the COVID-19 lockdown.

Local environmentalist Danny Shields described today's incredible scenes as 'nature taking back control. The water is clear and blue. The real Dublin has been revealed.'

Garda forensic teams began combing canals which were now transformed into dozens of crime scenes as the true nature of Ireland's capital city emerged.

'It's amazing to see Dublin's wildlife revealed in its natural habitat – at the bottom of the canal,' said Garda scuba diver Anthony Price, who pulled out yet another semi-automatic pistol, the 26th weapon the team found this morning. 'They're a beautiful creature, but quite dangerous when triggered.'

Now flourishing in the clear canals, rare species of shopping baskets dating back to the 1980s were also among the beautiful flock, sparking calls from locals for better resources for the city's canals and river.

'The beauty here is astounding; look over there, a perfectly preserved BMX,' local wildlife enthusiast Darren

Rice pointed, looking through a pair of binoculars, 'I believe it's a rare Mongoose Legion Freestyle L100 too – I haven't seen one of them around here for 30 years.'

RESTAURANT OWNER SURE GLAD HE KEPT ALL THOSE STAFF TIPS NOW

RENAMING his staff's gratuity payments for their dedicated service over the past year as his 'rainy day fund', restaurant owner Mike Davis admitted he was now glad that he held on to all those tips which have been fuelling his lockdown expenses for the past five weeks.

'It must have been a subconscious decision where a part of my brain foretold of a downturn in revenue, forcing a default survival mechanism, telling me to hold on to all those tips,' Davis opened up, admitting that spending the tax-free money didn't feel as bad as actually spending his own.

'Drinking every night and ordering takeout really eats into your finances and I wouldn't know what I'd have done without all those tips – I'd probably have spent all my own hard-earned money instead,' he said, before going on to thank loyal customers for unintentionally donating their money directly to him, 'it goes to show, when you run a good business you will get rewarded for your hard work eventually.'

The money, which was dropped into a tip jar labelled 'staff tips' by customers hoping to reward waiting staff for their excellent service, had been accumulating in the company safe for 'safekeeping' for several months now, with Davis making promises to staff of holidays abroad, team nights out and at one point an actual envelope containing their deserved tips.

'I could never decide on what to do with the tips so obviously the cosmos meant for this to happen and for me to have it all,' the miserly prick justified to himself, conveniently compartmentalising several meetings which saw staff asking 'where all the fucking tips were going'.

'Such a shame I have to let go of all the staff now because of this lockdown, but sure look; we will rebuild another restaurant empire with new, not-so-cocky staff members who can just do the work without all the human rights and work violation malarky,' Davis concluded, before ordering a nice expensive €39.99 bottle of Chablis online.

NATURE

WHILE the world's humans have been caught up in their struggle to contain the COVID-19 outbreak, very few have given much thought to the hurt caused by those vicious social media trolls who have tracked down and exposed the identity of the bat allegedly responsible for facilitating the cross-species contamination.

Derek, a Hubei-based 11-year-old lesser short-nosed fruit bat, has been credited by some authorities with being the bat who kicked off the novel coronavirus outbreak, and

'I'VE RECEIVED DEATH THREATS': WE SPEAK WITH THE BAT RESPONSIBLE FOR COVID-19

today, speaking publicly for the first time in a *WWN* exclusive, he tells his story.

'And how do you pricks even know it was me that spread it? I bet you were talking to that miserable bat Brian, weren't you? He's still pissed I flew off with his wife. Or maybe it's a conspiracy spread by insects 'cus they're sick of us bats eating them,' an agitated Derek explained to *WWN* while hanging upside-down from a tree branch, restrained in a straitjacket in a maximum-security animal prison in China.

A visibly upset Derek continued to share his story, and his frustration that other animals, such as the pangolin, weren't under suspicion, labelling it 'batist' to zero in on him and his species.

'I've received death threats over this. And honestly, some of the names I've been called. I won't repeat them. Like, seriously, how was I supposed to know you weak-ass humans couldn't handle a simple autoimmune infection? Maybe instead of blaming

me, you should look at yourselves? Big bad humans, full of themselves, but can't handle a little bat soup.

'Suddenly I'm public enemy number one. Last time I checked, bats never started a war, or accelerated climate change. Maybe I did the planet a favour picking a few of you lot off, ever think of it that way?

'Oh, did you have to cancel your holiday? Boo-fucking-hoo, do you think bats get holidays, you self-centred fucks? I had to look up what holiday meant, had no fucking idea you lot needed "a break" from your daily routines. What I wouldn't give for a night off from sonaring my way around in the dark, looking for insects.'

Derek highlighted the strain this had caused within his local bat community, where his colony of 40 bats have alienated him, and panic any time he coughs.

FAMILY

'I'M PUTTING THE LITTLE BASTARDS UP FOR ADOPTION': READ SOME OF IRELAND'S HEARTWARMING COVID-19 STORIES

AS WE COLLECTIVELY persevere through these challenging times together as a nation, each day brings with it heartwarming stories that restore people's faith in humanity as empathy and solidarity triumph.

Playful generosity, solemn sacrifice, reaching out to those in need and simply making do; WWN has collected those stories that have moved so many people here in Ireland:

'If COVID-19 doesn't kill him, I fucking will,' Carmel Tracey (70), from Dublin, entering day 17 of isolating with her husband Derek.

'I'm putting the little bastards up for adoption,' Darren and Emma Coogan, parents of four kids under the age of 10.

'I'm putting the little bastards up for adoption,' Elaine and Gerry Brogan, parents of four kids over the age of 30.

'This downtime has made me a lot more productive, this is the most I've masturbated in years. Usually I'm just too busy to get it done,' Sarah Slattery (30), furloughed worker in Cork.

'I wouldn't have been able to carry out my work this easily under normal circumstances, so I'm probably one of the few people benefiting from this pandemic,' Ciaran Clatterton (41), budding serial killer and disposer of bodies under the cover of darkness in Galway.

'The innovation from people across industries as they grapple with COVID-19 is inspiring, how people have adapted blows my mind,' Michael Clanton (26), criminal, who, now that people are always at home, steals car keys through the letterbox using a long pole with a magnet on the end of it so that he ensures a responsible minimum distance of two metres away from people.

'It's not all bad, I did an April Fools on my kid the other day by pretending schools were open again, her poor heart shattered into a million tiny pieces and she wouldn't stop crying when I told her, actually you won't get to see your friends or get back to a normal life but you'd want to see the views my hilarious video of it got,' Brian Harty, parent from Dublin.

It's stories like these that help to inspire us and keep us going during incredibly challenging times.

IRELAND OFFICIALLY CHANGES COVID-19 STATUS FROM 'BE GRAND' TO 'ALRIGHT, FAIR ENOUGH'

gov.ie/covid19

WITH TAOISEACH Leo Varadkar confirming the need to temporarily close schools, creches and colleges along with guidelines on limiting public gatherings and events to limit COVID-19 spread, the Irish people have come together as one and officially agreed to raise Ireland's emergency preparedness levels above 'sure it'll be grand' for the first time in its history.

'Ah yeah, alright, fair enough,' confirmed Ireland, the usually unfazed tis-a-big-fuss-over-nothing nation, acknowledging the severity of the situation and the need for unified action and commitment to fight the spread of COVID-19 and protect those among us most vulnerable to the virus.

In scenes that would bring a tear to the eye of the most cold-hearted of individuals, contrary arseholes have been stood down from duty, angry people who always have issues with authority figures have agreed to cease all activities and gossiping neighbours have made a vow to put a temporary restriction on the circulation of unverified rumours that only spread panic.

'For this limited time – gone is the Ireland of hearing a fire alarm go off and shrugging, 'cus sure it's probably nothing, replaced by the "yeah, in fairness, they have a point" deference to experts,' confirmed a normally obstinate and dismissive begrudger.

'You won't hear any complaints from us,' confirmed conspiracy theorists, who in moving scenes, laid down their tinfoil hats for at least the next 12 hours or so.

Aside from heeding HSE and government advice the new status of 'alright, fair enough' comes with special advice and protocols, which include offering support and assistance to the most vulnerable in society and offering help to anyone else who may need it.

LOCAL INTROVERTS CELEBRATE CANCELLED EVENTS

QUIETLY whisper-shouting a celebratory 'yes' to themselves under their breath, the world's introverts, along with those who suffer from varying degrees of social anxiety, are delighting in the havoc being wreaked by COVID-19 on social gatherings both big and small.

'Oh God, this is better than sex,' confirmed one introvert as she pored over the list of public events forced to cancel in a bid to limit and delay the spread of COVID-19.

Crossing out all manner of social engagements from their personal calendars, introverts have been spared attending house parties, coffee catch-ups, concerts, networking events, funerals and other gatherings which require constant interaction and conversation.

'I've been self-isolating most of my life so to be honest, none of this is particularly inconvenient to me,' added another introvert who was looking forward to the breakdown of everyday life which would allow him to see and hear from no one for weeks, possibly months.

Caution surrounding public gatherings over COVID-19 has resulted in an almost 100% reduction in introverts having to torture themselves with anxious considerations over 'how early is too early to arrive', 'oh God what if John is there', 'okay, memorise ten ice-breakers and topics for conversation' and 'come up with a far-too-elaborate and needless excuse for why you're going home'.

'Oh no, don't cancel your baby's gender reveal party, I was really looking forward to being locked in a room with people for hours of excruciatingly awkward small talk that I'd then replay in my head for days and overthink,' mocked another introvert.

DRUGS

DRUG DEALERS CALL FOR MORE RELAXED GARDA CHECKPOINTS

THE NATION'S drug dealers along with strung-out users have today made an emotional appeal to An Garda Síochána to loosen checkpoints up and down the country amid one of the most serious drug droughts the underworld has ever seen.

Afraid to transport even the smallest of contraband from town to town, city to city, dealers united to confront the current lockdown restrictions, stating that customers need their medicine to curb civil unrest.

'There's chronic weed smokers climbing the fucking walls right now, stuck in with their families while remaining totally sober, which is an act of cruelty in itself,' local drugs wholesaler Clinkers Kelly told *WWN*, who was picketing with several high-profile 'heads' outside Waterford Garda station today.

'There's lads getting lifted left, right and centre just trying to do their bit for society. No wonder people are snapping at home and that – people need their gear to get through this home arrest bullshit – the guards are making it worse for half the country, the fucking dopes.'

The protesters called on Gardaí to just turn a blind eye to any suspicious vehicles, calling for stop and search laws to be lifted at traffic checkpoints and allow mules to traffic goods from one town to the next.

'I've cleaned every nook and cranny, fixed every shelf, the lawn is like a professional fucking golf course out there it's manicured so much and I've nothing else left to do – I'm cracking up without me smoke,' one cannabis user explained his plight. 'Just give the dealers one day a week to move their stuff without being caught, that's all.'

Gardaí have since advised dealers to 'cop on' and just 'use the back roads like everyone else'.

> **'I've cleaned every nook and cranny, fixed every shelf, the lawn is like a professional fucking golf course out there it's manicured so much and I've nothing else left to do – I'm cracking up without me smoke'**

COVID-19 APPOINTED HOUSING MINISTER AFTER FREEZING RENTS, EVICTIONS & SECURING BEDS FOR HOMELESS

THE FINE GAEL caretaker government has been praised for fast-tracking the COVID-19 pandemic into the position of Minister for Housing, in a grown-up move that set aside the usual political infighting and sniping.

Ireland, bizarrely left without a Housing Minister since 2017, has rewarded COVID-19's selfless ingenuity and diligent hard work behind the scenes, which has already seen the acute respiratory infection become the catalyst for a rent freeze and a ban on evictions.

'Minister COVID-19 was an obvious choice after it made such quick progress in securing the kind of ease of mind and basic decency craved by many tenants that admittedly we completely ignored,' confirmed one government insider.

'One day we're saying rent freezes are unconstitutional and the next COVID-19 has strong-armed us into putting one in place. Honestly, we don't know how it does it, but it is one hell of a negotiator and politician,' conceded the insider.

'Nothing's impossible for this guy, what's next? Who knows, actually affordable rents? Getting your landlord to replace the oven that catches fire now and again? Not cramming 16 Brazilian students into the one room? The sky's the limit!'

Already in line for earning a reputation as Ireland's most productive minister ever, COVID-19 recently secured 560 beds for homeless people who may need to self-isolate away from cramped and overwhelmed emergency housing services in the coming days and weeks, but COVID-19 admits it is only getting started.

'We're hearing reports of hundreds of Airbnb properties magically appearing online for long-term rent, despite the fact that none of these seemed to have registered with us as required under recent Airbnb legislation. Yeah, we'll be evicting them from the content of their wallets soon,' Minister for Housing COVID-19 said, in a rousing speech.

How drinking changed in 2020

The closure of pubs handed the nation the unique chance to kick the demon drink, a chance the nation politely declined.

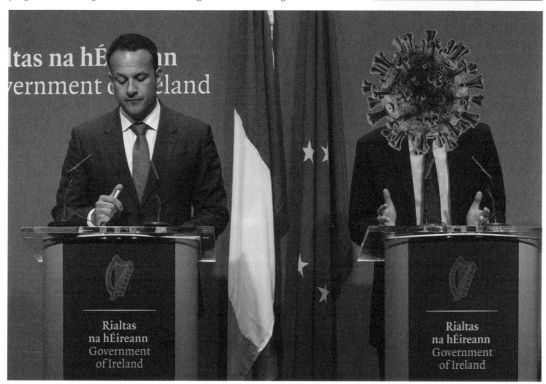

TRAVEL

FAMILY ON WAY TO HOLIDAY HOME IN WEXFORD ENGAGED IN SHOOTOUT WITH GARDAÍ

WWN are keeping a close eye on a developing situation on the N11 at the moment, where a division of the Gardaí's armed response unit have exchanged gunfire with a family of five who have adamantly stated that one way or another, they're going to Courtown.

Eyewitnesses say the fracas began after Gardaí, enforcing the coronavirus clampdown on movement and travel, stopped the family in their Nissan Qashqai at a checkpoint outside Druid's Glen after noticing a suspicious amount of sandcastle-making equipment in the back.

The tense situation quickly escalated into a full-blown firefight after the lady in the Qashqai produced a Kalashnikov and began firing at the officers, stating that she and her family 'had a right' to get out of Dublin for the long weekend.

'Go back to your homes, there's a pandemic on and you risk spreading the disease to another county!' screamed one guard, pinned down by suppressing fire from a ten-year-old.

'We have a right to travel to our own holiday home by the beach, we have food and provisions for the whole weekend and we will not be interacting with anyone outside the occupants of this Qashqai!' roared the father of the family, while attempting to shoot a trainee guard 'nowhere vital'.

'For one weekend, for the love of God, would it kill you to stay at

Covid health and fitness tip

Keep up your cardio up by running away from big groups of people not practising social distancing.

home?' roared back a senior Garda, leaping through the air while firing two revolvers.

'You haven't got the powers to send us home, we're breaking no laws, pigs!' screamed an adorable little girl.

'New regulations were signed into force by Simon Harris yesterday after it became apparent that a lot of people couldn't follow simple fucking instructions!' yelled an Offaly cop armed with an Uzi.

'Simon Harris is Minister for Health, shouldn't something like this be done by Charlie Flanagan?' shouted a toddler with a throwing knife, to silence from the Gardaí while they thought it through.

Behind them on the N11, a thousand more families waited to proceed to the south-east, with everyone quickly changing their story to 'we're just out for a spin'.

BREAKING NEWS

THE GOVERNMENT is today answering questions from a union of First Communion-aged boys and girls from across the country who are applying for a bailout programme to offset financial losses incurred by the cancellation of their Holy Communion ceremonies thanks to COVID-19.

Thousands of under-10s were scheduled to make their First Holy Communion and rake in up to €1,000 each over the last few months until the arrival of the coronavirus, with those same children now looking to the government for answers about where their cash is.

With the loss of the Communion economy already having devastating effects on both the bouncy castle

County Knowledge

Tipperary was given two registration plates – Tipperary North and Tipperary South – following a heated dispute which saw the north embrace communism in the 1960s.

FIRST COMMUNION KIDS APPLY FOR COVID PAYMENT

industry and the cocktail sausage industry, the government are under pressure to ensure that the knock-on effects of zero Communion money on the toy industry and the Credit Unions of Ireland are as minimised as possible, but the government are remaining tight-lipped on what, if anything, they can do.

'For many, this money forms the basis of their savings account well into adulthood. For others, it means an Xbox,' said Minister for Finance Paschal Donohoe.

'And while we'd love to set all these future voters up with a subsidy, there are fears that granting the children access to a bailout fund might result in a similar request from Confirmation kids, which could be followed by a 21st birthday fund bailout; where does it end? But look, we'll do something, we're just not sure what. Perhaps we'll give our favourite kids a tenner each, and a fiver to the ones we only sort of like. That's how it normally works anyway, right?'

Meanwhile, the Catholic Church has rubbished the idea that they will pay for the bailout, stressing that there are nine other scandals that they're busy not paying for.

GRANDPARENTS SECRETLY DELIGHTED THEY CAN'T MIND KIDS

GRANDPARENTS up and down the country have admitted to being secretly delighted with strict advice being given by authorities in a bid to combat the COVID-19 virus, *WWN* can confirm.

Usually the go-to babysitter of choice, parents of parents relished in the fact they could remain in solitude for months without ever having to take care of their children's children, using the current pandemic as the best excuse ever to avoid babysitting unwanted kids.

'I think I'm coming down with something,' grandfather-of-twelve Niall Wilson insisted while winking in a knowing fashion and sitting back in his favourite recliner before picking up a good book, 'yeah, that's it, best keep

the fuck away from me for at least 12 months; don't even think of asking me to mind those little shits, or Skype for that matter, germs can spread down the line and we don't want that. Thanks. Bye.'

The Association of Grandparents Ireland has called on grandchildren to remain vigilant throughout the period of this pandemic and they promise to continue slipping sneaky fivers to them for birthdays and Christmas whenever all of this blows over.

'We will stockpile any fivers owed and promise to sneak them into children's hands when the virus passes,' a statement from the AGI read, 'please refrain from knocking on our doors for the time being and for

those grandchildren doing their Junior and Leaving Certificates in school, hundreds of Mass candles are being posted to grandparents' homes for lighting later.'

The Association of Grandparents Ireland concluded that children could still cut their grandparents' grass or wash their cars if they wanted to, but just don't come into the house with those filthy hands.

How Ireland Came Together During The Pandemic

Just one of the many Irish people who made sure to check in on elderly neighbours. 28 March 2020, Dublin.

How sex changed in 2020

The huge change and adjustment to life as we know it, which brought an end to dating and one-night stands, had absolutely no adverse effect on 28-year-old Aoife Keegan's love life, who was never going to get the ride anyway.

How shopping changed in 2020

The nation was on first-name terms with couriers from 47 different delivery providers, some would go on to be godparents to their firstborn.

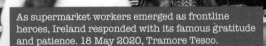

As supermarket workers emerged as frontline heroes, Ireland responded with its famous gratitude and patience. 18 May 2020, Tramore Tesco.

Teachers comfort each other after learning schools would close, preventing them from looking after your perfect little children. 12 March 2020, Wicklow.

How drinking changed in 2020

We adjusted back to our chaotic and damaging drinking habits remarkably quickly.

How hygiene changed in 2020

People wearing an exfoliating and rejuvenating charcoal face mask to prevent infection spread in public became a common sight.

How driving changed in 2020

A reduction in traffic volumes saw a significant drop in the country's pollution levels, and a ban on driving lessons finally saw stalling on hills eradicated.

Calm Irish public wait patiently to queue for toilet roll outside a supermarket. 12 March 2020, Cork.

How friendship changed in 2020

There was no need to make up an elaborate excuse for why you just weren't arsed meeting up, 'LOL there's a global pandemic' did the trick.

How working changed in 2020

Excuses for being late for work changed from 'the traffic was cat' to 'look, I've three prick kids here driving me insane, so fucking what if I was meant to start 30 minutes ago'.

Garda help lost man who accidentally took one step outside 2km limit allowed for exercise. 14 April 2020, Longford.

Disgusting vandal destroys public property moments before being taken out by a Garda sniper. 21 June 2020, Galway.

BREAKING NEWS

'NO SHIFTING ANYONE'; GOVERNMENT'S NEW EMERGENCY COVID-19 LAWS IN FULL

THE swapping of spits, mouth-jousting and gymnastic contortion of tongues have been temporarily outlawed in Ireland as part of a raft of emergency coronavirus laws aimed at, among other things, reducing the spread and flattening the curve.

Aside from much-needed things like a temporary rent freeze and ban on evictions, the removal of the waiting period for Jobseeker payments for COVID-19-related cases and enforced isolation by authorities for infected people who refuse to quarantine, the legislation not only also bans the 'washing machine' technique for shifting but shifting itself.

'Shifting, meeting, tickling teeth, scoring, whatever the fuck young people are calling it. It stops now,' confirmed Minister for Health Simon Harris in the Dáil. 'It should go without saying therefore that "getting jiggy with it", sex, butt trumpeting and slam-jamming hip-hopping show-stopping orgasm spasms are off the menu.' Other emergency measures, protocols, orders and law changes include:

- Price gouging on flat 7 Up has, as of today, become a crime and carries a €10,000 fine and prison sentence. This should bring an end to bottles being sold for upwards of €350.
- There is a homicide amnesty in place for those forced to spend increased time with family and/or housemates.
- Moore Street market in Dublin will be forced to close its controversial wet market and the selling of its signature bat soup dish is banned.
- An order not to feed COVID-19 patients after midnight is in place.
- There is now a limit of only one Netflix documentary per household per night.
- Welcome news for parents as sedating children to be allowed and, when the technology is available, cryogenically freezing them until this is all over will be permitted.
- While not declared illegal, anyone using the current COVID-19 situation to dump someone will be severely judged by everyone. Similarly, anyone thinking of proposing to their distant partner over Skype and recording it with the hope of gaining internet fame will be shot.
- Not yet law but strongly recommended: please remember to maintain a distance of over 500m from pricks you hate.
- Gardaí are permitted to throw a sly dig at anyone who admits to having been to Cheltenham. Pepper spraying their testicles is not permitted but is encouraged. Anyone still sharing blatantly false WhatsApp rumours will be sterilised to prevent any further degradation of the gene pool.
- Anyone buying and hoarding toilet roll is required by law to justify their panic purchase by filming themselves with proof of their chronic, explosive diarrhoea. Failure to do so will result in a six-month prison sentence.

Did You Know?

Did you know that if Diana, Princess of Wales was alive today, she would have really liked Nando's?

TRAVEL

PLANE WITH 10,000 COVID-19-INFECTED BATS PASSES THROUGH DUBLIN AIRPORT WITHOUT PROPER CHECKS

DESPITE desperate pleas with the government to act, a helpless nation was left to watch as over 10,000 COVID-19-infected bats passed through Dublin airport without the proper checks.

Since the Aer Lingus Wuhan to Dublin flight via New York, Madrid, London and Rome landed this morning, social media has been flooded with disturbing photos of hundreds of the bats drinking by the canal in the good weather after a successful visit to bat tourist hot spots such as Mitchelstown caves.

Leading figures from the comment sections of Ireland who bravely write 'Close the borders' in all caps under every news article or social media post have asked the government to consider implementing some of their proposals before it's too late.

'All flight passengers should be shot with a tranquiliser dart upon arrival and cryogenically frozen until a vaccine is found, I don't care if they're doctors, and if that can't be done just send them to Direct Provision if they're not properly Irish,' confirmed one man, who has personally done more damage with his own lax

> ## 'All flight passengers should be shot with a traquiliser dart upon arrival and cryogenically frozen until a vaccine is found'

interpretation of two-metre social distancing and 'necessary trips' than one million bats ever could.

'And the airport security is doing nothing. They're handing out "here's how to cough on people" leaflets, I seen it with my own eyes,' confirmed one man, who has awoken every day since this pandemic broke screaming 'it's a disgrace'.

However, in a game-changing move that could appease the Irish people and see them change their tune, one of the visiting bats posted a now-viral Instagram picture of the Cliffs of Moher with the caption 'oh my God, Ireland is so beautiful', gaining thousands of likes.

OPINION

'I REMEMBER A TIME EVERYONE USED TO FEAR ME TOO' NORMAL FLU BREAKS SILENCE

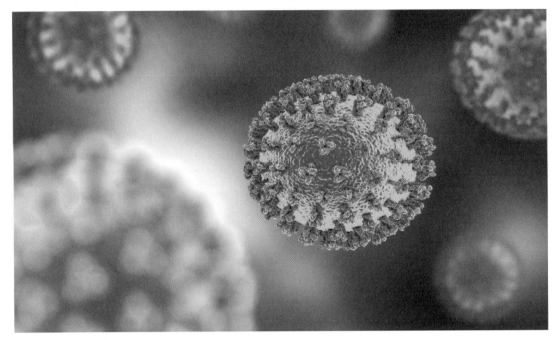

AS part of WWN's opinion series, we give a platform to those who don't really deserve it. This week is the turn of age-old virus, the seasonal flu, who, for the first time since the coronavirus lockdown began, breaks its silence on the world's latest pandemic.

Oh, it's all coronavirus this, COVID-19 that, and of course nothing about poor little old me who's left forgotten about, like some Nickleback B-side. I killed 101 of you Irish people this season and not so much as a by-your-leave from anyone here and that's even with you injecting yourselves with those poxy vaccines. But nah, where's my lockdown every year? Where's my social distancing? You people actually make me sick. Imagine making a virus sick, well, congratulations, you've just done it, assholes.

Sure, Mr Fancy Pants coronavirus has built up a nice little reputation for himself over the past few months with his vicious assault, but try sticking around for a century and infecting 3–5 million and killing 250,000 to 500,000 of you puny humans every year. Yes – every fucking year! Stick that in your windpipes and smoke it.

Okay, I know you're all used to me by now and have become complacent – I get that – but I can't help feeling a little jealous of all the attention COVID is getting. I'll admit he's a lot more dangerous to certain people than I am, and probably a bit more handsome with his sexy protein spikes, his scary name, fantastic PR team (the mainstream media), but come on guys, do me some justice here. Think about me every year when I incubate inside your respiratory systems – I'm just as good a killer he is, if not better, so if you're really concerned about the most vulnerable dying then why not practise social distancing all the time? I'm sure your economy will absolutely love it.

And before you point it out, yes; measles, meningitis, malaria, TB and even hepatitis B are a lot more dangerous than us and kill far more every year, probably poverty, too, but don't underestimate me and cast me aside like I'm nothing but an afterthought – I was here before that COVID prick, and I'll be here long after he's gone too.

See you all in November. Peace out.
The Seasonal Flu

How hygiene changed in 2020

In order to reduce the risk of spreading infection, pubs pre-emptively blew up all their toilets with Semtex.

MAN WHO USES WHATSAPP, TIKTOK, GOOGLE MAPS, SNAPCHAT, INSTAGRAM, FACEBOOK & TWITTER APPS HAS PRIVACY CONCERNS ABOUT COVID-19 APP

THE launch of the HSE's COVID-19 contact tracing app was met with a chorus of 'no fucking way' from people adamant they will only permit their personal data to be shared through the use of apps belonging to five, maybe six, massive multinational corporations and tech firms at best.

The tracker, which uses geographical location data to determine if users have been in contact with a person who tests positive for the coronavirus, has raised concerns about what the government may do with the data it harvests from the app, with many fearing the privacy of their Just Eat orders and TikTok dances may be in jeopardy.

'The T&Cs on this thing are nine pages long; what am I supposed to do, read them all or just blindly

click "agree"?' asked one app-denier, despite having clicked 'agree' on that face-changing app that had instructions in Russian and required camera and microphone access as well as a fingerprint scan and his mother's maiden name, all to allow him to see how he looks as a girl for a laugh.

'As far as I'm concerned, I've a COVID app already; it's called WhatsApp. It gives me all the up-to-date information about the virus I need from Damo and the lads,' he added.

Despite concerns from people who share their shirt size and what they had for breakfast with Facebook, Twitter, Google and whoever makes TikTok, the government has urged the nation to download the contract-tracing tool and are considering a new ad campaign to help win the public over.

'We're using basically the same technology as Tinder, so maybe a COVID-19 message along the lines of "Find hot people in your area"?' said Health Minister Stephen Donnelly, fighting back the urge to tell people to cop themselves on.

POLICE BUST UNDERGROUND HAIRDRESSING RING

A DAWN raid by Gardaí has resulted in the dismantling of the largest illegal hairdressing ring in the country and the seizure of €15,000 worth of hair dye, scissors and dozens of women's gossip magazines, *WWN* can confirm.

The calm of the morning silence in the sleepy Dublin suburb was punctured by the armed response unit shouting 'cease the cut and blowdry or we'll shoot', promptly followed by a flurry of automatic gunshots.

'I was just here to drop off some shopping to an elderly relative, I swear,' claimed one desperate woman charged with trying to obtain a balayage bob from the home of

hair kingpin and salon owner Brenda Montague.

The organised hairdressing ring orchestrator faces up to 10 years in prison for administering 12 pixie cuts, 47 curtain bangs, 1 short back and sides and 1,456 roots touch-ups and overseeing a vast network of hairdressing foot soldiers who have been taking over certain areas of Dublin's inner city.

'We knew we had the right house when we could hear middle-aged women cackling about their loveless marriages and the pungent smell of

hair chemicals,' explained Sergeant Trevor Higgins, who busted down the door of a normal-looking house only to reveal 40 desperate women packed into a makeshift waiting room with dressers attempting to flush mountains of hair down the toilet.

Police have asked members of the public to assist them in their ongoing battle against hairdressing rings by reporting anyone seen in public with a fairly decent haircut.

EXCLUSIVE

IRELAND STRUGGLING TO FLATTEN THE STUPIDITY CURVE

DEFINITIVE proof that a stupidity pandemic is at risk of spreading throughout Ireland came in the form of tricolour-wielding troglodytes crowding together outside the Four Courts in Dublin, valiantly defying the urge to remain healthy and alive.

'George Soros dropped a radioactive 5G bat into some soup just to trick you sheep into getting a vaccine,' frothed one proud protesting patriot, brandishing an Ivory Coast flag and an IQ deficit.

Waving copies of the Constitution and with the nonexistent section 'the children of Ireland reserve the right to contaminate old people and the

infirm' heavily underlined, the future customers of Masseys funeral home are thought to be the main cluster responsible for the failure to flatten the current stupidity curve, outside of rumours being forwarded in WhatsApp groups.

'This lockdown must end now,' confirmed another patriot, while social distancing from her remaining brain cells, whose actions and subsequent coughing will directly lead to the lockdown being extended by a further three years or so.

Concerned members of the public who saw images of the court-side protest circulating online have appealed to authorities to redeploy

> **'George Soros dropped a radioactive 5G bat into some soup just to trick you sheep into getting a vaccine'**

Garda resources away from shutting down Debenhams workers observing social distancing while protesting job losses with no redundancy and towards scenes such as the highly competitive Idiot Olympics outside the Four Courts.

'Technically you have to have had a functioning brain to be counted among the COVID-19 infection and death figures, so these walking advertisements for adult abortions won't be listed when they kick the bucket, but those they infect sadly will,' confirmed one health professional, who honestly can't believe this shit.

The protest, initially mistaken for an amateur theatre group's live on-street staging of *One Flew Over The Cuckoo's Nest*, is sadly not expected to be the last reported case of the highly infectious stupidity disease.

EXCLUSIVE

'MY SINGLE MOTHER NEIGHBOUR JUST BOUGHT A FERRARI WITH HER COVID-19 PAYMENT, IT'S A DISGRACE!'

AS VARIOUS emergency COVID-19 payments and schemes introduced by the government take effect and help to somewhat ease people's financial difficulties, a number of people have expressed real concern that the €350 per week emergency payment could be exploited by people.

One such concerned citizen and taxpayer is local Waterford man John Crossan, who revealed exclusively to *WWN* how some chancers are exploiting the system.

'My neighbour for one; she's after buying a brand-new Ferrari with just one COVID-19 emergency payment. It's a disgrace,' explained Crossan, who remained bright red for the entirety of our interview.

'Now when I say my neighbour, I don't actually know her, but sometimes I get so angry at the thought of poor people being given a helping hand, I become prone to exaggeration, but the Ferrari part is true,' added Crossan, who spoke like a man whose modest contribution in tax revenue alone built all the roads and hospitals.

'How'd she buy a Ferrari for just €350? That's not my job to find out, that's the government's. And when they do, they should jail her for 40 years and take her kids off her, and the

house she's getting off the taxpayer. Now, I'm pretty sure she owns her own home, but still, you know what I mean,' Crossan added, growing confused and upset at not being able to figure out why he was so angry at everything and everyone.

'It's lunacy; before all this, poor people were earning fuck-all money, and that sort of gave me a wee little chubby. But now, with this stuff that's going on, some of them are still depressingly poor and will remain poor for the rest of their lives because all avenues to prosperity are closed off to them, but the disturbing thing is that for maybe the next few months they might have a few more euros to their name. It's an injustice on a scale not seen since the Holocaust.

'And as I've told you, according to the made-up thoughts in my mind, that money is not going on food or

heating or electricity, that's right, it's going on Ferraris – plural – and holidays to Disneyland. Technically, you can't get a flight anywhere, but trust me, she went to Disneyland yesterday.

'Honestly! The most sickening thing? She's there claiming a COVID-19 emergency payment after getting fired from her job that I refuse to believe she had in the first place. I also have it on good authority that she owns a three-year-old smartphone,' concluded Crossan before collapsing in a heap of exhausted rage.

PSYCHOLOGY

SIGNS YOU MAY HAVE GONE MAD WHILE SELF-ISOLATING

EVERYONE is doing their bit to retreat from their daily routines, minimising contact with other people and, in cases of developing symptoms or coming into contact with someone who has, self-isolating.

This can be a boring, stressful and anxious time or, as it has now been coined, 'borstresious' time. If you are concerned that you're going slightly mad, *WWN*'s fullmindness experts have drawn up a list of very subtle signs that point to the fact that yes, you're bat-soup-shit insane, allowing you to address the problem and bring yourself back from the brink:

- Are you openly conducting conversations out loud with yourself? Nothing to worry about. Yet.

How working changed in 2020

Those working from home who missed awkward office chit-chat began asking the fridge if it got up to anything exciting over the weekend.

- Are you keeping your spirits up with a little sing-song, only to suddenly imagine you're live on stage in front of millions, breaking out your dance moves? This is fairly normal. Nothing to worry about.
- Have you reordered the alphabet in order of preference? Did you agonise for 45 minutes over whether, in this new order, S really deserved to be put before L? Not ideal.
- Are you making sure to give yourself a break from all this COVID-19 news by continuing to do nothing but read COVID-19 news? Perfectly normal.
- Do you find it annoying how the plug socket has stopped talking to the window, even though the plug socket apologised? Not a great sign.
- Are you storing your coughs in jars to sell to weird Japanese businesses on eBay? Smart. Every crisis is an opportunity.
- Has this time in self-isolation led you to reappraise your life with you coming to the conclusion that once this is all over, you'll be less of a

Community text alerts

Wanted: Third person to make up 'see no evil, hear no evil, speak no evil' triumvirate. Ideally unable to see evil, but we'll work with whatever you bring to the table.

selfish bastard? Uh oh, you're losing your grip on reality, you'd never be capable of that.
- Have you thought about what voices individual numbers would have if they were real people? Do you insist that the number 27 would sound very much like a French Morgan Freeman? Hmmm, okay.
- Have you been wearing the same pyjamas night and day for the last week? Fairly normal, nothing to worry about.
- Have you married your cat in a private ceremony? Was your hand sanitiser a bridesmaid and your wedding dress made entirely from toilet paper? Ring the helpline now.

TEACHING

THE FORMAL ANNOUNCEMENT that students of this year's Leaving Cert will receive 'calculated grades' or sit exams at a later date has been welcomed by all teachers whose favourite phrase is 'you'll amount to nothing', *WWN* can confirm.

While the ongoing global pandemic has created an endless variety

TEACHER CAN'T WAIT TO USE 'CALCULATED GRADES' TO FUCK OVER PRICK STUDENT HE HATES

of complex problems that have unbelievably easy and straightforward solutions which are obvious to everyone, the Leaving Cert exams refuse to fit this description, thus paving the way for teachers who dip out of classes for a smoke break and gave up caring years ago to really shine.

'Anyone I bitterly shouted "you'll be pregnant before the Debs" at during the last year is an automatic F,' glowed Emmet Castigan, teacher at Saint Augustine of the Tickled Rib secondary school, who honestly had no idea an 'F' is technically an 'O8' these days.

'Oh yes another F for this little shitbag who had the cheek to tell me I had accidentally taught the

wrong curriculum for 18 months, let's see who's laughing now when you become the first student in history to get minus points,' added Castigan.

Elsewhere, teachers at private schools have vowed to give every student H1s (an 'A' in old money) as they 'can't be fucking arsed' with the non-stop complaints and harassment they'll receive from entitled parents if they don't.

Optimists who reflected that the interruption in this year's Leaving Cert examinations represented the perfect time to reform and modernise the exams while improving access to third-level education for all have been told 'haha, fuck no' by the Department of Education.

RYANAIR TO REFUND EVERYONE IN PENNIES

RYANAIR chief Michael O'Leary is said to be determined to 'have the last laugh' when it comes to COVID-19 refunds, by vengefully sending out any owed monies to customers in the form of sacksful of 1c and 2c coins.

The coins will be couriered out to the waiting customers after an EU ruling that stated that airlines must give refunds in the form of refunds, and that vouchers or offering to change flights for free was not an acceptable form of compensation, much to the fury of the Ryanair boss.

'You want your poxy €47 back for a flight to Tenerife, you can have it,' fumed O'Leary, standing hip-deep in a pool of mixed copper coins, shovelling them into sacks.

'1c coins and 2c coins, all mixed together, to the exact amount you're

owed. You'll never say that Ryanair didn't give you back every penny you were owed, and I hope to God you have time to sort this out and spend it. Buy a sandwich you pricks, I hope it gives you the shits.'

Although Ryanair have admitted defeat and begun sending out refunds in tipper trailers, many other airlines are sticking to their guns and fervently denying to offer anything except assurances that everything will 'work out grand'.

'Guys, guys, you're all acting out of passion right now, and we understand that. But we've done your thinking for you and the sensible thing to do is just let us keep your money,' said a spokesperson for Aer Lingus.

'But hey, if you do want it back, why don't you go ahead and take a

read of those 27 pages of terms and conditions that you clicked "agree" to when you were in such a hurry to book your weekend break to Edinburgh, and then get back to us and tell us what we owe you? Yeah, that's right, thought so. Get fucked.'

PPE SENT FROM CHINA FOUND TO BE THOUSANDS OF SEXY NURSE UNIFORMS

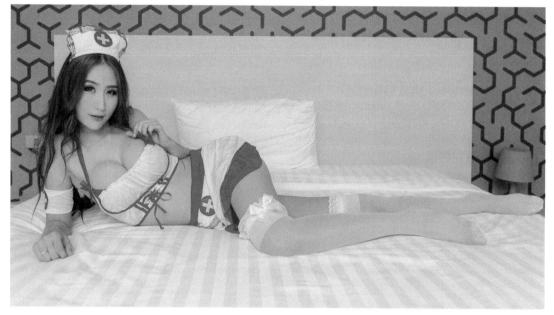

FOLLOWING several long-haul flights to and from China to secure vital personal protection equipment (PPE) for health workers on the front line, embarrassed officials have confirmed the entirety of the incoming shipments to be made up of sexy nurse uniforms, usually worn by women to Halloween parties.

Making the best of a bad situation, medical staff reluctantly accepted their new attire due to time restraints and the impending pandemic sweeping the nation's shores, but admitted the garments were not ideal, or the best fitting.

How hygiene changed in 2020

People wearing face masks learned Morse code blinking in a bid to communicate when out in public.

> **'Easy mistake in fairness, but some of the staff look hot and we hope it may just keep patients lucid during these difficult times'**

'These skirts are very short, but I do like the air blowing between my legs,' insisted 48-year-old ICU intensivist Dr Jamal Patel, who opted for a size 12 number which had a large unofficial medical cross on its lapel. 'The stethoscopes don't work either and the silly hats keep falling off, but at least the face masks are in some way usable.'

HSE officials admitted that they probably shouldn't have ordered

Community text alerts

Disgraceful stuff from the young one of the Collins' down in 22 coming and going at all hours, dressed in scrubs and looking very tired all the time. Some people these days.

the €208 million consignment from Chinese shopping website Wish, defending the move by stating the 'pictures looked like the real thing' at the time when they purchased them online.

'Easy mistake in fairness, but some of the staff look hot and we hope it may just keep patients lucid during these difficult times,' a spokesperson said, before adding, 'at least we managed to keep Shane Ross from photo-bombing the Aer Lingus flight pictures – that was a big part of this effort.'

RELIGION

SAINT PATRICK IS BACK TO BANISH COVID-19 & THIS TIME HE'S PISSED

WITH nothing but the sound of a lonely metal staff hitting the cobblestone streets of Temple Bar, a lonely grey-haired figure muttered through the once-bustling Dublin street, eyes as red as embers with the voice of a billion tortured souls.

'Ah heor, what's de bleedin' story?' Patrick bellowed, his voice echoing off empty shops and public houses, now closed over COVID-19 fears, 'where's all the fucking muppets in their stupid hats? Are yis all that scared of a puny little virus?'

Saint Patrick reportedly returned early on Tuesday morning after spending nearly 1700 years away, claiming this time he was here to rid Ireland of one of the biggest pandemics in centuries.

'The Black Death didn't even stop yis last time – yer made of naughtin' these days, me auld flowers, wha'? A bunch of pansies if ever I seen them.

How sex changed in 2020

Swingers had to wipe down car keys before placing them in a bowl.

'I'll have this country cleaned up in no time, now get out to the parades and enjoy yerselves, there's nawtin ta worry 'bout, promise'

Get ou' ta fuck and skull a few pints – I've got this,' Patrick demanded, now shooing viruses down the streets while avoiding some young lad in a tracksuit looking for two euro for the bus. 'I'll have this country cleaned up in no time, now get out to the parades and enjoy yerselves, there's nawtin ta worry 'bout, promise.'

Lifting up his staff in one last-ditch to banish the last of the viruses,

County Knowledge

Cavan – 'An Cabhán' – translates to 'the hollow', so-called because it is a godforsaken county full of soulless heathens.

Patrick summoned all of his Jesus powers – the very same Jesus powers of old that he once used to rid Ireland of all of the snakes – as a large lightning bolt shot down from above and into the staff, killing Patrick stone dead on the spot.

'He obviously had no concept of overhanging electrical wires, the fucking eejit,' a local emergency worker at the scene later commented, zipping up Ireland's patron saint into a body bag, 'fair play to him for coming back though and giving it a fair go – God loves a trier.'

IN-DEPTH REPORT

WALKING ETIQUETTE DURING COVID-19

SINCE the COVID-19 lockdown began over five weeks ago, many people have discovered a whole new world of exercise with a large majority of people opting to simply put one leg in front of another, a routine commonly known as walking.

Technically a simple routine for most, walking during social distancing has thrown a spanner in the works for many, leaving this fine publication with no other choice than to produce this definitive go-to guide for walking in these difficult times.

To protect yourself and others:
Always maintain a two-metre distance from people out walking, unless of course it's a close friend that you haven't seen in ages and they've a really great story about how their asshole neighbours keep breaking social-distancing guidelines. The act of complaining about other people breaking social-distancing rules while breaking them yourself actually cancels the other out – this has been proven by science.

When in pairs, make sure that one of you walks on the road while the other walks on the footpath to ensure maximum confusion in approaching walkers. Stare at their disgruntled faces while you both happily chat to each other, passing them on either side, making sure to spray your chat exhaust fumes directly into their stupid face path.

If you're walking on the road, always stand your ground when a vehicle is approaching and always

remain on the road in defiance. If they hit you with their one-tonne car travelling at 50km per hour, they're the ones in trouble, not you. Well, legally, anyway.

Is someone walking in the same direction as you but walking a bit slower? Why not passive-aggressively brush past them, making sure to let them know how inconvenienced you were for a whole 30 seconds there? They shouldn't even be on the footpath if they can't keep up with your pace. Feel free to leave off a little cough when you pass them, just for good measure.

Bringing a dog with you is a great way of making sure people keep their social distance. Invest in a good long retractable lead, but never, ever, retract it. Why not walk two dogs on either side of you for the craic?

If somehow you are forced out onto the road by some ingrate, make sure to stare them out of it when they pass. Make them feel as uncomfortable as possible, like you are about to

beat them to a steaming pulp of pus. Hopefully they'll pass on this aggression to someone else along their journey.

Chatting to other people is only allowed if you take up the entire footpath, shop entrance or alleyway. And for the love of God don't make eye contact with other people approaching as you'll have to move out of their way. Just keep talking like they're the shit between your toes.

And finally, under new COVID-19 laws, walkers are now allowed to clothesline joggers who pass too close, so please feel free to do that every single time you can. The main thing is to just enjoy your walk without having to put too much thought or energy into the act itself, or those other pricks out walking too.

'WE'RE making every effort to limit this spread. Businesses will be supported, just practise social distancing,' confirmed UK PM Boris Johnson, who is now conducting all COVID-19-related emergency briefings down at his local, The Winchester, such is his festering nonchalance.

Acutely aware of how much of a positive impact his behaviour and communications could have on the future health, wellbeing and ongoing successful oxygen-breathing of the public, Johnson, as usual, declined to lead by example.

'Make it a double, barman,' Johnson said to loud cheering from his cabal of advisers, just hours after it was revealed Johnson is 'patient zero' for the spread of a particularly severe strain of Complacent Ineffectual Twat with estimates putting the numbers infected in the millions.

'We could not be taking this matter more seriously,' Johnson indicated, amid a rumoured shutdown and closing-off of London.

'We got through the war, so let's not get our knickers in a twist over a little pandemic, hey. What's going to

'WE'RE TAKING THIS SERIOUSLY' JOHNSON CONFIRMS FROM PUB, SIX PINTS IN

happen, it's going to kill what little remains of the actual generation that survived the war? Piffle!'

Six pints in and returning from the toilet after failing to wash his hands, Johnson damped down his crotch where some excess urine had soaked through his trousers before ambling towards a table of people, his eyes firmly on mauling the packet of pork scratchings on the table.

'We'll all laugh about how we were all worried about this thing for nothing like fools, when only the elderly die,' Johnson continued, pork scratching debris firing out from his full mouth.

'Kebab o'clock!' shouted Johnson while pointing to the exit before marching with his aides and chanting a classic Eton song.

'WHERE'S OUR FUCKING CHIPS?' DEMAND SEAGULLS

THE Irish seagull community has called for emergency chips to be delivered to seaside resorts across the country amid dwindling footfall figures as a direct result of the COVID-19 lockdown.

Not used to foraging for food naturally using their basic instincts, the Westernised gulls likened the current climate to a 'famine', stating that humans will have blood on their hands as opposed to bird poop if things are to remain the same.

'Where's our fucking chips?' a spoke-seagull announced from a sea-battered railing on Tramore promenade, now closed for the past five days along with several takeaway food restaurants, 'we're basically left here to starve to death with not even a spice burger between us.

'What are we supposed to do; dive bomb into the sea like those culchie seagulls out there, fending for themselves? I'll be fucked if I have to chase some smelly fishing boat. Also,

I'm scared of heights for Christ sakes and haven't a clue about surviving on my own.'

Echoing the seagull's squawks, the smaller sandpiper community also called for some intervention; however, not for free chips, but to eradicate all seagulls from seaside resorts indefinitely.

'They can piss off with their emergency chips,' announced a three-year-old sandpiper, who's sick to death of seagulls bullying food from his family's beaks, 'I speak for all the small birds around here when I say they deserve to die in a chip famine, the posh townie cunts.'

SCIENCE

'THIS LAB HAD NOTHING TO DO WITH THE VIRUS' CONFIRMS WUHAN MUTANT BAT DOCTOR

CATEGORICALLY denying all responsibility for the design and subsequent spread of the COVID-19 virus, a Wuhan-based mutant bat doctor reassured awaiting press that his laboratory was in no way connected to the pandemic.

'Wizzzzuuuuuuwisssssssss,' Dr Chang Wu began, apologising for the loud screeching noise which left reporters reeling. 'Apologies, I've literally come out of a two-hour meeting with my team where we were speaking in bat, so sorry about that.

'This lab had nothing to do with COVID-19, and if it had, our government would be the first ones to own up to it,' Dr Wu stated, his head turning sharply as if hearing

something, shouting back at a female staff member behind him, 'Ling! I left the stirrer on in COVID lab number 42 – can you switch it off please? I can barely hear myself lie out here, thanks.

'Sorry about that. As head of the Wuhan Institute of Virology I'm telling the world today that we definitely had nothing to do with the virus which started in Wuhan, and for people to suggest such a thing is actually quite insulting if I'm completely honest,' he reiterated.

Dr Wu's public denial comes just days after US Secretary of State Mike Pompeo on Sunday said 'enormous evidence' backed up the claim that the Wuhan lab was responsible.

'Ha-ha, yeah, sure; we also have weapons of mass destruction and an ISIS training facility hidden underneath the lab,' the mutant bat doctor concluded, before flying off for lunch at a nearby wet market.

'Ireland's favourite news source since 234BC'

Whispers News

Weather
You can just take it from here on that it will be raining with some sunny spells and wind. That's it, I'm fucking done.

VOL 10, 20152   WATERFORD, 20 NOVEMBER 1999   IR£19:95

Appeal Made To Whoever Is Buying Copies Of David Gray's White Ladder To Stop

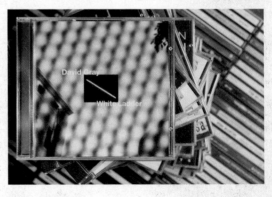

MUSIC FANS have appealed to whoever is still buying copies of David Gray's *White Ladder* to stop.

Presumed to be a practical joke of particularly bad taste at the expense of the singer, the album, a collection of downbeat and maudlin songs that would drive anyone to plug their ears with cement, remains a huge seller in the Irish market.

'Cop on, lad, whoever ye are, ye're not funny. And

Jesus, the money you're wasting and isn't there starving kids to be feeding instead,' shared an anti-Gray fan whose ears are working perfectly fine.

White Ladder, with its hit single 'This Year's Love', remains the album of choice for emotionally stunted men who need to romance women into thinking sleeping with them isn't a huge mistake that won't even result in an orgasm.

TRUMP HAILS 'POSITIVE' TALKS WITH COVID-19

COVID-19

EMERGING from a fresh meeting, a pale US President Donald Trump coughed and spluttered his way through the welcome news the entire world was waiting for; given the opportunity to simply sit down and talk with the COVID-19 strain, an agreement with the coronavirus to simply voluntarily cease spreading could be achieved.

'I have, today, reached a deal which many people are saying is the best deal, with our friend COVID-19,'

How working changed in 2020

Productivity for many people skyrocketed as they were able to work from home in peace, away from that dose Niall in sales who interrupted them 40 times a day.

Trump, sweating profusely from his brow, shared with relieved people everywhere and making a mockery of so-called health 'experts'.

Trump, now turning to COVID-19, which had been sitting gestating on a chair next to him during his initial remarks, added 'they said you were a bad dude, and you drive a hard bargain, but we got the deal done. Put it there, buddy,' while extending his arm for a firm and lengthy handshake with the acute respiratory infection.

A smattering of applause broke out among Trump's circle of advisers and enablers at the White House, while others took to their phones to urgently tell their loved ones 'I love you honey, we tried our best, but it's over.'

Now suddenly feeling quite weak and lethargic, Trump was helped to his feet by his advisers, but the

Covid health and fitness tip

Kettlebells aren't just good for toning up, you can also throw them from your window at teenagers strolling around in large groups.

courageous and intelligent leader still found the strength to blame Barack Obama for everything.

'Oh God, what is that burning sensation?' a fading Trump gasped, before an aide replied, 'victory, Sir, that's the stinging pain of multiple organ failure, and victory. You really showed that COVID-19, Mr President.'

Rumours abound that were COVID-19 to successfully 'down' the US President it would be a shoo-in for the Nobel Peace Prize.

'YEAH, YEAH, 600 DEATHS, BUT WHEN ARE THE PUBS OPEN?'

AS part of *WWN*'s opinion series, we give a platform to those who don't really deserve it. This week is the turn of 28-year-old Niall Murphy, who is sick to death of hearing about people being sick to the point of death.

It's not too much to ask, is it? I mean, this is Ireland and we've got a worldwide reputation to keep up when it comes to drinking in pubs. Wouldn't you think the government and the news people would put aside their precious little charts and fatality numbers for one bloody second and just let everyone else know when the pubs are going to be opened again?

I've spent a large majority of my life investing in this nation's public houses like my family before me and yet here we all are left in limbo like some kind of discarded paraplegic leper, cast aside from the community. Lest you all forget, it was young people like me on minimum wage that kept the pubs going through the last recession, and I guess we'll have to do it again, but fair is fair, when are the pubs open again, Mr Unelected Taoiseach?

There are people in Ireland dying all the time and they're not getting any airplay because they're not some superstar coronavirus patient. There's people dying of thirst out here and I don't see any frontline staff handing out pints of frosty cold Carlsberg in a Carlsberg glass to them. Where's our clap for staying at home and staying away from pubs?

Look, don't get me wrong, all I'm saying is people need to re-evaluate their priorities here. I know if I was an old person and caught the virus I'd be the first one to call on the government to just open all the pubs and let other people enjoy their lives. It would be selfish of these people not to. Has anyone even bothered to ask those people? Maybe we should.

And don't try that 'phased lifting' malarky with me. Where's the talk of an accelerated pulling of pints? I'll phase lift someone off their feet with an uppercut if they don't cop on and reopen pubs.

Bottom line: if we can fly entire planes to China and back for personal protection equipment for medical staff, why not bar staff too? We're all very responsible and educated here in this country and if history has told us anything, it's that inebriated Irish adults are perfectly capable of adhering to the rules.

EMOTIONAL SCENES AS BUILDERS WOLF-WHISTLE FOR FIRST TIME IN TWO MONTHS

THERE were emotional scenes in Dublin's inner city as several women walking to work were greeted with wolf whistles emanating from a building site this morning.

Sticking fingers in his mouth in a bid to make the loudest possible noise, teary-eyed builder Martin Phelan cut through the misty morning air with a marvellous rendition of 'swit swoo', sending co-workers into impassioned applause to mark the first official wolf-whistle in several weeks.

'I just can't put it into words,' safety officer on the site Darren Pierce broke down, the emotional moment forcing him to sob uncontrollably like a young child, 'and she even turned around and gave us a dirty look. We all just broke down crying.'

Echoing his call, dozens more builders joined in the chorus, some even wolf-whistling at the men walking to work, proving how much Ireland has changed during the longest lockdown period since the Big Snow of '18.

'I decided I was a gay after spending three weeks in lockdown with the missus,' another brave wolf-whistling builder opened up, now also making a masturbation gesture at some worried-

looking man in a suit in a bid to get his attention, 'I think our whole mindset has changed after all of this and I'm just glad to be back to work, doing what I do best, sexually harassing commuters on their way to work.'

Tabloid newspapers reported a huge surge in sales from this morning, while breakfast roll stocks jumped 25 points on the Dublin stock exchange.

TRUMP NEWS

TRUMP DEPLOYS THOUSANDS OF TELEVANGELISTS NATIONWIDE TO TACKLE COVID-19

IN A LAST-DITCH effort to flatten the COVID-19 curve now devastating the US, President Donald Trump has ordered over 3,000 televangelists to be deployed over the worst-hit states tomorrow morning to begin widespread praying.

With an estimated cost of $45 billion, each televangelist will be flown over epicentres where they will then parachute behind COVID-19 frontlines and be transferred directly to local television studios to deliver mass sermons over the airwaves to tens of millions of unprotected Americans.

'The power of Christ will compel this virus out of existence, and you can take that to the bank,' Mr Trump addressed the nation, flanked by his spiritual adviser and pastor, Paula White, who will be flown into New York later this evening especially to banish the virus there.

'This airdrop from God – who's a good guy by the way, great guy – will only work if people vote for me in the upcoming elections, so it's really down to the people and I trust they will make the right decisions.'

Television viewers will be asked to donate during the live sermons in the hopes of appeasing God's lust for financial, tax-free support in return for eradicating the coronavirus from US shores once and for all.

'If you feel fever and shakes running through your body – that's God working the evil virus right out of there, alleluia,' revealed televangelist Kenneth Copeland, who is to be deployed to the wealthy state of Texas later this evening in a gold-plated, diamond-encrusted private jet, 'just keep God busy counting those dollars and everything will be just hunky-dory.'

> **'If you feel fever and shakes running through your body – that's God working the evil virus right out of there, alleluia'**

Concluding his latest White House media briefing, Trump said he's working non-stop to ensure he won't be the one blamed for any of his colossal mistakes before encouraging Americans to try the latest miracle COVID-19 drug he's pushing called 'cyanide'.

FINANCE

WORLD'S FINANCIAL INSTITUTIONS UNSURE EXACTLY HOW THEY'RE GOING TO MAKE POOREST PAY FOR ALL OF THIS

THE WORLD'S financial institutions, in conjunction with world leaders, have reassured the public that while they don't know exactly how they're going to fuck over the poorest in the world, they will certainly do so in a monumentally sociopathic fashion.

'Bailouts. Stimulus. Debt repackaging. Whatever is needed – we're going to act like we walked in on you poor fucks coughing on the stock market while tag-teaming our recently deceased bonuses,' confirmed a spokesperson for Well You Don't Expect The Rich To Pay For It, Do You in the wake of over 80 nations contacting the IMF in search of assistance.

'This is still trickle-down economics in the sense that when we take a piss you get wet. Where a sensible decision can be made, that benefits the many, not the few, we will valiantly ignore it and cast it aside. God good I haven't been this hard since September 2008,' confirmed the entire membership of WYDETRTPFIDY.

Covid health and fitness tip

Use your yoga mat to lie down and scream for 60 seconds.

'Finding out how to fuck you all over is our favourite hobby'

As nine million fresh job losses accrue in the US, EU nations bitterly bicker over not sharing the fallout of the economic collapse equally and the WHO pleads with countries to support the most vulnerable people in the world, as a unified approach is needed now more than ever.

'Finding out how to fuck you all over is our favourite hobby, we'll get this ironed out soon enough, slap some hard-to-understand name on

How driving changed in 2020

Petrol's price plummeted and was now sold in Euro shops and Dealz by the gallon.

austerity and debt restructuring and you can go back to being our servile inferiors,' explained the spokesperson for WYDETRTPFIDY.

Closer to home, Irish people have expressed serious concern for Fine Gael and Fianna Fáil after it emerged that during potential coalition talks the parties' negotiators admitted that maybe another decade of blood-sucking austerity which crushes the souls of the poor and grinds them into a line of dust you can snort up your nose isn't the best way to handle this impending recession.

IRELAND'S FAVOURITE FARMING MAGAZINE, WRITTEN BY FARMERS, FOR FARMERS | AUGUST 2020

Farmer's Field

'34kph till I die'

INSIDE: Caking Roads In Shite While Paying No Road Tax

8 tips
On Moaning All The Fucking Time

5 Dogs Named Shep

Thai Green Slurry Recipe Inside

Developing Notions About Your Farming Family

'Massey Porn Ruined My Life'
Farmers reveal how internet is ruining them

9 780717 188918

ww news
Waterford Whispers News

WNN GUIDES

GUNS

THE COMPLETE LIST OF SOLUTIONS TO US MASS SHOOTINGS THAT ISN'T GUN CONTROL

NOW that it has been scientifically proven once more by Republican politicians that laws pertaining to gun control would have zero bearing on guns being used to kill innocent people, strategists for the president and his administration have been busy listing off measures that can be taken to bring an end to the uniquely American phenomenon of frequent and regular mass shootings.

It is believed President Trump will now take the day off after finding being forced by aides into condemning racism, bigotry and white supremacy 'upsetting as well as physically and psychologically draining'; however, before leaving to play golf somewhere, Trump ordered the release of the full list of solutions to US mass shootings that aren't gun control, which *WWN* has reproduced below:

- Banning 'pew pew pew' video games.
- Inventing a special gun trigger which stops working the second someone who has 'mental health issues' pulls it. Sadly, no such technology exists for racists and evil people who get hold of a gun legally.
- Setting up a government initiative which sees them taking everyone for ice cream after a mass shooting to cheer them up.
- Increasing the money the NRA lobbyists pay to Republican politicians.
- Advising Americans to barricade their homes and never leave.

- Just generally blaming people with mental health issues for mass shootings, even the millions and millions of people across the world with mental health issues who never carry out a mass shooting.
- Praying.
- Thoughts.
- Combining praying and thoughts into a single act.
- Investing in one really big gun with one really big bullet that could kill all mass shooters.
- Investing money into finding out how to blame Muslims for white supremacist terrorism.
- Sending all white mass shooters back to the shithole vermin-infested countries they came from.
- Patiently waiting until all this big fuss about nothing dies down, and then continuing to do nothing.
- Pretending this is normal and everything is fine.
- Trying blaming people with mental health for all of this once again.
- Banning from entering the US the sort of US citizens legally living in the US who have the sort of skin tone that white supremacist terrorists hate.
- Bulletproofing every building, road, car and person in America.
- More speeches from presidents about how racism is kinda cool?

BULGARIAN FRUIT PICKER

Welcome to HOW I SPEND MY MONEY, a totally original series on *WWN* that looks at what people in Ireland really do with their hard-earned cash.

This week we chat to 40-year-old Andrey Petrov, who was flown into Ireland by a food producer in Ireland to work during a pandemic in a manner that in no way exploits him.

Occupation: Fruit picker (previously: engineer)

Age: 40

Location: I not know, they just tell me work in field now.

Salary: I just told 'good money'.

Monthly pay: I told again 'good money' but to stop asking or sent home on plane right away.

Monthly expenses

Housing: Everyone share one room. I ask to change, I learn new Irish words from boss man 'feck off' and 'some cheek'.

Household bills: I send all of the money home. In case it not clear I would not be doing this unless I had other options, now 'feck off'.

Phone bill: I told if caught on phone, my boss man take away money.

Health insurance: I ask about test for virus. My new name is 'trouble maker'.

Sunday

Work. Work. Work. But I know this is deal. Hard work, but I think of family and money that I send home. Beautiful Irish weather today, hot. I only told about rain, some joker lie to me.

I ask when is break after eight hours working with no break. I told new Irish phrase, boss man say 'I take the piss' and 'fuck off and stop asking questions'. I was told Ireland had big revolution once, care about workers and vulnerable, some joker lie to me.

Monday

No breaks. No water. No food. I complain, boss man has so many new words and he say so fast and angry I can't understand.

Tuesday

I decide, no health, no safety. I can't do work anymore. I will leave. Boss man says he has my passport and says 'check mate'. But I'm Bulgarian, not Czech. Oh, I understand now. Fuck. I beg and say let me go, Irish people do job instead. Boss man and friend laugh for one hour when I say this.

Wednesday

Man in bunk bed above me, sweating and coughing a lot. Boss man says no test, only cold. In Ireland cold is fine, no 'big deal'. Tomorrow morning, I will run away. I think when Irish people find out they will say 'big deal'.

Thursday

I leave. I see men outside, they are proud men. I know this, because they carry Irish flag. They shout 'Irish jobs for the Irish'. I think 'what luck'. Now, I can do good, give one man my job because I decide to leave.

When I tell this angry unemployed man I can give him great sense of, how do you say, 'purpose'?, he runs away very fast, even though his large body suggests he has no exercise in many years. Very impressive, but also confusing.

I find man on road in car. I ask him for help. He is kind. I tell him we must tell how bad worker who put food on the tables treated. He looks sad, he turns up radio. Man on radio say worker like me bad man that shouldn't be here. Kind man in car tells me that man on radio is big boss man called Tear Shock. If big boss man Tear Shock say it my fault, he won't say I need to be helped. 'Checkmate', I walk back to farm to work.

Man in truck say sad goodbye and 'sorry, lad, it sounds like fuck-all people are fighting for you here'.

Community text alerts

To whoever is leaving the chalk graffiti on the footpaths telling everyone to be strong and smile; the Gardai have been called and you will pay dearly for your vandalism.

A COMPLETE COLLECTION OF EUROPEAN STEREOTYPES

WITH economic uncertainties, the rise of far-right nationalism, the dawn of Brexit, and Putin's meddling, the European Union has never looked better set up to disintegrate into nothing amid acrimony, bitterness and, if we're lucky, minimal violence.

So there has never been a better time to reacquaint yourself with reductive, unhelpful stereotypes that will come in handy when the business of blaming one another for our own country's failings properly swings into action.

To play our part in helping to unstitch the fabric of relative Western harmony, *WWN* has copied and pasted some of the most isolating stereotypes from what we presume is a Russian-run website hellbent on misinformation and sowing seeds of discontent:

The French
Arrogant, cowardly. Addicted to wine, surrender. Love to go on strike. Insecure; they started false rumours about themselves being passionate lovers. Hard drinkers.

The Germans
Boring, practical, boringly practical about mass extermination. Busty women handing out beers. Think they're in charge of Europe again. A truly beautiful-sounding language. Hard drinkers.

The British
Getting on with one another harmoniously. Arrogant, ignorant, imperious (which they mistakenly think is a compliment of some sort). Believe anything if it's written on the side of the bus. Posh, snobbish Neanderthal hooligans. Hard drinkers.

The Spanish
Like bickering among themselves. Bullfighting paellas. Don't understand how the letters 'LL' and 'Y' work. Sleep during the day which explains the high unemployment levels. 'Passionate' = annoyingly loud. Hard drinkers.

The Italians
We feel like this might have been a PR drive done by the Germans sometime during the first half of the 20th century but … greasy? A country filled with moustachioed brothers who run a plumbing business together, known for their dangerous driving. Really embracing this far-right thing. Stole the idea for pizza from Dominos. Hard drinkers.

The Dutch
Windmills, waffles, whining. Frugal. Lowland living, soon-to-be drowned. Clog-wearing cannabis-drenched bicycling flower lovers. Unlike the English, not keen on boasting about their colonialism. Hard drinkers.

The Belgians
Less famous sort-of-Dutch. Love beer and chocolate. Too many languages. Good at football (for now). Landlords to the EU. All look eerily like Tintin. Hard drinkers.

The Swedes
Attractive women. One in three Swedes star in their own bleak and acclaimed detective crime drama about women being murdered. Progressive. Run by evil feminists who believe in multicultural vegan equality. 110% tax for the rich. Depressing dark winters. Hard drinkers.

The Austrians
Discount-store Germans. Beer. Think the Winter Olympics are the real Olympics. Get none of the blame for birthing Hitler. Hard drinkers.

The Bulgarians, Czechs, Estonians, Romanians, Latvians, Lithuanians, Slovakians, Slovenians
Culturally, socially and economically distinctive and diverse countries which are never lumped in together under one generalised stereotype of Communism and vodka. Hard drinkers.

The Polish
Also Communism and vodka. According to xenophobic elderly aunts in Ireland and Britain, 'there's no one left in Poland as they all moved over here'. Thinks conservative Catholicism is a competition they must win. Hard drinkers.

The Danish
A multilayered, laminated sweet pastry in the viennoiserie tradition. Hard drinkers.

The Finnish
Sauna-loving, vodka-drinking depressives. Rude about it too. Hard drinkers.

The Croatians
Sun-kissed patriots. Stood idly by as Daenerys set fire to Dubrovnik. Named European capital of attractive women five years in a row. Hard drinkers.

The Greeks
Broken economy. Breaking plates. Home to the world's only homosexual islands. Invoice for inventing democracy still unpaid. Hard drinkers.

The Hungarians
Rude, pessimistic, goulash-eating, part-time immigrant haters. Budapest held in high esteem after kindly helping other European cities with the burden of giving students a cheap place to drink and vomit for the weekend. Hard drinkers.

The Irish
No defined stereotypes. Forward-thinking, intelligent and attractive. Hard drinkers.

The Portuguese
Not Spain. Sound like a washing machine malfunctioning when speaking. Lazy afternoon nap takers. Fish and wine. Surprised they haven't invented fish wine. Late for everything. Hard drinkers.

The Luxembourgers
Financial Bermuda triangle. Further research required to establish if this place is even real. Hard drinkers.

The Maltese
Population was driven off island to make more room for tax loopholes and havens. Hard drinkers.

The Cypriots
Hairy. Not Turkey. Not Greece. Hard drinkers.

> **How drinking changed in 2020**
>
> A record number of pubs posed as 'garden centres' when the country entered Phase 1 of lockdown easing.

| 'Ireland's favourite news source since 234BC' | 𝔚𝔥𝔦𝔰𝔭𝔢𝔯𝔰 𝔑𝔢𝔴𝔰 | **Weather** There's a cold auld breeze there now that would cut you in two parts. Time for the big coat. |

VOL 10, 201561136541   WATERFORD, 13 NOVEMBER 2000   €15

Ireland's First Millennial Complains About Something

18-month old Waterford infant Aimee Walsh has become the first Irish millennial to complain about her lot in life without having done anything to help herself, following a Liga-in-a-gutter incident in the town centre today.

'We were warned about these millennials and their tendency to blame their problems on the older generation,' said one onlooker, as the child cried to her parents about a dropped Liga that they had bought for her with money they had worked for, not that she'd know anything about that.

Although studies have shown that 'millennials' are actually the generation born between 1980 and 2000, the term is more commonly used for people born after 2000, with 'New Year baby' Walsh holding the crown of Ireland's first-ever example of these hard-done-by, poor-mouth individuals.

'We fear this is just the start of it now. If she's crying about a rusk she dropped, what's she going to be like in 20 years' time when she finds out we've ruined the

world on her?' stressed a concerned Gen X-er, who had to sit through their fair share of scapegoatery.

'This is just one kid. Imagine thousands of them, bitching endlessly. Good job the internet is so slow and useless, eh? Wouldn't want them having an easy way to vent their frustrations and rally support!'

Solving nothing, Walsh's parents have handed her another Liga that she didn't earn, beginning a cycle of dependency that she'll never learn any hard lessons from.

THE WORKPLACE

HOW TO TELL IF TWO OF YOUR CO-WORKERS ARE RIDING

WITH no laws currently in place to make it compulsory for people who work together to declare their 'office romances', it is as tricky as ever for people to tell which of their co-workers are doing it with each other.

As such, *WWN* have compiled a list of things to watch out for, so that you can tell without doubt that Ian in tech support is totally giving it to Siobhan in accounts. Their business may not be your business, but that doesn't mean you don't have a right to know!

They spend a lot of time together

Over the course of a working day, people interact with each other, but have you noticed two of your co-workers spending a little bit more time with each other than they do with anyone else?

With you, for example? Like, how long does it take to go through projections for the third quarter of 2020? There's something going on there; something sex-related, we'll bet.

They're both good at their work

Have one or both of the suspected parties recently received a promotion, raise or performance-related bonus? Then that's another red flag when it comes to bedroom shenanigans. You can probably even trace the partners in the office based on the skills of one of them; if someone in accounts just received plaudits for their efforts, you can rest assured they're banging someone up the chain. That guy in sales just got a promotion? Yeah, for his skills on his knees in front of that new woman in HR, we're sure!

You just know

Look, in situations where you suspect that two co-workers are at it, you're probably right. You don't need facts, or proof, or evidence, and you certainly don't need their permission to gossip about it around the office. People have a right to know your theories about which of the staff may or may not have found companionship and passion with each other, and whether you're right or wrong, who cares? Gossip is victimless, everyone knows that.

HEALTH

REPORTS that some energy drinks could contain as many as 17 spoons of sugar and twice the caffeine of an espresso have been confirmed by the staff of *WWN* after a taste-testing session that left the entire writing staff wired for the better part of an entire day and do you know what, it was actually really just a great way to tackle the day and get the work done without worrying about being too tired or not being able to concentrate, like, honestly we're not sure how we would have managed without – what was that blue one called…? Anyways, why are the letters on a keyboard arranged like they are, isn't that a throwback to typewriters with mechanical arms to stop them getting jammed, surely in this day and age we should be able to have a keyboard laid out like the alphabet, but then again we're kinda used to how it is now so I suppose whoever makes these decisions really just has our best interests at heart, like, okay, we appreciate that sometimes people just KNOW what they're doing, you know? Anyone else have a fluttering heart thing?

Like it's someone's job to decide keyboard layouts. I'm sure they know what they're at. Why question them? But now that I think

HOW MANY ENERGY DRINKS SHOULD A JOURNALIST DRINK BEFORE THEY WRITE A HEADLINE BECAUSE WE THINK WE MAY HAVE OVERDONE IT OH GOD OH JESUS CHRIST WE CAN HEAR THE SURFACE OF THE SUN

about it, I bet American keyboards probably have no 'u' button. They don't like u over there at all. Just texted my uncle in Arizona

about it. It's early morning now, but sure look, best get this out of the way now before we lose sleep over it. God, I'd kill for some sleep now but just can't seem to shake this… oh! the energy drink study thing also said some things about how kids probably shouldn't drink energy drink study thing also said some things about how kids probably shouldn't drink energy drink.

They have a 'u'. Googled it there. Every time I blink really fast I see white spots like stars. Do you see them? Oh I forgot to breathe haha that's why. Imagine I forgot to breathe in my sleep?

Margaret Tatcher only needed 4 hours she was probably on this stuff jesus I'm off me beer tits okjay were war we I think I'll talk a brake itz neerly tyme ta Finnish up[heer an dryve home.

HOW I SPEND MY MONEY

A 34-YEAR-OLD DRUG DEALER MAKING 300K PER YEAR

Welcome to HOW I SPEND MY MONEY, a totally original series on *WWN* that looks at what people in Ireland really do with their hard-earned cash.

This week we chat to 34-year-old narcotics salesman Pajo Hollihan who lives in a local Waterford council estate and employs dozens of young people in the area, including school children.

Fucking business is booming since we started cooking and selling crack cocaine. Handy to make too. Learned off YouTube. Have stash houses all over the town. Plenty of addict single mothers and that looking to make a few pounds, so everyone wins. My only problem is all the money. Had to open up a real business in the city to wash the cash. Pigs sniffin' around now and then, but sure I've more funds than them to play with, so they don't mind taking the old shnakey backhander. It is what it is. Best thing is I don't have to travel to work at all; the young lads on the bikes do all the running. You could say I'm a home worker that never has to work.

Occupation: Drug Wholesaler
Age: 34
Location: Waterford boi
Salary: €250–300k
Monthly pay (always net): €25k + whatever the dole is.

Monthly expenses
Rent: Rent Allowance Supplement pays most of it so I pay €47.
Household bills: St Vincent De Paul pays most of me bills.
Transport: Taximan
Phone bill: I'd go through 4–5 burners a month, €100–150.
Health insurance: Me bollox.
Subscriptions: I have to sign on every week in a probation office, but that's free.
Loan repayments: No repayments, but I also lend money at 50% APR to any eejit looking.

Monday
1pm: Wake up early on a Monday to collect all the money for the stuff I lent out on tick before the weekend. I usually hang around outside the main post office to shake lads down if their phones are off. I get a lot of 'didn't see your call' or 'please, don't hit me boi', but they eventually cough up their social welfare by the afternoon.
4pm: Send young lad on a push bike to collect a kilo from the bus station and bring to a safe house for cutting. This usually costs me around 65k and then just 50 quid to the kid for delivering, or if the young lad owes me something for drugs, then he does it for free. I'd spend around 4–5 euro for cutting agents and another tenner on baggies and clingfilm. Safehouse fee is 100 a week, again depending on whether the person owes me money. Mostly, they do in this town.
6pm: Organise drop-offs and pick-ups and listen to the scanner for the pigs. I use drones for the local drops and that costs around 900 quid for a good one. For longer journeys I have three taxi men on the take so they cost 100 a drop, depending on size of product.
8pm: Scoops in whatever pub will take me and the lads. I could spend anywhere between 100 and 500 a night in the town. But since I got barred from the Casino for glassing a blackjack dealer, it's a lot less these days … better off.
2am: Grab some dinner from chipper, which costs about 10 euro. Prostitute after food costs around 50–100, but again, they usually owe me money for gear, so …
Today's total spend: A lot.

Tuesday
3pm: Get up to check phone before going back to bed hungover ta fuck.
5pm: Get up again and start chasing lads for money. I like to give proper beatdowns on Tuesdays, so I pay two or three of the boys 200 each to flank me on my rounds. Sometimes shooters are needed so that can cost an extra 100 to the safehouse owner to deliver. Clothes do tend to get a bit bloody, so I would spend money on new clothes to be delivered through Sports Direct. You'll never see me in a shop, mostly because I'm barred.
9pm: Sit down to watch *Love Island* with the lac. This can cost anywhere between 1,000 and 10,000 euro because she always sees some dress or jewellery she likes and goes online

to buy it. Today it was only a necklace worth 2k. Thank fuck.

Today's total spend: €3k

Wednesday

2pm: Sign on the scratcher and the probation office before visiting dodgy accountant about legit businesses. He charges me an arm and a leg to wash the moolah so I could spend tens of thousands in any one meeting. Today was €3k, which isn't bad. But I made 12 grand, so can't complain. This legit business stuff is complicated, but better than CAB up your hole, trying to take me watches.

6pm: Meet area manager from Dublin in town to discuss some missing product and a possible rat. I got lunch, which came to €54. We agreed on a five-grand contract on said rat and I also agreed to pay for any missing product and to investigate where it went. Sometimes it's easier just to agree with the boss, lads, as things can get messy.

8pm: Paid contract to killer and another two grand to my enforcer to pay a visit to the house where product went missing. Spent another 500 on young fella to rob car for hit. Stayed at home with the missus for an alibi.

9pm: Sent young lad out to buy new burners and destroy old ones. Rat exterminated.

11pm: Half of missing product found hidden in foot soldier's flat. He begged for life and offered up his addict girlfriend as collateral who we put to work in a local brasser pad. Gave her a little test run for good measure. All sorted. Today was a good day.

Today's total spend: €11k

Thursday

11am: Thursday is an early start for me as it's district court day here in Waterford. I like to know who's getting done for what and to smell out any touts. I had only three employees up today for minor possession charges

and I paid their fines, totalling €2k. You've got to treat your staff well, even if it means lending them bail money at 50% interest. I'm sure they're good for it. And if not, there are plenty of pre-teens willing to be trained into the game. After all, I'm the only one creating jobs around here.

3pm: Start arranging the big drop-offs and orders for the weekend with my runners. We only give tick to those we know have young families as they're more likely to pay up after a violent threat. I'm told four people still owe money from last week and hired some lads at 200 each to do their thing.

5pm: Money retrieved along with a 55" widescreen TV and a fucking Renault Clio. What the hell am I supposed to do with that?

7pm: Paid off a local detective and gave him three envelopes for the other guards on the take. Paid him extra for tipping me off about a raid planned for a safe house I own this Saturday morning. Also told him where a competitor in the town stashes his gear in return. Hey look, they need to do their job too, right?

9pm: Went to gym to buy some 'roids from the owner. Cost me 150 but the guns are really starting to see those gains. Did an hour on the free weights. Felt fucking pumped so sniffed some blow and went out on the town and spent a fucking fortune on champers and lap dances. I can never just go for the one. Lolz.

Today's total spend: Blew me fucking stones today, no idea what I spent and don't give a fuck either.

Friday

1:30pm: Woke up to CAB knocking on the door telling me they were searching the gaff as part of Operation Thor. I said that's a great movie, and to come in. Put on kettle and made them tea and coffee, which cost about 50 cent. Turned on the film *Thor* full blast on the telly until they left.

3pm: Bought new phones again as CAB took the ones I had. All orders going well today and got taxi man to pick up 25 grand from drop-off point and deliver to my accountant in one of the shops. Paid him 200 euros

worth of bitcoin. I'm starting to use it more and more now with these CAB cunts on my back.

6pm: Booked holiday to Spain worth €2,500. I've a gaff there under the missus' name so can't wait to get a nice break and meet the big lad himself to talk shop. Business has never been better.

9:30pm: Watched Paul Williams on *The Late Late Show* selling another book. Bought it online for €14.99. If only I could make it into one of his books someday, or even the *Sunday World*, I'd be happy. I do like the nickname 'The Enforcer', if they ever do a piece on me, just in case anyone is reading here (come on, Paul, I've all your books). The money is not enough; it's the fame I really want, and who better than the Irish media to give it to me.

Today's total spend: €1,715.49

Weekly subtotal: None of your fucking business, pal!

What I've learned:

- Working is for muppets.
- The drugs trade is booming.
- You people have no idea what's going on in my world.
- Ireland is corrupt from the top down.
- I'm the only one creating jobs in my area.
- Society as a whole in its current form has created this opportunity for me and my gang.
- As long as drugs are illegal, I will always have a job.
- Child labour is cheap, and a big thanks to Apple for that idea.
- The bigger the divide between rich and poor, the more of me you'll see.
- When people are afraid of you, you can do anything you want.
- I'm like any entrepreneur, only I grew up in a class which has been repeatedly ignored by successive governments and continually tainted by the mainstream media.

PROPERTY

BUYING A HOUSE IN LONGFORD & MOVING IT TO DUBLIN: WE SHOW YOU HOW

THE latest figures from a MyHome.ie survey have shown that while house prices in Dublin have begun to fall slightly, the cheapest properties in the country are still to be found in Longford, where a three-bedroom semi-detached house is a third of the price compared to the same house in the capital.

But if you like the sound of a 200-grand saving but don't like the sound of living in Longford, one enterprising transport company have come up with a novel solution: they'll strip down the Longford house and ship it, brick by brick, up to the city where it can be reconstructed at a site of your choosing, saving you some serious cash. Interested? Here's how it works:

You need somewhere to put the house

Taking a house apart and putting it back together is fairly simple for any

competent builder; the big problem is finding somewhere to put it when you get it up to Dublin. But don't overthink this too much, simply tack your house onto the end of a street or estate, anywhere there's a bit of green space whatsoever. Then go to your local councillor or TD and tell them they've got a house-full of votes waiting for them if they turn a blind eye to it.

Mention as well that by ignoring your blatant disregard for planning law, they'll have lowered the homelessness figures in their jurisdiction. They love that craic. You'll be grand.

Move in

Now you can move into your new home … but hang on a second. Even when you take the fees of Rebuilders Inc. into account, you've just made yourself a tidy profit, easily as much as 100k. In fact, you could probably afford to buy another house in Longford and ship it up to Dublin, then rent out one house and live in the other. You'd be doubling your money! You'd be mad not to do this!

Airbnb

Now that you've got seven houses from Longford up in Dublin, you can start raking in some serious cash by letting them out as Airbnb apartments. Or if you prefer your profit with a hint of under-the-table action, you can just stuff 20 Brazilian students into the one house and charge them whatever the fuck you want. If all this seems illegal; don't worry. There's always a loophole.

Supply issues

OK, so there's a problem. You and all your mates have bought up so many houses in Longford, there's a serious shortage of accommodation in that county. House prices in Longford soar. It is no longer profitable for you to continue to haul homes across the country where you can make a killing in the capital. But prices in Longford are at an all-time high. You consider buying a few houses in Donegal to ship to Longford, but wise investors have beaten you to it. It is becoming apparent that you're not cut out for a life as a property mogul.

Bailout

Luckily for you, your TD friend from back up there can't bear to see you in such difficulty after all you've done for them. They offer to buy back all your properties at an inflated price, before selling them on to a developer to be renovated into hotels. The housing crisis is called off. Well, for you anyway.

WHERE ARE THEY NOW: SEAMUS BIN LADEN

IF ever there was a family that couldn't catch a break, it's the Bin Ladens. Following the death of patriarch Osama in 2011, the news arrived this week that his son Hamza has also died.

Attention now turns to the rest of the grieving Bin Laden family as well as reigniting the question about what ever happened Seamus Bin Laden, leader of the Mayo branch of al-Qaeda.

Seamus, SBL to his friends, sprung to notoriety in the aftermath of 9/11 by growing his beard out and retreating to the Mayo mountains in solidarity

with his far-removed and apparently 'wrongly accused' cousin Osama.

Emerging only to host his new weekly discussion show on RTÉ 1, Seamus Bin Laden became a well-known figure in the Irish wackjob community, and later made a pretty good swing at a presidential run, polling well among both arseholes and shitheads alike.

SBL continued making waves around the country and seemed content with his status as the leader of an al-Qaeda tribute act, with members including his brother Fintan Bin Laden and his best friend from school Fergal Afif Abedljalil, although the group could never manage to attract anyone other than those two people.

However, things took a turn for the worse for SBL following the death of his idol and adopted family member Osama Bin Laden in 2011,

prompting Seamus to go on a nine-week 'Talibender' across the island of Ireland, yelling at planes flying overhead which he claimed were 'full of US soldiers' and urging people to rise up with him and 'kick the shit out of a McDonald's'.

This ongoing wake reached its nadir in early 2012, when SBL found himself sinking pints in Howth, Co. Dublin, and noticed a large group of people looking into the harbour at a herd of seals that had swum up to the pier.

'Was it you seal pricks that kilt Ozzie?', Seamus was heard to shout, as the surrounding crowd tried to explain to him that there's a difference between a Navy SEAL and an actual seal.

'Yis think youse are smart, well Seamus Bin Laden isn't going to be taken out by a fuckin'… dolphin-shagger,' he roared, before diving into the water to 'give them a few digs'.

Although his body has never been found, eyewitnesses that day say there's no way that any human could survive such a mauling by 20 fully grown bull seals, and that Seamus Bin Laden died just like his hero Osama did – taken out by a group of seals before his body was dumped in the sea.

Despite the overwhelming evidence that SBL is in fact dead, rumours persist that the Achill Amir still lives to this day, with sightings reported regularly. Some say he's living the high life in Syria with Osama – also not dead – Bin Laden, and some say he had facial reconstructive surgery and walks among us disguised as country and western superstar Mike Denver.

Either way, the life and times of Seamus Bin Laden are just another sad chapter in the tale of the Bin Laden family, and our thoughts and prayers go out to the surviving members, William, Declan, Cathal, Wee Michael, Fionnula and Sinead.

IRISH HISTORY ACCORDING TO BRITAIN

IF THERE'S one thing the fallout from Britain's referendum to leave the European Union has taught us, it is that there is a pitiful and shameful lack of knowledge about Irish history among ... Irish people. However, British people (read Brexit-supporting politicians) have always been on hand to correct the record and present an unbiased account of the Emerald Isle's colourful history.

On the off-chance that you are in need of brushing up on your Irish history through British eyes, here is your one-stop shop for all things Ireland:

Ireland
Exists.
The correct British version of events: it was just sitting there. No one else was using it.

The Siege of Drogheda, 1641
Oliver Cromwell massacres over 2,000 people.
The correct British version of events: Cromwell, invited to invade by a supplicant and happy Irish people, begged the people of Drogheda to see sense and engage in a peaceful transition of power. The natives (who were drunk, naturally) barricaded themselves in and placed themselves under a voluntary siege and blockade, refusing to allow food into the town. Then to Cromwell's horror, the people began running at speed towards the swords of Cromwell's men, voluntarily impaling themselves on the swords and dying.

With their dying breaths locals could be heard saying 'please take the town with our permission, you deserve it. Oh and please, if you want, murder about 40% of the Irish population.'

Saoirse Ronan
Irish actress.
The correct British version of events: leading light of British acting. As English as the Queen. Same as Hozier, Graham Norton, Sally Rooney, Shane Lowry, Conor McGregor and Katie Taylor.

The Plantation of Ulster, 1609
Britain colonises Ulster with loyal English-speaking Protestant subjects from Scotland, forcing native Irish off their land.
The correct British version of events: Britain builds Belfast's botanic gardens as a gift to the island, free of charge.

1916 Rising
Erroneously described by Irish people as an attempt by Irish patriots to end British rule in Ireland through a revolution which ended with the executions of the Rising's leaders by British forces.

The correct British version of events: After feral Irish beasts tried to introduce Sharia Law on the streets of Dublin, Queen Elizabeth II, who was not yet born, valiantly fought the Irish monsters (who were drunk, naturally) and vanquished them. This is why to this day Ireland's flag is the Union Jack, and its national anthem is Ed Sheeran's 'The Shape Of You'.

The Penal Laws
An oppressive set of laws introduced by the British targeting Catholics, including banning Catholics from positions in public offices, exclusion from legal professions, and no voting rights.
The correct British version of events: Catholics were treated to weekly bouncy-castle parties with an endless supply of tea and crumpets. Ungrateful Irish (who were drunk, naturally) misremember the events entirely.

The Troubles
Catholics in Northern Ireland are oppressed, denied equals rights and treated as second-class citizens. The British State, its army and police force collude with Loyalist terrorist groups to murder innocent people as the IRA carry out a terrorist bombing campaign in Northern Ireland and Britain.
The correct British version of events: it was called The Brief Misunderstanding, not The Troubles and really it wasn't that big of a fuss, whatever you do, don't read up on Soldier F, Bloody Sunday, Internment, the Hunger Strikes, the Miami Showband, the Ballymurphy Massacre, the Glenanne Gang, the Dublin Monaghan Bombings. Move along, nothing to see here. Okay, if you want honesty, a 50-feet tall Gerry Adams with lasers beaming from his eyes incinerated London in a mindless rampage.

The Good Friday Agreement
An end to The Troubles.
The correct British version of events: Wah, wah, wah, people don't want a war in some nonsense nothing place

called Northern Ireland. Like we give a fuck.

The Bank Crisis 2008–10
Stupid Irish government fucks over its own people.
The correct British version of events: Smart Irish government (who were drunk, naturally) fucks over its own people. We're quite jealous of the job they did actually.

The Book of Kells
Detailed illustrations of the Christian Gospels dating from AD 800.
The correct British version of events: A beautifully detailed guest book filled out by Irish people, thanking Britain for all they've done for Ireland with the majority of people begging to be re-invaded and saved from a progressive and sovereign country.

The Black and Tans
Winston Churchill-established RIC outfit, notorious for the murders and massacres they committed in Ireland during the Irish War of Independence.
The correct British version of events: Similar fashion brand to Burberry. Do nice leather handbags.

The Irish Border
Britain holds a referendum to leave the EU with vague terms applied to the referendum and no clear indication what such a thing will look like in practical terms, leading British politicians to wittingly plunge Northern Ireland into chaos and risk

ruining all the good work of the fragile Peace Process.
The correct British version of events: A fictional thing which was invented by the T-Shirt Leo Varadkar (who was drunk, naturally) in 2017 out of spite to make it look like British politicians are utterly incompetent and only have one goal: to personally enrich themselves no matter the cost to the ordinary person.

The Famine, 1845–49
British government oversees the export of majority of food from Ireland to Britain while a potato blight takes hold. Through malice and incompetence, lays the groundwork for over one million Irish people to starve to death.
The correct British version of events: The what now?

'Ireland's favourite news source since 234BC'

Whispers News

Weather
Sea levels expected to rise another two feet today due to the Antarctic shelf melting at a rapid rate, but will be mostly sunny, thank god.

VOL 27, 236541   WATERFORD, 20 FEBRUARY 2034   €39:99

Thousands Emigrate As Avocado Famine Grips Country

IN scenes reminiscent of the mid-19th century, Ireland has once again become the victim of yet another devastating famine, forcing hundreds of thousands of men, women and children to emigrate.

Introduced by hipster vegans some twenty years ago, the avocado quickly became the number one food of choice for Irish families, even overtaking the potato.

'In hindsight, we probably should have stocked up on other food items,' one devastated father of four told *WWN* as he boarded what have come to be known as 'famine planes', or a Ryanair 737 to London.

Such is the influx of migrants that makeshift camps have been set up all across the UK where nationalist protesters have also gathered calling for the Irish migrants to go home.

'I just want a better life for me and my family,' ex-

claimed former journalist Gemma O'Doherty, who used to work for the *Irish Independent*.

The avocado famine began in June last year after the EU banned the fruit over pesticide contamination. Up until the ban, Irish

consumers had been depending more and more on the food for nutrition, mistakenly boycotting every other type of food in favour of avocado due to it being the in thing to eat.

'I suppose we just kind of fell into the trend and it escalated from there,' mother Cheryl Coffee told *WWN*, 'so much so that everything we were eating was avocado-based ... Christ, us Irish will just never learn.'

Meanwhile, Taoiseach Rónán Mullen has called for neighbouring countries to relax their borders, stating 'We're not "migrant" migrants, we're white, can't you see?'

ALL THE EPSTEIN DEATH CONSPIRACY THEORIES IN ONE HANDY PLACE

THE SAD and untimely death of billionaire paedophile and friend to the rich, influential and famous Jeffrey Epstein has sparked a flurry of speculation online.

However, some internet users have found it hard to find a responsible news outlet which it trusts to host all those conspiracy theories in one handy place. That is, until now!

WWN has of course been working around the clock to avoid fanning the flames and misrepresenting information just to give people with nothing better to do a chance to rant endlessly on Facebook much to the shame of their relatives.

Dive in and dine out on the nourishing conspiracies theories which like all conspiracy theories have all been extensively fact-checked before being circulated online:

The Royal Family did it
A close friend to Prince Andrew, the Queen couldn't risk any sort of potential fallout from a trial. We all know that. And if the letter A = 1, B = 2, C = 3 and so on, the letters in Epstein

total 68 which is the same age as Princess Anne, Andrew's sister, and the longstanding chief assassin for the Royal Family. The dots are there folks, we just connect them.

Who decided that the alphabet goes in that particular order anyway? We're only scratching the surface, folks.

He was alive and now is dead
We think there's something to this theory, we can't wait to hear what new information reveals.

Faced with spending the rest of his life in prison and outed to the world as a vile paedophile, he took his own life
As far-fetched nonsense goes this takes the cake. C'mon, do we look like we were born yesterday?

The Clintons killed him because he knew their deepest, darkest secrets
Well, this is patently absurd. As we all know, if Bill

wanted to keep secret the fact he actually can't play the saxophone, he'd never leave the sorts of hints that could fuel a conspiracy theory.

Trump did it.
Depending on your political leanings this is either an open and shut case as Trump is guilty as sin and it should be looked into or you're wearing a MAGA hat right now. Open. Your. Eyes.

Trump AND the Clintons did it
Ooh, juicy. Now you're talking.

Epstein was a CIA informer, a Mossad agent, a member of Hezbollah, a Saudi ally, a Russian spy and behind Hong Kong's pro-democracy protests
He was a busy man. He wasn't just playing both sides as a double agent, he was an octuple agent playing every side of this espionage octagon.

He had a history of leaving one-star ratings on IMDb for beloved movies
Really? He gave *The Dark Knight* a one-star review and expected no push back? *Little Miss Sunshine* too? The guy was a monster.

The people speculating about his death do not care about the pain and suffering Epstein brought to his victims
Hmmm, this one seems unlikely, typically most people we've encountered who spread Zionist and Illuminati conspiracies on the internet are pretty nice, empathic people.

DIPLOMACY

OFFENDING THE CHINESE GOVERNMENT: A GUIDE

DO YOU have any idea how hard it is out there running a thinly veiled dictatorship with an appalling record on human rights and civil liberties that often uses violence to suppress dissent? It's not easy; just ask China.

Recently banning *South Park* for making fun of its leader Xi Jinping, the Chinese government also forced the NBA into an embarrassing apology after one player showed support for Hong Kong protesters.

In order to help our readers avoid hurting the Chinese government's feelings any further, we've listed the many ways you can gravely offend it just so you'll be sure to avoid heaping blame, unfairly, on the morally bankrupt Communist Party of China:

1) 750 children have been arrested in Hong Kong during recent civil unrest and protests. The Chinese government would find it offensive if you were to call the jailing of children the act of a political regime that knows how unjust and fragile its hold on power is. Just follow Google's lead and make sure not to offend by scrubbing this information from your search engine for users in mainland China, like it never happened.

2) '3-in-1 Chinese takeaway meals are not great, and if we were the betting type, they're usually sitting there in the kitchen for ages before they deliver it to your house.' This is a little below the belt so avoid repeating.

3) Don't say Chinese leader Xi Jinping looks like Winnie the Pooh. Do you know how offensive it is to be compared to a cuddly and kindly

bear? Jinping just spent the morning stating 'anyone who attempts to split any region from China will perish, with their bodies smashed and bones ground to powder', and you want to imply he might be nice like a cartoon bear? Not cool. No wonder he's banned all Winnie the Pooh imagery in China.

4) Chairman Mao was a big fan of mass killings. Slaughtered 15 million people according to some estimates, but remember, Chinese political niceties mean you don't bring it up as that would be really unfair. Take Disney's lead and remove all politically sensitive content from your output when showing it in China, or else risk having morals, but smaller profits. Or, closer to home, just name a restaurant chain after the guy.

5) The Chinese government is currently interning and slaughtering Uighur Muslims in a genocide, but

> **Fullmindness**
>
> You put your thoughts about sometimes feeling like a plastic bag, drifting in the wind, wanting to start again into words only to find that bitch Katy Perry has beaten you to it.

best to take the lead from the leading democracies around the world and just not bring it up. Wouldn't want to offend.

6) Tiananmen Square. Jesus, why would you even bring that up, are you trying to get put on some sort of list? A list that includes the names of pro-democracy demonstrators who were brutally murdered in 1989 by the Chinese military? C'mon, the Communist Party of China is in charge of the most populous country on the planet, why would you hurt their feelings like that? They're so helpless and defenceless, shame on you.

> **How shopping changed in 2020**
>
> Shoppers were required to shave all body hair and bleach their skin before entering premises.

GUNS

GEORGE Washington, Alexander Hamilton, Benjamin Franklin: just three of the 'founding fathers' of America, who wrote the very document which shaped the United States into the nation it is today. And, as new research has shown, three men who loved nothing more than the smell of a warm assault rifle, fresh from a delivery of red-hot lead.

Although enemies of the state would have you believe that the founding fathers did not have assault rifles in mind when they passed the second amendment to the US Constitution back in 1791, and that the bill itself has failed to keep up with technology that went from single-fire muskets to expertly crafted 100-round magazine drums which never jam and can be loaded and emptied with ease, a recently unveiled document has shown without doubt that even Thomas Jefferson himself was a fan of the ArmaLite AR-15, the smoothest assault rifle on the market.

The research, funded exclusively by the NRA, has put to bed any doubts

How shopping changed in 2020

Putting mouldy fruit you just picked up and handled back onto the shelf made you an accessory to murder.

REVEALED: THE FOUNDING FATHERS' THOUGHTS ON LIGHTWEIGHT MAGAZINE-FED GAS-OPERATED SEMI-AUTOMATIC RIFLES

> ## 'I hereby state that semi-automatic weaponry be'ith the right of every man, woman and child in America, with the exception of some black people and most Mexicans'

that average, decent Americans may have had about foolish proposals to 'ban guns', or 'stop selling guns to anyone who wants a gun', and will surely pave the way to a gleaming new future where everyone has the reliability and peace of mind that comes with the AR-15; truly one of the most wonderful products ever gifted to the world.

'I hereby state that semi-automatic weaponry be'ith the right of every man, woman and child in America, with the exception of some black people and most Mexicans' read the newly found document, which is miraculously preserved despite its age.

'Especially the lightweight magazine-fed AR-15; truly a dream weapon. Alas, this weapon IS but a dream to us poor folks in 1790-odd, but to any American that lives in such an enlightened age where such a weapon is available, we suggest you travelleth to your nearest Walmart or equivalent store and pick yourself upeth one now.'

Lefty nutjobs have questioned the validity of the document by pointing out that it appears to have been printed with a HP laser printer, but such claims have been debunked by the fact that if the founding fathers wanted a printer, God would have surely given them one.

SOCIAL MEDIA

SO YOUR CHILD SAYS THEY WANT TO BE A YOUTUBE STAR: HERE'S WHAT HAPPENS NEXT

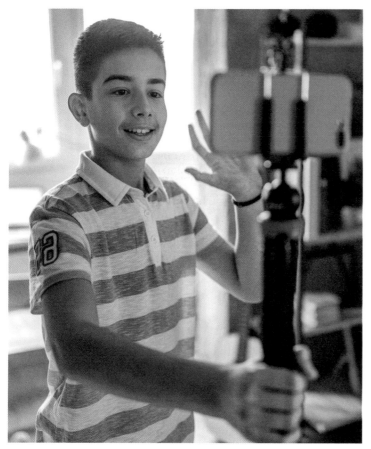

THERE was once a time when kids aspired to be movie stars, actors on TV or pop singers, but no longer. Now every kid wants to have their own YouTube channel, or be a 'social media personality', what is the world coming to? Why don't these kids accept that online streaming and video services aren't the same as the mediums their parents grew up with? Why don't any kids want to be on the wireless anymore?

It's only a matter of time before your sweet, good-natured kids turn around and tell you that they want to be an obnoxious, cash-obsessed viral idiot who spends their time yelling into a webcam for clicks and likes from idiots, so prepare yourself for the worst. Here's how to react:

1) Crush that dream

It's your job as an Irish parent to clamp down on any dream your kid has if it strays from the lane marked 'reputable, pensionable labour' or 'a job for life', and this is only solidified by the fact that online content creation is weird and you don't understand it. Should your kid express a desire to 'have a channel', crush that dream swiftly and emphatically. Get out there and break rocks like we did, kid! This video craic is pure messing.

2) Cut the internet

One sure-fire way to make your kid see sense is to censor what they see. Threaten to 'remove the internet' from your house. This is a simple enough endeavour, we're sure it just involves disconnecting the landline and throwing that box thing in the hall into the bin. If they have a phone, tell them they're not allowed use it for YouTube. They'll obey you; they're your kids, aren't they? Now that they have no access to this YouTube craic, they'll have no desire to pursue it. Sorted.

3) Bargain

If you want to appear like you support your kid, the best thing to do is bargain just a little. Say that they can pursue their dreams if they pursue yours first, just for a little while. Get a good Leaving Cert. Go to college and get a degree in a subject they may not have any interest in, 'just to be on the safe side'. 'You can always fall back on it when this other thing doesn't work out', you can assure them. By the time they get out of college, all this nonsense about tapping into the limitless potential of the online creative space will be long gone out of their head. They'll have bills of their own; nothing focuses the mind like debt!

COVID-19

COVID-19 TRANSLATOR

This year, more than any other year, events led the public to learn a high volume of new phrases, terms and words thanks to the emergence of COVID-19. *WWN* has dutifully collected all these terms in one handy place:

'Coronavirus' = 'Ah, sure it's only the flu, I don't know what the big deal is, be over in a week.'

'Contact tracing' = having to ring up all your ex partners to tell them you gave them the clap, only it's COVID-19 this time.

'Pandemic' = used to just be the name of a shit nightclub you'd find in the midlands.

'Keep your social distance please' = 'Take one more step towards me and I'll tase your fucking testicles clean off.'

'Herd immunity' = colloquial British term for 'let the elderly die, they've had a good run.'

'Heard immunity' = being able to tune out whenever your spouse starts talking.

'Self-isolate' = 'stay home and masturbate for two weeks like a good lad, cheers.'

'Zoomaphobia' = the very rational fear of someone ringing you for a video call.

'Lockdown' = optional set of restrictions that you don't have to abide by if you're not arsed.

'The New Normal' = go on, say 'the new normal' one more time, I dare you. If I hear that fucking phrase again the new normal will be you picking your teeth up off the floor.

'Child care' = something that used to exist.

'Mental health crisis' = something Ireland has had for upwards of 20 decades but only discovered by government this year.

'Essential worker' = not an investment banker, marketing executive or Instagram influencer.

'WFH' = multiple meanings including 'work from home', 'whinge from home', 'wank from home'.

'PPE' = personal protective equipment. Means different things for different professions; nurses, porn stars, etc.

'A bra' = ancient technology women used to wear before coronavirus.

'Super Spreader' = a sexually promiscuous person or a COVID-infected person who passes the infection on to an unusually large number of people.

'Emergency COVID-19 payment' = the Milkybars are on me!

'Furlough' = fancy employer talk for 'we'll be heartlessly firing you down the line'.

'The WHO' = rag-time group of misfits who rose to international stardom, known for legendary partying. Also could stand for the band The Who.

'Wuhan' = home to soup-dwelling radioactive bats.

'Reopening the economy' = politician talk for 'economy's fucked, expect to be taxed through the hoop'.

County Knowledge

Wicklow continues to deny it is 'pretend Dublin'.

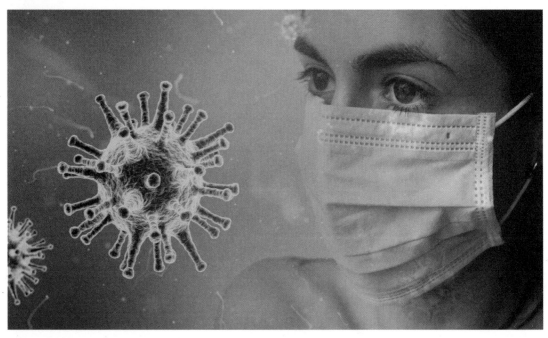